THE PRIVATE LIFE OF WARREN HASTINGS

THE PRIVATE LIFE OF WARREN HASTINGS

FIRST GOVERNOR GENERAL OF INDIA

CHARLES LAWSON

GYAN

Published by

Gyan Publishing House
5, Ansari Road
Daryaganj, New Delhi-110002
Phone: 011-47034999, 9811692060
E-mail: books@gyanbooks.com

Distribution Network
gyanbooks.com
India, USA, Canada, UK, Australia

ISBN: 978-93-7316-059-7 (PB)

First Published, 1895

2nd Impression 2025

Printed at: Gyan Press, Delhi.

THE PRIVATE LIFE OF WARREN HASTINGS
Author: CHARLES LAWSON

THE PRIVATE LIFE
OF
WARREN HASTINGS

Swan Electric Engraving C°

Warren Hastings.

Painted by Sir Thomas Lawrence P.R.A.

Engraved by W. Fry

THE PRIVATE LIFE

OF

WARREN HASTINGS

First Governor-General of India

BY

SIR CHARLES LAWSON

Fellow of the University of Madras, etc.

With 3 Photogravure Portraits and 78 Illustrations and Facsimiles

London

SWAN SONNENSCHEIN & CO

NEW YORK: MACMILLAN & CO

1895

PREFACE

DURING the century which has now passed since Warren Hastings was acquitted of the charges brought against him by the House of Commons, posterity has endorsed the remark of the Prince Regent to the Allied Sovereigns, that he was "one of the most deserving, and, at the same time, one of the worst used men in the Empire." Shortly after the conclusion of his trial he disappeared from public view, yet his name has a greater attraction for modern students of Indian history than has that of any one of his twenty eminent successors in the office of Governor-General. He made a successful appeal for national sympathy when he exclaimed to his accusers: "I gave you all, and you have rewarded me with confiscation, disgrace, and a life of impeachment!" His end was peace; but he went to his grave conscious that full reparation had not been made for the grievous wrongs inflicted upon him. Posterity shares that feeling, and regrets that "one of the greatest men that England ever produced" was the victim of implacable prejudice. Of late years his public life has been scrutinised anew, and without bias, by many writers who have done honour to his memory; but his private life has not, perhaps, engaged as much attention as it deserves; and I have been encouraged to give in the present volume the chief contents of a paper that I contributed in July, 1892, to the *Journal of Indian Art and Industry*, together with additional information which I have gleaned since that date from his kinsfolk, from his private papers in the British Museum, and from other sources.

My grateful acknowledgments are due to Miss Marian Winter, of Worton House, Steeple Aston, Oxfordshire, for permitting me to see Hastings' private diary, and for affording me the opportunity of reproducing the engravings, which he once owned, of the trial scene at Westminster Hall, and of his portrait by Sir Joshua Reynolds. I am also much indebted to the Rev. Warren Hastings, M.A., of Churchill, Oxfordshire, to Miss A. C. Hastings, of Martley, Worcestershire, and to Mr. Warren Hastings Woodman-Hastings, of Stubhill, near Twining, Worcestershire, for particulars about the Hastings family, as well as to the Earl of Rosebery, K.G., Viscount Cross, G.C.B., General Sir Charles D'Oyly, Bart., of Newlands, Blandford, Dorsetshire, the late Sir George Scharf, K.C.B., Director of the National Portrait Gallery, the Hon. Henry Dudley Ryder, of Messrs. Coutts & Co., the Rev. Arthur Grisewood, M.A., Rector of Daylesford, and Mr. George Murray Smith, of 40, Park Lane, London, for various communications which they have very kindly made to me with regard to subjects that are alluded to in this book.

C. L.

LONDON, *July*, 1895.

CONTENTS

LIST OF ILLUSTRATIONS

THE PRIVATE LIFE OF WARREN HASTINGS

CHAPTER I

A WORCESTERSHIRE FAMILY

It is conjectured that Warren Hastings was descended from a Danish sea-king, who was vanquished by King Alfred of England, after a long career of what in our days would be called piracy; but one need not go so far back to establish his claim to belong to an old county family. Ethelbald, King of the Mercians, made a grant of the ford in the dale, called Daylesford, to Begia, "a servant of God," for the erection and support of a monastery, which is supposed to have been destroyed during the Heptarchy. In 874 Wereford, Bishop of Worcester, gave six manses in Daylesford to Ceolwulf, King of the Mercians, on easy conditions, for his own and three successive lives. A hundred years later, when the land had reverted to the Bishop of Worcester, it was conveyed to Æthelred, King of England, who gave it to Alfere, Earl of Mercia, by whom it was made over to his brother, Athelstan, for his life. About the time of the Norman invasion the land was seized by Agelwice, Abbot of Evesham, who, however, had to restore it to the Bishop of Worcester. Otto, the grabbing brother of the Conqueror, then possessed himself of the property; but eventually the Bishop established his superior right to it. A notice of Daylesford was duly entered in the Conqueror's Survey, known as the Domesday Book.

At this period Astrope de Hastings held lands at Fecko, in

Warwickshire, and from him descended John Hastings, Baron of Abergavenny, created Earl of Pembroke. The Earls of Pembroke married thrice into the Royal Family; but for "five generations," it is recorded, the "father never saw the son, nor the son the father," owing to the sons being born posthumously. John Hastings, last Earl of Pembroke of that creation, died without issue, and the Earldom thereupon reverted to the Crown, and the Barony of Abergavenny went by marriage to another family. From another branch of the Hastings family sprang the Earls of Huntingdon. In the reign of Henry II. Milo de Hastings held land at Daylesford from the Bishop of Worcester; and either he, or a relative of the same name, "Sir Miles Hastings of Daylesford com: Wigorn," resided there during the reign of Edward I. The head of the family thus became lord of the manor of Daylesford. The son and heir of the second Milo, or Miles, namely, John Hastings of Daylesford in Worcester, and of Telford in Oxfordshire, married a daughter of Thomas Penyston, or Pynaston; the son and heir of this John Hastings married a daughter of Sir Richard York, Kt., of York; and the succeeding son and heir, Simon Hastings, died, aged eighty-two, at Daylesford in 1627, and was buried in the parish church. His tomb bears the following inscription:—

Doth marvel, reader, that I here do lye
Who might have made this church my canopy?
Why, 'tis no wonder. Should a strong-built story
Hinder my corps in mounting to its glory?
My parting soul forbad it; and withall
Charg'd me to chuse this place of buriall,
That this my tomb each passenger might tell
They must expect the sound of passing bell.
Eightie two years compleat my days did make
Before my mother earth me home did take,
And when her right in all mankind she leave
Heaven to the blest my purest earth receive.

In the year 1834, shortly before her death, Lady Charlotte Fitz Gerald gave to her niece, Maria, Marchioness of Bute, various papers relating to her family, including the following letter, dated 9th March, 1804, from Warren Hastings; and in October, 1852, Lady Bute made a copy of this letter for Sir

John D'Oyly, and stated, in a note, that she did "not know to whom it is addressed":—

My dear Friend,—I am much gratified, from a better principle, I trust, than that of pride, by the honor which the Countess of Moira has done me, in the question which she has desired you to propose to me, namely, "When my ancestors settled in Worcestershire?" The only authority to which I can at present have recourse for the solution of this question, is Dr. Nash's history of Worcestershire. This book contains many detailed particulars of the family, and among the rest this passage: "In the reign of Henry 2nd, Milo de Hastings held three hides of land in Daylesford of the Bishop of Worcester, for which he owed suit to the court of Blockley, and hundred of Winborewater." In another place it says, Astrope Hastings "held lands at Fecko in Warwickshire of the Bishop of Worcester, so early as the reign of the Conqueror, or very soon afterward." As the distance of time between the death of William the Conqueror, at which period A. de H. settled in Warwickshire, and the commencement of the reign of Henry the 2nd is but sixty-seven years, it is most probable that Milo de Hastings was the first of the line that settled in Worcestershire; that is, in that part of the county which afterwards became the property and fixed residence of the family through many centuries; and in this opinion I am confirmed by my recollection of a genealogical table copied (I believe) from the record of a visitation made in the reign of James 1st, in which the first name inscribed upon it is stated to be descended from Milo de Hastings. Hence it appears that my ancestors first settled in Worcestershire between the years 1154 and 1189.

Dr. Nash, relying on the authority of Penyston Hastings, my grandfather, derives the pedigree of the family from "Hastings the Dane." Whatever splendour it might boast from so remote an antiquity, and so distinguished a progenitor, it has lain in great obscurity ever since the reign of Charles 1st, when (according to the historian) "John Hastings having spent four manors in defence of the King, conveyed Telford" (one of those in Oxfordshire) "to Speaker Lenthall," to save the rest of his estate. I should be happy if my genealogy could be traced to any ramification, however distant, that could bring it into an affinity with a family so illustrious as that branch of it to which the Countess of Moira belongs, and with a lady, for whom I may be allowed, though personally unknown to her, to say, that I entertain a very high respect; and I did once take some pains, and with very able assistance, to explore it, but without success. I wish too that I could call you my cousin; but I want no heraldry to tell me that you are my friend, and I hope you know with equal assurance, that I am,

Most sincerely and affectionately yours,

WARREN HASTINGS.

A daughter of Simon Hastings married W. M. Gardiner, of Lagham, Surrey, son of Sir William Gardiner, Kt., "whose heir he was." The younger Gardiner died "ye fift of January, Ao 1632," aged thirty-two, at Daylesford, and the slab placed to his memory, close to the Communion Table, bears a brass plate, on which he is represented in the costume of the period of James I. The following quaint inscription, on brass plates, runs around the edges of the slab :—

> A full carowse (vain world) let those drink up
> That like thy sweetes : I did but kisse ye cup ;
> Thy best I tasted and dislik'd ; for when
> Thy enjoy'd pleasures doe but weary man
> What will thy labors doe. This made mee soone
> To seeke for rest before my age's noone.
> Should any blame my haste let it suffice,
> I went to bed betimes, betimes to rise.

During the Civil War Hastings of Daylesford vied with other Worcestershire gentlemen in making sacrifices first for Charles I., and, after that King's execution, for his fugitive son and heir. He joined the Royal Army as a volunteer ; he sold his estate in Oxfordshire ; he heavily mortgaged his property in Worcestershire ; he parted with his plate in order to find money for the Royal exchequer ; and, after disposing of half of his possessions for "the cause," he ransomed himself by making over most of the remaining half to Speaker Lenthall, of Cromwell's Parliament. He was thus beggared by his fidelity to his King and to the King's son ; and, when the latter was restored to the throne, he made the family no compensation for the great losses which it had loyally sustained on his father's and his own behalf.

According to an old record, in which the name of the family is spelt in a variety of ways, the living of Daylesford was bestowed as follows between 1281 and 1701 :—

Year.	*Patron.*	*Incumbent.*
1281	Thos. de Hastynge	Thos. de Cursen.
1302	Prior et Con. Wor.	Wustan de Wygon.
1305	do.	Willis de Shireborn.
1325	Rolandus de Hastynge	Ds. Wills Trybe.
1335	Thos. Hastynge de Daylesford	Henricus Motte.
1364	Rex ratione custodie heredis	Philippus Haym.
1399	Laurentii de Hastynge defuncti... ...	Henricus Bovere.
1419	Thos. Hastynge	Johannes Coleshull.
1481	Edwardus Hasting	Ricardus Bilhowey.

Year.	Patron.	Incumbent.
1482	Edwardus Hasting	Will'us Atkinson.
1488	do.	Mauricius Berthram, A.M.
1490	do.	Will'us Vincent.
1491	do.	Will'us Lake.
1525	Joh. Hastyngs	Joh. Haddington.
1543	do.	Ricardus Ireland.
1593	Simon de Hastyngs	Georgius Osboldston, A.M.
1645	Carolus rex ratione memoris etatis Joh. de Hastynge	Johannus Wyld.
1646	do. do. do. ...	Tho. Bunce, A.M.
1661	Johannus Hastings	Johannus Stephens.
1679	Franc. Russell (Baronettus)	Com. Withom, A.M.
1690	Penyston Hastings	Carolus Penyston, A.M.
1701	do.	Penyston Hastings, A.B.

Penyston Hastings, the patron in 1701, had two sons, the elder of whom was Samuel Hastings, and the younger was the above-mentioned Penyston Hastings, A.B., the Incumbent. The elder branch of the family is still largely represented, and Sir James Stephen was in error, therefore, when he stated in his *Story of Nuncomar* that Warren Hastings "was the last descendant of the family to which he belonged."

Samuel Hastings had a son, William Hastings, who resided at Shipton-under-Whichwood, in Worcestershire, and died, leaving a son, James Hastings, who lived in Hanover Square, London, and died in 1768, aged sixty-three, leaving a son, also named James, in holy orders. This Rev. James Hastings, M.A., had fifteen children; became Rector of Martley, in Worcestershire, and died in 1856, at the patriarchal age of one hundred. The eldest of his seven daughters, Joanna Hastings, born in 1782, died in 1886, aged one hundred and four. The second of his eight sons, John Paget, entered the Church, became Curate of Martley; went to India as a Chaplain in the East India Company's service, and had a son, Warren Hastings, who died at Ferruckabad, in the Bengal Presidency, in 1838, aged twenty.

The Rector's fourth son was Vice-Admiral Sir Thomas Hastings, K.C.B., of Titley Court, Herefordshire. This distinguished officer was a Lieutenant on board H.M.'s ship *Undaunted*, when Napoleon was conveyed in that vessel to Elba; and he wrote the following letter from that island to his family in England :—

No pen can do justice to the rapturous joy with which we were received by the inhabitants of Marseilles, a town whose trade had particularly suffered from our exertions to destroy it, on the 16th of April, when we returned from a short cruise to our old station at that port. The day before we had learnt from a fisherman that some great change was expected. On that morning we observed the white flag flying on all the forts with the English united; this induced us to stand close in, when a deputation of the inhabitants came on board with the Mayor, and invited us to anchor, and informed us of the joyful intelligence of peace, and the downfall of the disturber of the world—Bonaparte. To describe the immoderate exclamations of enthusiastic joy would be impossible. The air re-echoed with cries of "*Vive le roi!*" "*Vive Louis XVIII.!*" "*Vive l'Anglais!*" At 12 we

ADMIRAL SIR THOMAS HASTINGS, K.C.B.

saluted, and anchored. It was strange to view those very people who had so short a time before been employed doing each other all possible mischief, now rushing into each other's arms, and embracing with a more than fraternal warmth.

We remained at Marseilles till 23rd of April, when we received orders to sail for Frejus to take the ci-devant Emperor to Elba. On the 24th we arrived, and on the 27th everything was arranged for his embarkation. This mighty enemy of England preferred trusting himself in the hands of those very people whom he had so often stigmatised as being destitute of honour and principle to those over whom he had reigned, and so often led to victory and glory. On his way down he had met with no insult except at Avignon, where the people hung his effigy by the wayside, and called out to see the tyrant. He was escorted by a regiment of Austrian Hussars, and accompanied by a Russian Marshal, and Colonel Campbell of the Guards.

At Frejus he remained two days, and on the night of the 28th left that place to embark. The road was lined with Hussars, and a square was formed on the beach around the boat. At half-past 8, he embarked in the utmost silence, which was only interrupted by a trumpet march. The sea was peacefully calm, and the whole scene was fully impressive.

Deserted by all his Generals but two, as well as the greater part of his domestics, ever fearing for his safety, he throws himself on board a frigate belonging to that country whose deadly enmity he justly merited. There he is received with all the honours due to a Sovereign Prince, which, to do him justice, he was fully alive to, and he observed the English were indeed noble and generous enemies. It behoves me to say that the unbending fortitude and the noble firmness with which he bears the reverse of circumstances does at least command respect; and could we divest ourselves of the idea that the murderer of d'Enghien, A. Wright, etc., etc., stood before us, we might soon rise into admiration. The same night we weighed anchor, and made sail. During a long passage of six days he assumed an affability which certainly did not appear natural to him. His height is five feet five inches, inclining to fatness, which makes him appear inactive and unwieldy, his eyes are grey and extremely penetrating. The expression of his countenance is by no means agreeable, and his conversation is general, and on all subjects he seems well informed. His attention seems to have been much turned to naval affairs, as his remarks on that head were extremely apt and pertinent. I was appointed one of the Commissioners for taking possession of the island, and rendering the flag independent, and therefore, on our drawing near, I quitted the ship with Count Clamon and General Count Drouet, and went through all the necessary ceremonies, after which we returned, and found the ship nearly in the port of Ferrara. Next day his flag, which is an odd one, being white with red diagonal stripes and three bars, which he says should indicate his wish to cultivate Industry, Harmony, and Peace, was hoisted, and a salute of twenty-one guns by the *Undaunted* took place, followed by all Forts. At two o'clock the procession was ready, when he stepped into the boat, the guns were manned, and as soon as he cleared the ship a royal salute was commenced. The style we rowed into the Mole was, first the Emperor's boats with Marine Guards and Officers, and the Officers of his household; afterwards a concourse of shore boats with music, people strewing flowers and cheering our landing. He was received by the Municipality, who presented the city keys, made of gold, on a plate of silver. Then we marched in the greatest order, the streets being lined with troops and strewed with flowers, the air re-echoing with cries of "*l'Empereur!*" "*Vive Napoleon le Grand!*" The greatest scene of hypocrisy was now to be performed. On entering the Church, the Te Deum was sung; and the disturber of the world, this scourge of nations, knelt down at the altar of that God he had so often denied, and into Whose presence he had hurled so many unwarned and unexpected victims. I had borne everything else with patience, and those honours paid were certainly due to him as a sovereign; but to observe the sanctified veil he drew over his face called to my remembrance that the greatest and most complicated villain was at this moment before my eyes, and awakened in my breast sentiments far from being friendly. This mass over, we proceeded to the house arranged for Napoleon's palace, where all the forms of allegiance were observed. We thus ended our most extraordinary voyage !

The Admiral founded the gunnery ship *Excellent*, and died in 1872, aged eighty-seven.

The Rector's fifth son, William Warren Hastings, had ten children, the eldest of whom, Warren Burrows Hastings, Rector of Ludford, Lincolnshire, died in 1871, leaving five children, the eldest of whom is the Rev. Warren Hastings, M.A., of Cavendish College, Cambridge, now Curate of Churchill—the birthplace of his famous kinsman and namesake—and chief

THE REV. WARREN HASTINGS, M.A.

living representative in the male line of the old family of Hastings of Daylesford. Before he entered the Church the Rev. Warren Hastings was a keen soldier, and he held a commission as Lieutenant in the 4th Battalion of the Worcestershire Regiment, and also one in the Cambridge University Volunteers. After he was ordained he made the modern grand tour of the world, *viâ* America, Japan, China, and India. He arrived at Denver, in the United States, early in November, 1892 ; and he was promptly interviewed by a reporter of the local *Republican*, with the result that the following paragraph appeared the next morning in that journal :—

"Warren Hastings, England," is upon the register at the Metropole Hotel. It is a classical name—Warren Hastings. That name has cut a prominent figure in English history. The Warren Hastings of old was Governor-General of India. He ruled that province with autocratic sway. When he returned to England he was impeached for cruelty to the natives. Edmund Burke, the celebrated English orator, was his prosecutor. His accusation of Hastings is one of the most eloquent speeches of the world. Burke was assisted in his prosecution by Fox and Sheridan. That was in 1786. Warren Hastings was small and delicate. His relative, who is now in Denver, is tall, robust, and of athletic build. He is a clergyman of the Church of England. He was formerly a Lieutenant in the Army. He is a graduate of Cambridge, a cultivated and affable Englishman. He is very much impressed with the architectural beauty and the business push of Denver.

SIR CHARLES HASTINGS, M.D.

The Rector's sixth son, Sir Charles Hastings, M.D., D.C.L., will always occupy a prominent place among Worcestershire worthies. He was born in 1793; and, having entered the medical profession, he settled as a practitioner in the city of Worcester in 1818, the year of the death of his eminent relative at Daylesford. In 1832 he took the initiative in establishing the Midland Medical and Surgical Association at Worcester, and commenced the publication of that Society's *Journal*. He occupied the post of Secretary and mainspring of this Society for eleven years, when he was prevailed upon to accept the position of President and Treasurer. The Society's influence increased so steadily under his care that, in 1856, it was somewhat reluctantly resolved to exchange its provincial for a national status, and it was then re-named The British Medical Association, and its office was removed from Worcester to the metropolis. Dr. Charles Hastings was unanimously elected President and Treasurer of the new Society, and he retained the former office, and discharged its duties with unabated zeal until his death in 1866, at the age of seventy-three. He was created a Knight Bachelor, and he was the recipient of honours from numerous scientific and philanthropic societies. At the meeting at Chester, of the British Medical Association, shortly after his death, it was stated by the new President, that, "in every relation of life Sir Charles Hastings was a man to be loved, to be respected, and, I may say, to be venerated." Later in the year, at the annual meeting of the British Association for the Advancement of Science, the venerable Lord Brougham, having referred to the "great position and distinguished fame" of Sir Charles Hastings in the medical profession, and to his "kindness and humanity in the exercise" of his duties as a physician, proceeded to say that "his labours in the investigation of physical science, and as founder of the Natural History Society of Worcestershire, showed how little his studies were confined to the profession of which he was so distinguished an ornament." The British Medical Association founded a Hastings medal in honour of its first President, to be awarded for eminent service to medical science by any member of the medical profession in any country. The latest recipient of the medal is Dr. Lawson Tait, the famous physician of Birmingham. The Association, as a further mark of respect for its founder, had his head engraved on its seal.

Sir Charles Hastings left a son, George Woodyatt Hastings, who founded the above-mentioned British Association for the Advancement of Science, and for several years represented the Eastern Division of Worcestershire in Parliament. The Rector's seventh son and tenth child, named Decimus, entered the Navy, and, like his brother, Sir Thomas Hastings, attained the rank of Vice-Admiral. The Rector's eighth son, Henry James Hastings, entered the Church, succeeded his father as Rector of Martley, became Honorary Canon of Worcester, and Rural Dean, and died in 1875, aged seventy-eight, leaving a son, the Rev. John Parsons Hastings, the present Rector and patron of Martley.

Francis Decimus Hastings, the seventh son and tenth child of the Rev. James Hastings, Rector and patron of Martley, and patron also of Areley Regis, was born at Betterley, near Ludlow, of which parish his father was then Rector, in October, 1795, and went to sea in 1807, or in the twelfth year of his age. He was a midshipman of H.M. ship *Amethyst* when she was wrecked in Plymouth Sound. He saw a great deal of active service on the coast of Spain, during the Peninsular War, as an officer of the frigate *Iris*. He then went on the *San Domingo* to the North American station, and saw more active service. In March, 1814, he was promoted, after examination, to be Lieutenant, and served in the *Charwell* for a time, and then joined the *Icarus*, of which his brother Thomas was First Lieutenant, on the South American station. Later on he served in the West Indies, where his health broke down, and he was placed on half-pay in 1821, at the age of twenty-six. Being conscious of the defects in his education, owing to his early removal from school, he now read for some months with his brother Henry; then entered as an undergraduate of Trinity College, Cambridge; passed a most creditable examination, and graduated B.A. In 1824 he was appointed First Lieutenant in the *Stag*, which vessel he often commanded during the absence of the Captain, Sir Thomas Troubridge, M.P. for Sandwich. In 1832 he was transferred to the *Excellent* as First Lieutenant to his brother, Captain Sir Thomas Hastings, K.C.B. He was promoted to Commander in 1840. and appointed to the *Edinburgh*. During the Syrian war of that year he showed signal bravery and good judgment, and was complimented in despatches for his "coolness and gallantry." At the bombardment of Acre he commanded the *Edinburgh*, and was severely wounded. He was then promoted to be Captain, and received a gold medal from the Turkish Government, and the war medal from the Admiralty. But, owing to his health having been permanently impaired by wounds and hardships, he had now to relinquish active service. In 1859 he was promoted to be Rear Admiral, and was advanced to the rank of Vice-Admiral in 1865. He married twice, but had no family. He died on the 21st of May, 1869. He was then a churchwarden of St. Stephen's Church, Barbourne, and on the 30th idem, being the Sunday after his funeral, reference was made to him in a sermon that was preached in that church by the Rev. T. G. Curtler, M.A. The preacher chose for his text Ephesians iv. 25—"Speak every man truth with his neighbour,

ADMIRAL DECIMUS HASTINGS.

for we are members one of another"—in order to enforce his argument that "truthfulness of character" peculiarly distinguished the deceased Admiral. He described him as—

A man with a keen and intelligent interest in the affairs of the time, keeping abreast of the questions of the day (whether religious or secular), having strong views of his own, but never colouring a fact to make it favour his own way of thinking, or favour another way less ; a man never forward to express opinion, but expressing it simply and directly when reasonably formed and called for ; one, in spite of some natural impatience (the result, it may be, of the bodily disease which had distressed him long, and to which he at last succumbed), ever striving to understand, and give due weight to the argument of an opponent ; one ready to acknowledge, and glad to see success where himself had foreboded failure—such an one, to the best of my belief, was he who is gone, and such an one is eminently a truthful man.

And now as regards the younger branch of the family of Penyston Hastings, the penultimate owner of Daylesford. The Rev. G. R. Gleig, Chaplain-General, states in his *Memoirs of Warren Hastings*, that his hero's grandfather was the second son of Samuel, last lord of the manor; that the benefice was a poor one; that, like others in his situation, the Rector "preferred to share his indigence with a partner, rather than suffer it alone: so he married, and had two sons, the elder, named Howard, born in 1711, the younger, called Pynaston, in 1715." Mr. Gleig was under a misapprehension; for the name of the lord of the manor referred to was Penyston, he having been named after his mother's family, the Penystons of Coggs, in Oxfordshire; and he gave his name to his second son, whom he presented to the living in 1701. It is recorded in the old Parish Register at Daylesford, which is in a bad condition, that—

> The Revd. Mr. Penyston Hastings Clerke Batchelor of Arts was inducted into ye Parish Church of Daylsford in ye Diocess of Worcester ye 15th day of November 1701 and did ye Sunday next following in ye said parish church read ye morning and evening prayer of ye Church of England and did give his unfeigned assent and consent to ye Book of Common Prayer and did likewise read ye same day in ye time of divine service ye 39 Articles of ye Church of England and gave his unfeigned assent and consent to ye same and likewise did do and perform everything required of him by ye Act of Uniformity made ye 14th of ye Reign of King Charles ye 2nd.

The elder son, Howard, obtained employment in the Customs in London, and prospered, for it appears from a statement in the British Museum of a case by Messrs. Way & Shepherd, Solicitors, for the opinion of Mr. John Madocks, of Lincoln's Inn, Barrister-at-Law, which bears date the 1st of November, 1780, that, on the 12th of June, 1747, Howard Hastings, then of the parish of St. James's, Westminster, executed a will by which he left an annuity of £20 to his father, the Rev. Penyston Hastings, of Daylesford; an annuity of £5, both to his aunt, Honor Hastings, and to his sister, Elizabeth Hastings, such annuities to be increased in each case to £10 after his father's death; and an annuity of £50 to his wife Jane, daughter of the

Rev. Moses Terry, of Lincoln, on condition that she vested all her property in trust during her life for the said Mr. Terry and his wife, and after their decease in trust for his nephew, Warren Hastings. He gave his niece, Anne Hastings, all his right to interest on £2,000 old South Sea Annuities, assigned to him by John Chadwick, of London, in trust, for the payment of an annuity of £60 to Jane Houghton, of the Cross Keys Tavern, Covent Garden ; and he gave his niece an annuity of £20 during the life of the said Jane Houghton, or until such time as she became possessed of the said £2,000 stock. He expressed his desire that she would relinquish her right to interest in two houses in Cheltenham—namely, the Plough Inn and an adjoining house—to her brother, Warren Hastings. He gave William, Duke of Cleveland and Southampton, "the best horse and all the fowling pieces" that he was possessed of; and he bequeathed his diamond ring to Miss Mary Vane. He stated that he was entitled to an annuity of £200 during the life, and also to the sum of £2,000 on the death of the Duke. He gave his nephew, Warren Hastings, an annuity of £40, "which, with the nett produce of the Cheltenham estate," he desired might be applied towards the said nephew's maintenance and education. He gave all his real and personal estate, excepting the £2,000 South Sea Stock, to his executors for the payment of the above-mentioned legacies, and he directed that any surplus that might remain after such payment should be invested in Government securities, until his nephew, Warren Hastings, attained the age of twenty-one, when the accumulation should be paid over to him. Should his nephew not reach that age, then the surplus was to be paid to his niece, Anne. He stated that as the Hon. Henry Vane—nephew of the Duke of Cleveland, who afterwards became Viscount Barnard and Earl of Darlington—had often done him the honour to profess a great friendship for him, and a desire to serve him on account of some service that he, the testator, had done for him and his family, he took the liberty to recommend his nephew, Warren Hastings, to his care and protection. He also said that if he might presume to beg a favour of Lady Grace, it was that she would take his niece, Anne Hastings, under her ladyship's protection. He appointed the Hon. Henry Vane, Henry Vane the younger, Fairmadoc Peniston, of Cornwell, in the county of Gloucester, and Joseph Creswicke, his executors.

Howard Hastings died in 1749, without revoking or altering his will; Joseph Creswicke, then sole surviving executor, died in 1772; William, Duke of Cleveland, died in 1774; and the majority of the beneficiaries in the will—excepting Warren Hastings and his sister—died before 1780. It was alleged that during the period of twenty-three years that he survived the testator, Joseph Creswicke had either received, or by his wilful neglect had failed to receive, the annuity of £200 due to the estate by the Duke of Cleveland, and that his, Joseph Creswicke's, executors had failed to recover the £2,000 due on the Duke's death, from his executor, the Earl of Darlington. It was estimated that the sum which should have been received from the Duke by way of annuity during the period that he survived Howard Hastings amounted, without interest, to £5,000, irrespective of the £2,000 payable on the Duke's death. It was proposed, therefore, to take action on behalf of Warren Hastings, then Governor of Bengal, and Anne his sister, married to John Woodman, in order to make the executors of Joseph Creswicke account for the payment, or non-payment, of these sums. The solicitors anticipated that the learned counsel might ask "why so much time had been suffered to elapse," and they therefore suggested that, "from the important business in which Mr. Hastings and his friends have been engaged on, they had not time to think of it." Mr. Madocks gave it as his opinion that the lapse of time was no bar to the proposed suit, and he explained the course which should be pursued. He pointed out, however, that the "materials" for the case were not stated. "I presume," he added, "it must have been under some deed of agreement between Howard Hastings and the Duke of Cleveland." He enquired if any one had the deed, "as it ought to be stated in the bill to be submitted to the Court."

There is in the British Museum a draft, running to nine large pages, of the first portion of a petition in Chancery to Edward, Lord Thurlow, then Lord Chancellor, in which "Warren Hastings, of Bengal, in the East Indies, Esquire," and "John Woodman, of the parish of St. James, in the City and Liberty of Westminster, in the County of Middlesex, Esquire, and Ann, his Wife, late Ann Hastings," state that Howard Hastings "was in his lifetime, and at the time of his death, seized of, and well entitled unto a very considerable real estate, and also possessed of considerable personal estate, consisting of Household Goods and Furniture, Plate, Linen, China, Books, ready money in the public funds, Bond notes, Mortgage Leases for years, and other personal Estate." The particulars of his will were then recapitulated, and the petitioners proceeded to say that some time after the testator's death the Hon. Henry Vane, and Henry Vane the younger, and Fairmadoc Peniston renounced the probate and proof of the will which was then proved by Joseph Creswicke. The latter portion of the petition has not been preserved. Here, apparently, the matter rested. Presumably the deed of agreement could not be found, and nothing is now known of the nature of the service which was rendered by Howard Hastings to William, Duke of Cleveland (grandson of King Charles the Second by Barbara Villiers), Hereditary Chief Butler of England, Receiver-General of Profits of the Seals in the King's Bench and Common Pleas, and Comptroller of the Seal and Green Wax Office. There was obviously a divergence of opinion between him and the Duke as to the latter's liability in honour and in law to pay the annuity; and as his bequests appear to have been dependent to a great extent on the receipt by his executors of that annuity, much disappointment must have been caused to Warren Hastings and the other prospective beneficiaries under his will.

CHAPTER II

BIRTH AND EDUCATION

ACCORDING to Mr. Gleig, the second son and namesake of the Rev. Penyston Hastings was married in 1730, when "he could not have been more than fifteen years of age," to Hester Warren, daughter of Mr. Warren, proprietor of a small estate, called Stubhill, near Twining, in Gloucestershire, and "the consequences of a connection formed so improvidently were such as never fail to ensue in such cases. The young couple soon began to experience the extremity of remorse and destitution. How they managed to subsist at all I am quite at a loss to conceive. . . . Yet they did live together for two years, during which his wife presented her boy-husband with two children. . . . Warren Hastings was born on the 6th December, 1732, and his mother died a few days afterwards. . . . His father seems to have quitted Churchill almost immediately on the decease of his wife." Lord Macaulay took it for granted that Mr. Gleig had authority for his assertions; and, in his famous essay, he stated that young Pynaston was an "idle, worthless boy." But though, as Warren Hastings remarked many years afterwards to E. B. Impey, "there was not much in my father's history that would be worth repeating," Penyston Hastings was not a "boy" in 1730. The reduced facsimile which I give overleaf of the entry in the register of Churchill of the baptism of the future Governor-General shows that, at the date mentioned therein, namely 1732, the father of the infant was recognised by the minister and churchwardens of the parish as a man in holy orders.

Mr. Warren Hastings Woodman-Hastings, grandson of Warren Hastings' sister, who inherited, and now resides on the Stubhill estate, informs me that his great-grandfather, the so-called "boy," was the eldest of four children, and was born at

Cornwell, in Gloucestershire, in 1704; being followed by Priscilla, born at Cornwell, in 1706; Howard, born at Daylesford, in 1711; and Samuel, born at Daylesford, in 1715. The Rector named his eldest son after himself, and educated him for the Church. Eventually he sent the youth to Balliol College, Oxford, where he matriculated. The following is the entry in the admission book of the College: "March 26th, 1724. *Penistone Hastings filius unicus Penistoni Hastings Clericus de Daleford in agro Worcestien: admissus est communarius.*" As the Rector had three sons at this date, it is supposed that *unicus* in the entry was a clerical error, as *primus* would have been

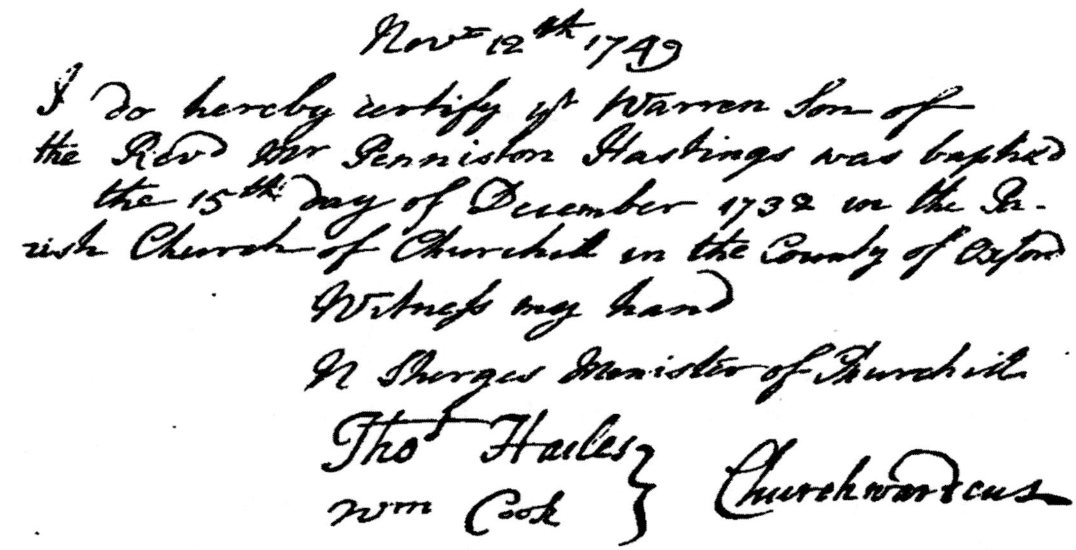
Novr 12th 1749
I do hereby certify yt Warren Son of
the Revd Mr Penniston Hastings was baptized
the 15th day of December 1732 in the Pa-
rish Church of Churchill in the County of Oxford
Witness my hand
N Burges Minister of Churchill.
Thos Hailes } Churchwardens
Wm Cook }

more correct. The presentations for degrees are carefully entered in the College bursar's books, and the lists for 1724 and for several succeeding years have been searched in vain for proof that Penyston graduated at Balliol. Nor is it known when, or where he was ordained; but it is evident that, in 1730, he was a good deal older than "fifteen." In Foster's *Alumni Oxoniensis* he is described as "s. Penyston, of Daylesford, co. Worcester cler:" and it is stated that he "matriculated at Balliol on the 28th March, 1724, aged sixteen." Hester, his wife, was not a young girl, as she is described by Gleig and others, when she married; for, according to her great-grandson, she was baptized in the parish church of Twining in 1705, and she was therefore five-and-twenty at the date of her marriage.

Some light is thrown on the position of the Warren family by the draft of a curious petition to Lord King, Baron of Orkham, Lord High Chancellor of England, dated the 3rd of November, 1733, and bearing the signature of W. Lane, which is in the British Museum. In this document, which was amended by order of the Court, on the 7th of December, 1734, John Warren, of Tyning, in the county of Gloucester, as "their Uncle and next friend," moved the Court on behalf of "your Orator and Oratrix," Warren Hastings and Ann Hastings, to institute an inquiry into the disposal of moneys that belonged to their mother, Hester Hastings. It sets forth that Hester Hastings was entitled before her marriage to £220, "which was coming or belonging to her out of a copyhold estate at Cheltenham," and "likewise to a considerable sum of money from the estate of John Fletcher, late of Exchange Alley, London," by virtue of his will, dated the 23rd September, 1721; that by an agreement entered into before her marriage with Penyston Hastings, of Church Hill, in the county of Oxford, clerk, dated 29th July, 1730, the latter covenanted that all moneys which she was then in possession of, or might hereafter become entitled to, by will or otherwise, should be "conveyed or lodged" in the hands of Thomas Warren, her brother, and Ann Warren, her mother, for the use of her, the said Hester, for life; and that should the said Penyston survive her, then that he should have the interest of her fortune during his life, and, after his decease, that such fortune should be divided equally between their issue. It then alleges that the said Penyston Hastings, father of the "Orator and Oratrix," having contracted many debts with his uncle, Harry Gardner, his father, Penyston Hastings, of "Darlsford," in the county of Worcester, clerk, and "diverse others," had "lately withdrawn himself from his habitation to some distant place, and left your Orator and Oratrix wholly unregarded and unprovided for by him." It accuses him of having "combined and confederated" with his uncle, father, Thomas Warren, and Ann Warren, to "defeat the said marriage agreement," by assigning away the moneys accruing from his wife's fortune towards the payment of his own debts; and it declares that the creditors were consequently interrupting, diverting, and misapplying the money that was in trust ; and were thereby defeating the purposes of the trust "contrary to equity and good conscience." It prays, therefore, that Penyston Hastings the elder, Penyston Hastings the younger, and Harry Gardner may be restrained from receiving any part of the income derivable from Hester's estate, and that "some provision and allowance might be made for your Orator's and Oratrix's maintenance." In conclusion, it begs that the case may be heard "before this High and Honourable Court."

THE BIRTHPLACE OF WARREN HASTINGS.

I am unable to say whether the petition was ever presented ; but, as Warren Hastings preserved the draft until the eighty-fifth year after it was prepared, probably he attached importance to the statements that it embodies.

It may be supposed by the reader of Gleig and some other writers that Warren Hastings was born in a hovel, when his father was in the "extreme of destitution"; but it will be seen from my sketch that his birthplace is a substantially built, fairly commodious, and well-situated house, which no curate now-a-days should mind occupying. A tablet has been placed in front of the house by Earl Ducie, who has also had a memorial erected on a green near the house, in honour of "William Smith, Father of British Geology," who was born at Churchill in 1769, and died at Northampton in 1839.

Three years previous to the birth of Warren Hastings, his great-grandfather, Samuel Hastings, was compelled by pecuniary embarrassment to sell the Daylesford estate to Mr. Jacob Knight, a London merchant. With this gentleman the Rector (grandfather of Warren) subsequently engaged in litigation over the tithes, which proved so costly that he was constrained to move to Churchill, and reside there. He did not, however,

resign his small benefice, which he held for fifty-one years. He then died, in 1752, and was buried in Daylesford churchyard.

Warren Hastings remained at Churchill, under the care of his grandfather, until his eighth year. The locality still answers to the description which William of Malmesbury gave of it some seven hundred years ago, as "a land rich in corn, productive of fruits in some parts by the sole favour of nature, in others by the art of cultivation, enticing even the loss to industry by the prospect of a hundredfold return." Close to Churchill is a rivulet. In after-life Hastings said to a friend :—

To lie beside the margin of that stream and muse was one of my favourite recreations ; and there, one bright summer's day, when I was

scarcely seven years old, I well remember that I first formed the determination to purchase back Daylesford. I was then literally dependent upon those whose condition scarcely raised them above the pressure of absolute want; yet somehow or another, the child's dream, as it did not appear unreasonable at the moment so in after years it never faded away. God knows there were periods in my career, when to accomplish that, or any other object of honourable ambition, seemed to be impossible, but I have lived to accomplish it. And though, perhaps, few public men have had more right than I to complain of the world's usage, I can never express sufficient gratitude to the kind Providence which permits me to pass the evening of a long and I **trust not a useless life, amid scenes that are endeared to me by so many personal as well as traditional associations."**

Westminster School.

Green"

The boy was removed by his uncle Howard (who, as has been said, obtained employment in the Customs in London) from the village school at Churchill when he was eight years old; was placed for two years at a preparatory school at Newington, near London, where he was well taught, but ill fed;

and at ten was transferred to Westminster School, where he remained upwards of six years. This famous School was founded by Queen Elizabeth in 1560, and established in old monastic buildings, which it still occupies, to the south of Westminster Abbey, which has always stood in the relation of chapel to the School. Additions have been made and some improvements effected in the present century ; but, in most respects,

THE GREAT SCHOOLROOM, WESTMINSTER, BEFORE RECENT ALTERATIONS.

the School still wears an aspect closely resembling what it did when the delicate little orphan from Churchill was consigned to the tender mercies of his schoolmates, and subjected to the severe discipline, rough accommodation, and short commons that were the lot of a boarder. Shortly before he joined the School the venerable granary of the "monks of old," which had been used since 1560 as the school dormitory, was pulled down, and on its site, to the right of the gateway, a new dormitory was built, which contained one spacious room in which the lads commanded few of the necessaries of comfort, and opportunities for privacy that render the cubicles of modern schools so agreeable. The old gateway is unchanged, except that it is now dwarfed, when viewed from Little Dean's Yard, by the majestic Victoria Tower of the Houses of Parliament in the background, and that a few more names of old boys have been carved on its stones. The walls, windows, and roof of the Great Schoolroom remain substantially as they were a century since; but, in the interior of the room, the lower part of the wall has been wainscoted with unpolished and carved oak. The "shell," or apse, at the north end of the room has also been wainscoted, and provided with a daïs, on which the canopied chair of the Head Master, and, on each side of it, eleven chairs for the Monitorial Council are arranged. The arms of the Founder and of twelve Head Masters adorn the curved wall of the shell; and the arms of old boys who achieved distinction in after life, with their names, and the dates of birth and death, are painted on the wainscot of the shell and around the room. The Warren Hastings shield, showing the "manche," or sleeve,[1] which he adopted as an heraldic emblem, is close to the Head Master's

[1] Miss A. C. Hastings, of Martley, a member of the family, has informed me that "William, son of Samuel, must have had the mermaid crest," which he transmitted to his descendants now living. "It is a fact that when Warren Hastings became Governor-General he had no crest, so he ordered search to be made as to what crest he ought to take. The Huntingdon family are descended from an heiress of the Earls of Pembroke—Margaret de Hastings, who took the Hastings coat-of-arms with her into the Huntingdon family, but not the crest. The Huntingdon crest is a bull's head. Warren Hastings adopted that with the Hastings' manche." In a sheet of facsimiles of the coats-of-arms carried by the nobility and gentry at the battle of Hastings in 1066, there is depicted a manche, or sleeve, painted black, instead of red as the Huntingdon and Hastings' families have it.

chair, and is near the shields of Thomas Pelham, Duke of Newcastle; William Cowper; Charles Montagu, Earl of Halifax; Charles Wentworth, Marquis of Rockingham; John Locke; William Murray, Earl of Mansfield; John Dryden; William Pulteney, Earl of Bath; Francis Attenbury; Henry Fitzmaurice, Marquis of Lansdowne; Sir Christopher Wren, etc. Immediately in front of the Head Master's chair is an ancient oak table, blackened by time, and much notched, containing a drawer, in which repose now, as was the case in Hastings' time, neatly made birches wherewith to convey striking arguments to disorderly, or indolent lads. An iron bar, from which once hung a curtain that divided the upper from the lower school, still

The Rod Drawer

remains, and the chief cook of the School continues every Shrove Tuesday to hurl a pancake over it, in conformity with the custom of the "Pancake Grease," the origin of which has yet to be discovered.[1] The College Hall is at an inconvenient

[1] The following paragraph appeared in the *Daily Telegraph*, 27th February, 1895:—

"'Tossing the pancake' is a custom too ancient and too popular at Westminster School to be forgotten on Shrove Tuesday, and the traditions of the institution were accordingly duly observed. Shortly after twelve o'clock a small procession, headed by one of the Abbey vergers carrying a silver wand, and in which the cook, arrayed in white, holding in his right hand a large frying-pan containing a newly made pancake, was a prominent figure, left the kitchen, and advanced to the door of the great school. Knocking thrice, according to time-honoured custom, the inquiry was made, 'Who demands admittance?' when the reply was given, 'The cook.' The bar which separates the upper from the lower school had in the meantime been drawn out, and all the boys were congregated behind the barrier.

distance from the Schoolroom, and is reached through the cloisters of the Abbey. It was built nearly five hundred years ago, contiguous to the Jerusalem Chamber of the Abbey; and it has undergone no alteration since Hastings dined and supped at its massive oak tables, which are said to have been made

from the timbers of wrecked vessels of the Spanish Armada.

At the age of fourteen and a half Hastings competed for a King's

---

On admission the cook and his attendants advanced midway up the hall, and the former, whirling the frying-pan three times round his head, dexterously hurled the pancake amid the crowd of expectant youngsters, who scrambled for its possession. Master Guy Simonds, son of Captain Simonds, chief officer of the Metropolitan Fire Brigade, had the good fortune to secure the largest piece, and immediately ran off to the Deanery to claim the usual reward of a guinea. The cook became entitled to a similar sum."

Scholarship in the School, and he came out, on the 27th May, 1747, at the top of the following list of successful candidates, which forms one of the curiosities in the School Library :—

ELECTI IN SCHOLAM WESTMONASTERIJ.

	Nomen.	*Parentela.*	*Comitatus.*	*Oppidum.*	*Ætas.*
1.	Warrenus Hastings	Filius Pennistoni	Oxoniensis	Churchilliæ	14
2.	Bartholomæus Wall	,, Jacobi	Essexiæ	Staffordiæ	14
3.	Henricus Toundrow	,, Thomæ	Staffordiæ	Burtoniæ	14
4.	Elijah Impey	,, Elijæ	Middlesexiæ	Hammersmithiæ	14
5.	Justius Alt	,, Justii	Middlesexiæ	Londini	14
6.	Robertus Andrews	,, Roberti	Middlesexiæ	Londini	14
7.	Jacobus Bensley	,, Jacobi	Suffolciæ	Hennamiæ	14
8.	Daniel Shipton	,, Johannes	Hertfordiæ	Watfordiæ	15
9.	Johannes Hales	,, Thomæ	Cantii	Bishopsbourniæ	14
10.	Nathaniel Hume	,, Jacobi	Oxoniensis	Oxonii	14
11.	Andreas Burnaby	,, Andreæ	Leicestriæ	Ashfordiæ	14
12.	Georgius Smalridge	,, Philippi	Castrensis	Christlestoniæ	14
13.	Thomas Hebbes	,, Johannis	Middlesexiæ	Londini	14
14.	Guilielmus Wasey	,, Gulielmi	Middlesexiæ	Londini	13
15.	Philippus Williams	,, Lewellini	Glamorganiæ	Diffliniæ	14

It is noticeable that in the above list only five of the fifteen lads whose names are given belonged to the county of Middlesex. Two came from Oxfordshire, and one each from Essex, Staffordshire, Suffolk, Hertfordshire, Kent, Leicestershire, Chester, and Glamorganshire.

It appears from the register that among Hastings' many schoolfellows at Westminster were the following notable persons: the above-mentioned Elijah Impey, Chief Justice of Calcutta; the poets Charles Churchill and William Cowper; Henry Fitzmaurice, Lord Shelburne, afterwards Marquis of Lansdowne; George Hobart, third Earl of Buckinghamshire; F. Vane, M.P. for Durham; Hamilton Boyle, Earl of Cork and Orrery, and High Steward of the University of Oxford; John Warren, Archdeacon of Worcester; A. Burnaby, Archdeacon of Leicester; Thomas MacGwire, Attorney-General of North Carolina; Ralph Barnes, Archdeacon of Totnes; Philip Duval, Canon of Windsor; Paston Gould, Colonel of the 20th Foot; John Marsden, Prebendary of York; John Hinchcliffe, for a few months Head Master of Westminster School, then Master of Trinity College, Cambridge, and finally Bishop of Peterborough; Samuel Smith, Head Master of Westminster School and Prebendary of Westminster Abbey; George Colman, dramatist, translator, and joint proprietor of Covent Garden Theatre; Nathaniel Hume, Canon of Sarum; William Digby, Dean first of Worcester, and then of Durham; etc.

The most noteworthy memorial of Hastings at the School is a silver cup, or *poculum*, of large size and great weight, called the "Warren Hastings Cup," which was presented in 1777, for the use of the King's Scholars of St. Peter's College, by Hastings and other "old boys" then residing in India, in token of their undiminished attachment for their School. On one

THE WARREN HASTINGS CUP.

side of the cup the arms of the School (without the motto, "*Dat Deus incrementum*") are engraved, and the other side bears the following inscription: "*Alumnis Regiis Scholæ Westmon: ipsi plerique Alumni, D.D.D.*," beneath which are the names: Warren Hastings, Elijah Impey, Geo. Templer, Edw. Hay, Joh. Wombwell, Gul. Markham, Joh. White, Ch. Benezet, Pet. Touchet, Rob. Holt, Joh. Scawen, Joh. Williams, Alex. Macleod, R. S. Perreau, Edw. Bengough, G. C. Meyer, Car. Cooper, Geo. Arbuthnot, F. Pierard, Car. Mouatt, Gul. Franklin, and Gual. Hawkes.

In 1801 Sir Elijah Impey attended the election dinner in the College Hall, and the Rev. Mr. Wingfield, under-master, afterwards Prebendary of Worcester, composed some Latin verses in honour of the distinguished guest, which were recited by Edward Goodenough, captain of the School, afterwards Dean of Wells. The following is E. B. Impey's translation of the lines :—

Welcome ! old brother Westminster, to these
Time-honoured walls : our Lars and Lemures
Hail thee a pilgrim worthy of their shrine,
True to thy pledge : for lo ! yon pledge is thine.
Wafted on Hooghly's tide, from far Bengal,
Yon tankard tells of old St. Peter's Hall ;
Tells of thy plighted faith, and blameless truth
In age redeem'd the promise of thy youth :
That mimic tusk, from elephantine bone,
Chang'd to a silvery lustre not its own,
Those thinking heads on solemn draughts intent,
Their lithe probosces into handles bent
Invite thy grasp. Then toast Elisa's name,
Drink deep : A "Floreat" to our Royal dame !
Yet thou no more gratuitous canst share
The rich carouse : for lo ! 'tis reckon'd there,
Whate'er of glory in the gift may be
Graces the giver, and reverts to thee.

Hastings worked hard, and gave such good promise by his attainments in classics of reflecting honour on the School, that, when his uncle died, and his guardian and distant kinsman, Mr. Chiswick, a Director of the East India Company, resolved to send him to India, and with that object decided on removing him, at the age of sixteen, from school, the Head Master, Dr. Nicholls, interposed. Hastings commenced his autobiography when he was an old man, but wearied of the task after filling four pages. Those pages were found among his papers after his death, and have been shown to me by Miss Marian Winter, of Worton House, Steeple Aston, Oxfordshire, grand-niece of Mrs. Hastings. In the earlier part of this fragment Hastings said :—

My uncle Howard, to whom I am indebted for my education, and for every other care of me which good principle unimpelled by natural affection could dictate, died in the year 1748. I was soon after taken from school. I hazard the imputation of vanity in yielding to the sense of gratitude and justice which is due to the memory of my ever revered master, Dr. Nicholls, to relate that, when I waited upon him to inform him of that purpose of my guardian, he, in the most delicate manner, remonstrated against it, adding that, if the necessity of my circumstances was the only course requiring my removal, and I should continue at school, he would undertake that it should be no expense to me. I have been told that many similar instances of his bounty were carried into effect. I could not profit by it.

Mr. Chiswick was a practical man as became a man of business. He may have cherished admiration, out of office hours, for the ancient classics in the abstract; but his experience warned him that a knowledge of book-keeping and proficiency in penmanship would be more advantageous to a young "writer" in the Company's service than familiarity with Homer, and sympathy with Horace. The learned Doctor, on the other hand, entertained a profound respect for the ladder by which he had mounted to eminence in the educational world; and it pained him to part with a remarkably clever pupil. Had Mr. Chiswick permitted his ward to accept the Doctor's generous offer, Warren Hastings may have proceeded to Oxford, or Cambridge, and have eventually returned as a master to Westminster. But Mr. Chiswick was not to be deterred from his purpose, and Hastings left the School in obedience to his guardian's wishes.

Mr. Chiswick placed young Hastings with Mr. Thomas Smith, writing master of Christ's Hospital—or the Blue Coat School—for private instruction in accounts and caligraphy; and, in due course, Hastings obtained a certificate from that gentleman, of which the following is a reduced facsimile:—

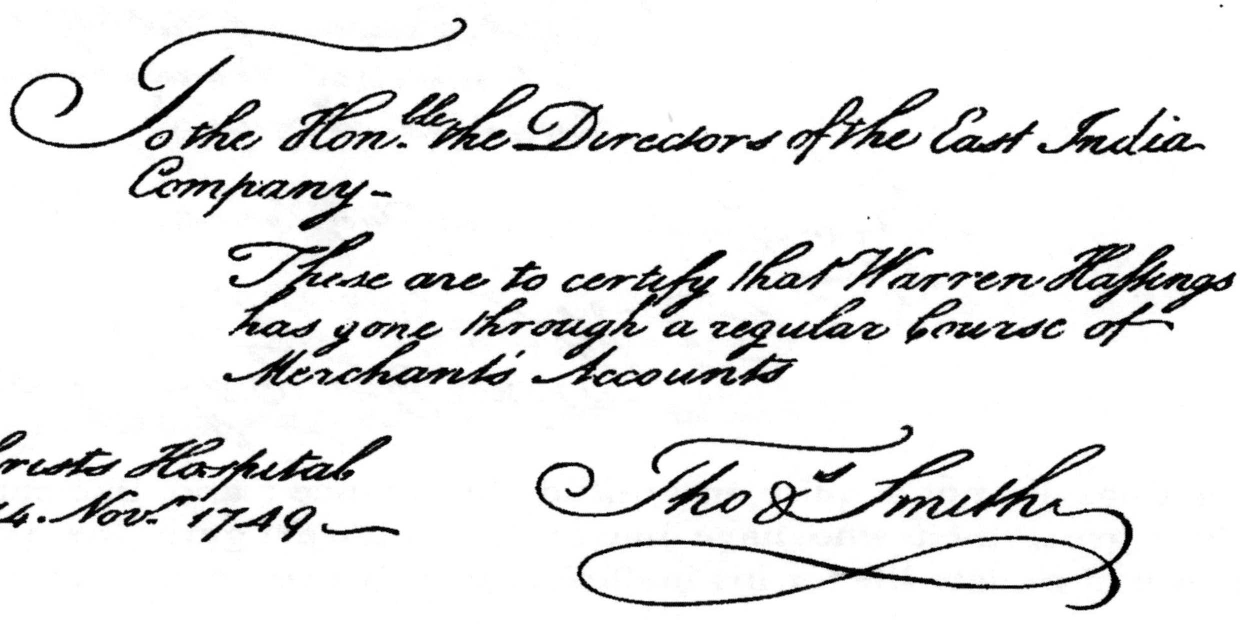
To the Hon.ble the Directors of the East India Company—

These are to certify that Warren Hastings has gone through a regular Course of Merchants' Accounts

Christs Hospital
14. Nov.r 1749—

Tho.s Smith

It will be seen that Mr. Smith testified that his pupil had "gone through a regular course of Merchants' Accounts." But

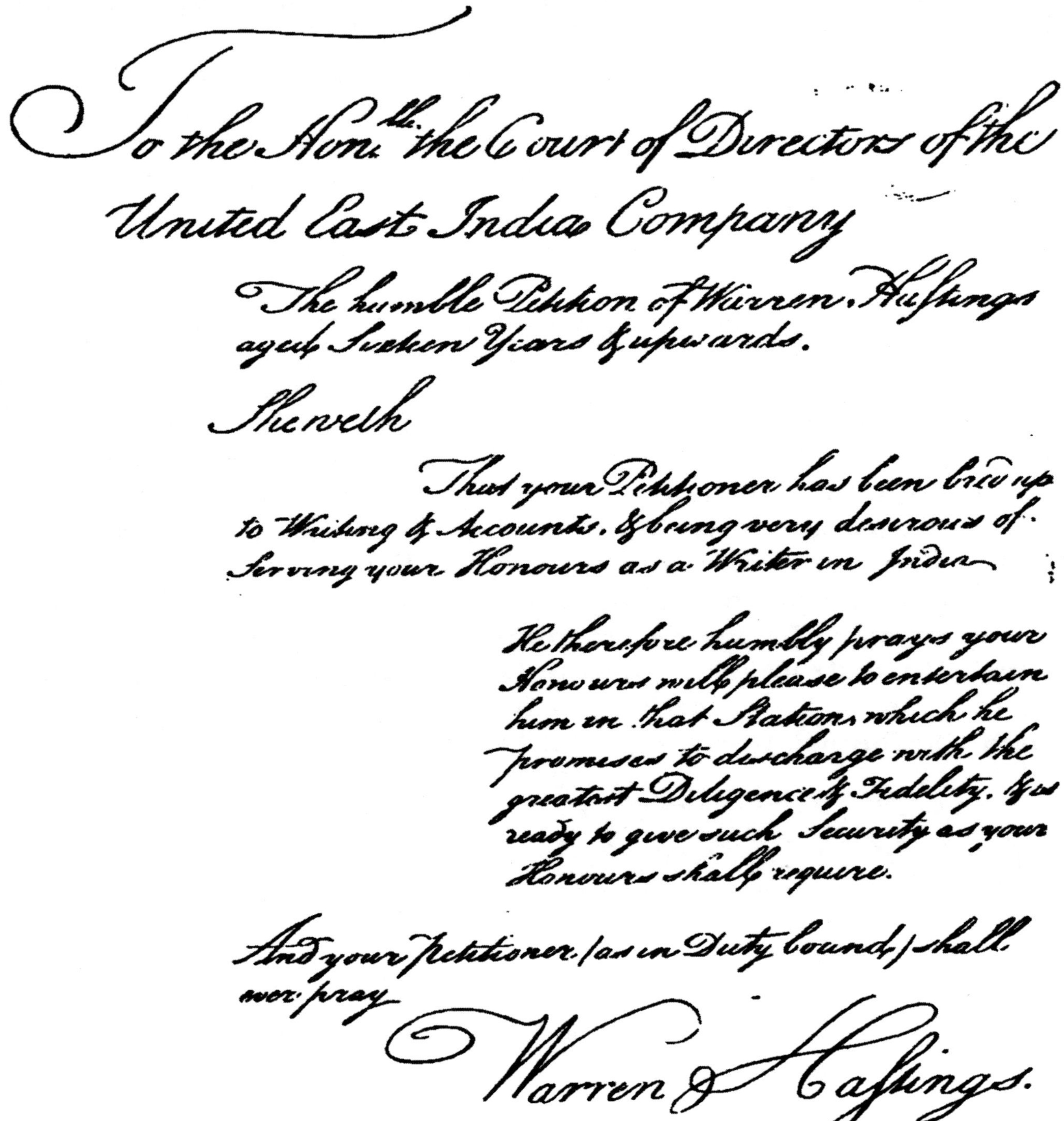
To the Hon.ble the Court of Directors of the United East India Company

The humble Petition of Warren Hastings aged Sixteen Years & upwards.

Sheweth

That your Petitioner has been bred up to Writing & Accounts, & being very desirous of Serving your Honours as a Writer in India

He therefore humbly prays your Honours will please to entertain him in that Station, which he promises to discharge with the greatest Diligence & Fidelity, & is ready to give such Security as your Honours shall require.

And your Petitioner (as in Duty bound) shall ever pray

Warren Hastings.

Hastings did not acquire an aptitude for finance ; and, like some other great men who have had a soul above figures, he paid dearly in private life for his inefficiency in this respect. He was, however, indebted to the precepts and example of Mr. Smith for the excellence of his handwriting. In after-life he conducted a very large official and private correspondence; and the many specimens of his letters, and of the duplicates that he made, which are still in existence, show that it was habitual with him to dispense with an amanuensis, and to write so that he who ran might read.

Hastings now made an application to the Court of Directors of the East India Company for employment. It will be observed, from the reduced facsimile of his "humble petition" which is given on the opposite page, that he stated that he was "aged sixteen and upwards"; represented that he had "been bred up to Writing and Accounts"; and that, "being very desirous of serving" their "Honours as a Writer in India," he prayed them "to entertain him in that Station," which he promised "to discharge with the greatest Diligence and Fidelity." He also said that he was ready to give such security as their Honours might require. The writership was obtained, and Hastings embarked without delay for Calcutta, where he arrived in January, 1750, a few days after completing his seventeenth year.

CHAPTER III

HIS INDIAN CAREER AND RETURN HOME

IT would be foreign to my present purpose to sketch the official career of Warren Hastings, which has been discussed so amply from time to time by Mill, Gleig, Macaulay, Stephen, Strachey,[1]

[1] On the 25th February, 1892, *The Times* reviewed Sir John Strachey's monograph, "Hastings and the Rohilla War" (Oxford, at the Clarendon Press), and remarked: "The average Englishman's knowledge of Indian history is for the most part derived from a single source—Macaulay's two celebrated Essays on Clive and Warren Hastings. . . . Unfortunately, Macaulay, though his knowledge of some Indian topics was direct and profound, relied mainly for his historical facts on Mill's History of British India, a work which, as Sir Henry Maine said of English classical literature towards the end of last century, 'is saturated with party politics.' Of James Mill, Sir James Stephen has written that 'his want of accuracy was nothing to his bad faith.' Such was one of Macaulay's authorities; another source of his inspiration was the glowing eloquence of Burke, whose 'sleepless humanity,' as Lord Rosebery finely calls it, was not controlled by a too scrupulous accuracy, nor inconsistent with the rancour and scurrility of a fish-wife. From these sophisticated palettes Macaulay borrowed the colours with which he drew his well-known picture of Warren Hastings. Sir James Stephen has shown, in his masterly work on *The Story of Nuncomar and the Impeachment of Warren Hastings*, how false was the colour, and how distorted the perspective of one portion of Macaulay's picture. . . . Sir John Strachey has now done signal service to the memory of a great Englishman, and to the intelligent and dispassionate study of Indian history by setting forth in detail the grounds of the conclusions here stated, and examining the whole question afresh. . . . To say that he has vindicated Warren Hastings against the invectives of Burke and the other managers of the famous Impeachment, against the calumnies and inaccuracies of Mill, against the involuntary misrepresentations of Macaulay, is to say little. He has re-written an important chapter of Indian history, and exemplified the true spirit in which that history should be written. But it is all in vain, we fear. History has little chance against rhetoric, and Indian history has never been made interesting to English readers except by rhetoric. In spite of all that Sir James Stephen did some years ago, and all that Sir John Strachey has done now, Macaulay will still hold the field, and his

Trotter, Lyall, Keene, Busteed, and Malleson.[1] I will, therefore, only say that, after remaining two years in Calcutta, he was posted to Cossimbazar, and was employed "in making bargains for stuffs with native brokers." In 1756 he married the widow of Captain Campbell, of the Company's service, who bore him two children—a daughter, who lived but nineteen days, and a son, who was sent home for education, but died very young. Mrs. Hastings died at Cossimbazar, when her husband was Resident at that station, shortly after the birth of her son. There was some resemblance between her fate and that of her husband's mother; but very little is known about the period of his life with which she was associated. He was summoned to Calcutta in 1761, in his twenty-ninth year, as a Member of Council; and in 1764 he returned to England, after an absence of fourteen years, having realized a "very moderate fortune," the greater part of which he left in Bengal, in view to obtaining a high rate of interest. He was generous to such relatives as he found in England—too generous, as it proved, for his own comfort, since his investments in Bengal proved so ill-advised that he lost all the savings that he had left behind him. He found that the widow of his uncle Howard was in poor circumstances, and he purchased an annuity of £200 a year for her.

---

picture of Warren Hastings will still be accepted as authentic by that body of readers who care less for truth than for effect."

[1] On the 19th January, 1895, the *Saturday Review* acknowledged in very appreciative terms the "public service" which Colonel G. B. Malleson, C.S.I., had rendered by writing his *Life of Warren Hastings*, and remarked: "The time has, in truth, come for a Life of Warren Hastings which shall fairly represent the materials now existing for it. Sir James Stephen's examination of the great judicial episode in Hastings' Indian career, Sir John Strachey's scrutiny of the most striking of his military undertakings, Dr. Busteed's researches into the social aspects of Calcutta life in the last century, Sir Charles Lawson's monograph on the years at Daylesford, and Mr. Forrest's three volumes of selections from the Bengal records from 1772 to 1785, have supplied a new body of evidence which required to be sifted by a master's hand. Colonel Malleson has now, with patient labour, accomplished for Warren Hastings' life as a whole what Sir James Stephen and Sir John Strachey effected for particular incidents of his public career. . . . This book forms a fitting continuation of many acts of redress which Colonel Malleson has secured for names worthy of honour, but done to death by slanderous tongues."

His sister had married Mr. Woodman, who subsequently became steward to the Duke of Bridgewater; and to her he made a present of £1,000.

He made the acquaintance of Dr. Johnson about this time, and the lexicographer formed a high opinion of him. In a letter which he wrote to him after his return to Calcutta, dated the 30th March, 1774, Dr. Johnson remarked:—

> Though I have had but little personal knowledge of you, I have had enough to make me wish for more; and though it is now a long time since I was honoured by your visit, I had too much pleasure from it to forget it. By those whom we delight to remember we are unwilling to be forgotten; and therefore I cannot omit this opportunity of reviving myself in your memory by a letter which you will receive from the hands of my friend Mr. Chambers, a man whose purity of manners and vigour of mind are sufficient to make everything welcome that he brings. . . . That he is going to live where you govern, may justly alleviate the regret of parting; and the hope of seeing both him and you again, which I am not willing to mingle with doubt, must at present comfort as it can, Sir,
>
> Your most humble servant,
>
> SAM. JOHNSON.

On the 20th December of the same year, Dr. Johnson forwarded to the Governor-General a copy of his *Journey to the Western Islands of Scotland*, and said:—

> Being informed that by the departure of a ship there is now an opportunity of writing to Bengal, I am unwilling to slip out of your memory by my own negligence, and therefore take the liberty of reminding you of my existence by sending you a book which is not yet made publick. I have lately visited a region less remote, and less illustrious than India, which afforded some occasions for speculation. What occurred to me I have put into the volume, of which I beg your acceptance. Men in your station seldom have presents totally disinterested. My book is received, let me now make my request. There is, Sir, somewhere within your government, a young adventurer, one Chauncy Lawrence, whose father is one of my oldest friends. Be pleased to show the young man what countenance is fit, whether he wants to be restrained by your authority, or encouraged by your favour. His father is now President of the College of Physicians, a man venerable for his knowledge, and more venerable for his virtue. I wish you a prosperous government, a safe return, and a long enjoyment of plenty and tranquillity.

In July, 1776, Dr. Johnson remarked in a letter to Mr. Fowke that, "I live in a reciprocation of civilities with Mr. Hastings."

Warren Hastings Esq.r
GOVERNOR GENERAL of BENGAL, &c. &c.

In the opinion of Mr. Boswell,[1] Hastings was "a man whose regard reflects dignity even upon Johnson—a man the extent of whose abilities was equal to that of his power; and who, by those who are fortunate enough to know him in private life, is admired for his literature and taste, and beloved for the candour, moderation, and mildness of his character." This was written in 1791, while Hastings was still on his trial at Westminster Hall; and it was prompted by the compliance of Hastings with Boswell's request for permission to see and publish three letters which Hastings treasured as mementoes of Johnson. Hastings forwarded the letters to Boswell on the 2nd December, 1790, from his house in Park Lane; and, in a covering letter, he explained that "my veneration for your great and good friend, Dr. Johnson, and the pride, or I hope something of a better sentiment, which I indulged in possessing such memorials of his good-will towards me," had induced him to bind these three letters, "which I believe were all that I ever received from Dr. Johnson," in "a parcel containing other papers, and labelled with the titles appertaining to them."

After four years of inactivity at home, he was compelled by pecuniary embarrassment to solicit re-employment in India. The Directors knew his worth, and appointed him second in Council in the Government of Mr. Du Pré, at Madras, at the age of thirty-seven. They informed the Madras Government that—

> Mr. Warren Hastings, a gentleman who has served us many years upon the Bengal establishment with great ability and unblemished character, offering himself to be employed again in our service, we have, from a consideration of his just merits and general knowledge of the Company's affairs, been induced to appoint him one of the members of our Council at your Presidency, and to station him next below Mr. Du Pré. He will proceed in one of the Coast and Bay ships, by which you will be advertised of such further directions as may be necessary concerning his appointment.

Outfit allowances were not yet granted to Governors and Councillors; and Hastings, it is said, "was forced to borrow money for his outfit, but he did not withdraw any portion of the

[1] *The Life of Samuel Johnson, LL.D.*, by James Boswell, edited by Percy Fitzgerald, M.A., vol. ii. London: Swan Sonnenschein, Lowrey & Co., 1888.

sum which he had appropriated to the relief of his distressed relations."

Hastings secured a cabin on board the *Duke of Grafton*. The following list of her passengers is preserved in the India Office :—

For Madras: Warren Hastings, Esq. (Deputy Governor of Fort St. George), the Rev. A. Salmon, Lieutenant John Searle, John Charles Maclin (Writer), William Syce (Cadet), Acton Wollaston (Cadet), Travers Danver Taylor (Cadet), Hugh Dilkes Harding (Cadet), Clement Higginbotham (Cadet), Ralph Winstanley Wood (Cadet).

For Bengal: Mr. and Mrs. Imhoff and child, Mrs. and Miss Thompson, Miss Pearce, John Moulton (Free Mariner), Daniel Redmond, Thomas de B. McLaughlin, Philip de Lisle, Benjamin Whitehead (Cadet), Thomas Reynolds (Cadet), Hugh Munro (Cadet), John Jefferson (Cadet), James Denty (Cadet), George Douglas (Cadet), George Anderson Eastland (Cadet), William Nassau Green (Cadet), the Honourable Frederick Stewart (Writer), Adam Callender, Esq. (Captain of Infantry), Archibald Ramsay, Charles Barber, Thomas Hatch, Philip Coates, Richard Long, John Hicks (Ship's Carpenter), Hugh Burridge, and Henry Griffith (servants); and Sukey, Maria, and Rose (native maid servants).

Hastings entered upon the duties which devolved upon him at Fort St. George with characteristic ardour. He was chiefly engaged as export warehouse-keeper, *ex officio*, and the experience that he had gained in a similar capacity in Bengal enabled him to check abuses, and to promote the best interests of the Company's trade. His success commended him to the authorities at the India House; and, two and a half years after he arrived in Madras, he was offered, and accepted, the Governorship of Bengal. He was ambitious of occupying a more influential and lucrative sphere of action than presented itself at Fort St. George; but he did not leave Madras without regret, for "I never did business," he wrote, "with men of as much candour, or in general of better disposition" than his colleagues in the local Council. He had lived "with much comfort" among "the people of this settlement"; and "I am flattered with the assurance that I shall leave more who are sorry than who are glad that they lose me." His relations with Mr. Du Pré, the Governor of Madras, had been of a most friendly nature, and he assured a Director of the East India Company that he was happy in leaving that gentleman in the chair. "I hope," he kindly added, "the Directors will encourage him to continue in it. His abilities are very great, and if equalled by any quality it is by his unwearied assiduity and application."

In a letter to Sir George Colebrooke, which he wrote on the voyage from Madras to Calcutta, he remarked that "the uncommon abilities and unwearied application of Mr. Du Pré left me little room to exert myself beyond the limits of my own particular department":—

> As to the rest of my conduct, I must content myself with the humble merit of having made it my study to give every support in my power to the measures pursued by the President, and to contribute my share to the good understanding which I had the happiness to see reign at the Board during the whole time that I was a member of it. I cannot wish myself a better fortune than to be seconded by men equally disposed to support and co-operate with me, and equally satisfied with the rectitude and propriety of my conduct.

His last official act in Madras was to write, on the 31st January, 1772, to Mr. Du Pré to formally advise him of his "appointment to the Government of the Company's affairs in Bengal," and his approaching departure "to my allotted station." He then said:—

> Having performed the duties of respect in that address, permit me, Sir, now to indulge the sentiments of my heart, in expressing the personal concern which I feel in losing, with your presence, the hopes which I had conceived of being admitted to a share of your confidence and friendship. The distance to which I shall shortly be removed almost wholly deprives me of so pleasing a prospect, at the same time that it furnishes me with the means of offering you this declaration of my esteem, without hazarding the imputation or suspicion of flattery.
>
> I hope still to be honoured with a place in your remembrance as a person who would have esteemed it a happiness to have devoted his best services to the support of your welfare. I, on my part, shall never forget the many instances which I have received of your kindness, nor yet the very great and amiable qualities which eminently distinguished your character, especially the sincerity and candour of your expressions, and the gentleness of your manners. These are virtues which in private life will always command love and respect; but in persons of your elevated sphere are the best endowments in the gift of Heaven, and the source of blessings to mankind.

Hastings was overwhelmed with work in his new position in Calcutta, but he continued to cultivate the friendship of his former chief at Madras. On the 8th October, 1772, he wrote to assure Mr. Du Pré that he would consider it as a misfortune were he to lose the pleasure of hearing from him, "for I can truly assure you that I receive more comfort from your letters than from any written thing on this side of the Cape, or perhaps on the other."

> I confess I am interested enough to wish you may change your mind and stay another year, because if you do, I know it will be from motives that will do you credit, and because I shall be, or think myself, secure of having added to my present perplexities a share in those of Fort St. George. I cannot help thinking that you may receive an invitation from the Directors to remain, as they have let their resentment drop so lightly, and have yet thought of no person for your successor.

Mr. Du Pré vacated his appointment in the following February, and wrote a letter of farewell from Madras to Hastings, who, in the course of a long reply, said :—

> I am happy in the assurances which you give me of your friendship, and thankful for the promise of your support. My own heart tells me that I have a just claim to the former, and I shall endeavour by every means to maintain my claim to it until I am so fortunate as to meet you in England. I know not whether my pride is not as much interested as my fortune in the opinion which you may entertain of my conduct. I shall contrive from time to time to submit it to you, and shall be obliged to you for your advice and unreserved sentiments upon it.
>
> I remember hearing you declare you would lead a country life, and have no more concern in public business. I hope, and am not altogether selfish in hoping it, that you will not adhere to this resolution. But whatever line you may make your choice, may you be happy, loved, honoured, and esteemed as much as I think you deserve.

Hastings made suitable acknowledgments for his promotion to the friends who had interested themselves on his behalf. To Lord Shelburne he wrote :—

> The Court of Directors have since been pleased to confer upon me the government of their possessions in Bengal—an honour equally unsolicited and unexpected on my part. By whatever means it has fallen to my lot, there is a degree of confidence implied in the manner of it, which claims a more than ordinary share of my attention to the very weighty affairs of that presidency. You will permit me to say, my Lord, that you have furnished an additional motive to my ambition, in the desire which I feel to merit the good opinion which your Lordship has already been pleased to express of me.

In a letter to Sir George Colebroke, a Director, Hastings said :—

I feel too sensibly the weak ground on which my interest stands, unless supported by the most wary conduct in the administration of the very weighty affairs entrusted to my charge; and I know too well both the proneness which people in general have to misrepresent the actions of those in authority, and the too great readiness with people at home to credit implicitly such misrepresentations. It is impossible to avoid errors; and there are cases in government in which it may be necessary to adopt expedients which are not to be justified on such principles as the public can be the judges of.

He then promised to have the good of the Company always at heart.

Soon after he had assumed office, the Directors of the East India Company wrote to the President and Council of Fort William:—

We wish we could refute the observation that almost every attempt made by us and our administration at your Presidency for the reform of abuses has rather increased them, and added to the miseries of the country we are anxious to protect and cherish. Are not the tenants more oppressed and wretched? Are our investments improved? Has not the raw silk and cocoons been raised upon us fifty per cent. in price? When oppression pervades the whole country, when youths have been suffered with impunity to exercise sovereign jurisdiction over the natives, and to acquire rapid fortunes by monopolising commerce, it cannot be a wonder to us, or yourselves, that native merchants do not come forward to contract with the Company, that the manufactures find their way through foreign channels, or that our investments are at once enormously dear and of debased quality. . . . It is, therefore, our resolution to aim at the root of those evils. Our President, Mr. Hastings, we trust, will set the example of temperance, economy, and application; and upon this we are sensible much will depend. And here we take occasion to indulge in the pleasure we have in acknowledging Mr. Hastings' services upon the coast of Coromandel in constructing, with equal labour and ability, the plan which has so much improved our investments there; and as we are persuaded he will persevere in the same laudable pursuit through every branch of our affairs in Bengal, he in return may depend on the steady support and favour of his employers.

In the year 1773 the Indian Regulation Act was passed in Parliament, at the instance of Lord North; and Bengal, which had previously ranked as a Presidency under Madras, and before Bombay, was constituted the chief and over-ruling province. Its Governor was at the same time made Governor-General of the three Presidencies, and Hastings was promoted to the new office. With him was associated a Council of four, namely, Mr. Richard

Barwell,[1] of the Company's Bengal Civil service; with Mr. Philip Francis, General (afterwards Sir) John Clavering, and Colonel the Hon. George Monson, who were sent out from England. Fortified by the complacent assurance that human nature is the same everywhere, the new arrivals tested Oriental men and Oriental things by Occidental standards, and passed judgment thereon with a light heart and heroic platitudes, little realizing that the longer Europeans live in, work for, and sympathise with India, the more should they realize the magnitude and difficulty of the task of grafting Western upon Eastern modes of thought, feeling, and practice. Instead of giving respectful consideration to the local experience which had been laboriously accumulated by Hastings and Barwell, they systematically ignored it; and, priding themselves on their open minds, and their freedom from race prejudice, they habitually placed the Governor-General in a minority, and unhesitatingly brought his authority into contempt.

On the 14th December, 1774, Hastings wrote a demi-official letter to Lord North, thanked him for his new appointment, and alluded to the chronic feud in the Council, in consequence of the unconciliatory proceedings of the persons who had been selected by the Premier to assist in carrying his plans into execution. On the same day he addressed the following letter to the Earl of Rochford:—

---

[1] Richard Barwell was the son of William Barwell, Governor of Bengal, 1748, and afterwards a Director of the East India Company. He was born at Calcutta in 1741, and was educated in England. He obtained a writership on the Bengal establishment in 1756, and was appointed a member of the Bengal Council in 1774. Two years later he married Miss Sanderson, the "reigning beauty of Calcutta." He retired in 1780, and is said to have returned to England "with one of the largest fortunes ever accumulated in India." In 1781 he purchased from the Earl of Scarborough, for £102,500, the estate of Stansted in Sussex (eight miles from Chichester); and during the five following years he expended a large sum of money in enlarging the house, and beautifying the grounds, with the aid of Bonomi, James Wyatt, and "Capability Brown." In 1784 he entered Parliament as member for St. Ives, and in 1796 he was returned for Winchelsea, but he resigned his seat a few months later. He died at Stansted in 1804, aged sixty-three, and the estate was sold by Sir Elijah Impey and his other trustees. (See *Dict. National Biog.*)

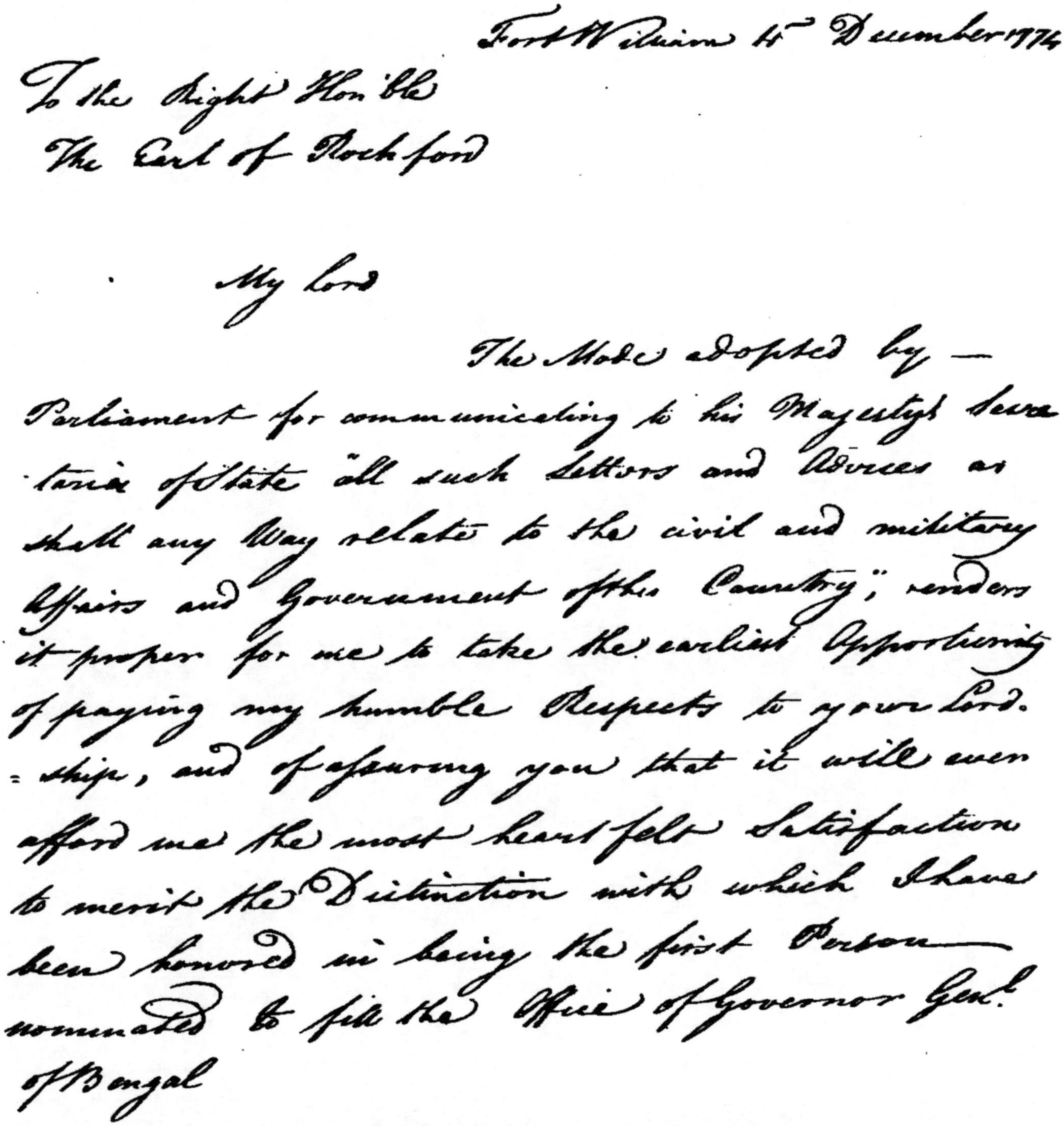
Fort William 15 December 1774

To the Right Hon'ble
The Earl of Rochford

My Lord

The Mode adopted by — Parliament for communicating to his Majesty's Secretaries of State "all such Letters and Advices as shall any Way relate to the civil and military Affairs and Government of this Country"; renders it proper for me to take the earliest Opportunity of paying my humble Respects to your Lordship, and of assuring you that it will ever afford me the most heartfelt Satisfaction to merit the Distinction with which I have been honored in being the first Person nominated to fill the Office of Governor Genl. of Bengal

FIRST PAGE OF HASTINGS' LETTER TO THE SECRETARY OF STATE.
(*Reduced size.*)

[*Face page* 42.

enough to meet with the Approbation of my Sovereign and his Ministers, I shall in that Approbation find a Comfort equal to the Grief & Anxiety which must continue to agitate me till the Question is determined either for or against me. Permit me however to observe, without deviating from the Intention of this Address, that the Question is of great Magnitude and Importance, involving the future Progress or Decline of an Empire, and of its Commerce, most essential to the Prosperity of Great Britain.

I have the Honor to be
with the greatest Respect
My Lord
Your most obedient
and most faithful
Servant
Warren Hastings.

FOURTH PAGE OF HASTINGS' LETTER TO THE SECRETARY OF STATE.
(*Reduced size.*)

[*Face page* 43.

The mode adopted by Parliament for communicating to His Majesty's Secretaries of State "all such Letters and Advices as shall any way relate to the civil and military Affairs and Government of this Country," renders it proper for me to take the earliest Opportunity of paying my humble Respects to your Lordship, and of assuring you that it will ever afford me the most heartfelt Satisfaction to merit the Distinction with which I have been honored in being the first Person nominated to fill the Office of Governor-General of Bengal.

My past conduct in the several appointments held under the Company will, I hope, prove to your Lordship the zeal which has actuated me for the service of my Country, as well as the Moderation and Circumspection with which I have at all times endeavoured to conduct myself. Your Lordship will, therefore, do me the justice to believe that every event which occasions difference of opinion between me and the members joined with me in the Administration must give me the deepest concern, especially in the very commencement of the new Government. The Rise and Progress of such difference your Lordship will find distinctly marked in the dispatches now sent home, which will be officially laid before you by the Court of Directors. To these despatches I shall entirely trust for the Defence of my Conduct in those matters which have been objected to me as faulty, though attended with consequences the most beneficial for the Company and the Nation. I shall abstain in this Letter from every species of Accusation against those who have occasioned the Distraction of our Councils, lamenting that they did not bring that conciliatory Spirit with them with which they found me ready to meet them, and which might have tended to heal any Differences incident to a Diversity of Opinion.

If the Decision of my Superiors on these Disputes shall disappoint the Expectations which I may have been too sanguine in indulging, I shall receive it with becoming Resignation, and with the consolation of having acted for the best. But should I be happy enough to meet with the Approbation of my Sovereign and his Ministers, I shall in that Approbation find a comfort equal to the Grief and Anxiety which must continue to agitate me till the Question is determined either for or against me. Permit me, however, to observe, without deviating from the Intention of this Address, that the Question is of great Magnitude and Importance, involving the future Progress or Decline of an Empire, and of its Commerce, most essential to the Prosperity of Great Britain. I have, &c.

Hastings had been delicate from childhood, and he was but a youth when he first landed in India. Yet his first period of uninterrupted service in Bengal extended to fourteen years, and his second period was almost as long. He held the office of Governor of Bengal for two, and that of Governor-General of India for eleven years. He was, while filling the latter appointment, thwarted at every turn by those who should have relieved him of many of the cares of State that devolved upon him. He had not only to direct the administration of the province immediately under his own control, but he had to keep a vigilant watch over the proceedings of the subordinate Governments of Madras and Bombay. He was overwhelmed with official duties, and no sooner had he extricated the State from one grave difficulty than other troubles demanded his earnest attention; and all the time he had to combat the chronic malice of his Council, and the narrow suspicion of the Court of Directors. It is marvellous that his health stood the strain of the life that he led, for in his day there were no Himalayan Capuas for jaded Europeans to flee to for the recuperation of body and mind, and the monotony of their existence in the damp heat of Bengal was not broken by daily whiffs of news from the outside world. Yet exile had its compensations; and Hastings found great solace in the society of his wife Marian (whom he had married in 1777), and received from her sympathy a constant incentive to exertion. When, therefore, she was compelled to return to Europe, his life lost its chief charm, and he set his mind on the resignation of his Proconsulate. In 1784 he had at times felt, as he stated, "miserably bad"; but in September, 1785, he wrote from Benares to his wife, and said:—

> I am indeed in far better health than I was at this season of last year; but the best health that I gain, or can hope to gain in India, is but a palliative acquired with continual sacrifice and unmanly attentions. I want a multitude of aids to cure me thoroughly, all of which may be included in two comprehensive but comfortable terms, a hard frost and my own fireside.

Early in 1785 he wrote to the Court of Directors, and resigned his appointment. On the 1st of February he gave over charge to the Council, and took leave of its members. He then embarked in the *Barrington*; and on the 7th idem—the birthday of his wife—he saw the last of India. The following were his fellow-passengers: Mr. John Shore, Colonel Toone, Colonel Popham, Major Tooney, Major Lands, Captain Green, Captain John Scott, Dr. C. Francis, and Mr. David Anderson. There were also twenty-five soldiers of H.M.'s 73rd Regiment. No mention is made in the ship's log at the India Office of lady passengers. He had a pleasant voyage, "without bad weather, in a clean and tight ship, with officers of skill and attention, and even of science; a society that I loved; and a rapid course." He employed his leisure on board in drawing up a retrospect of his administration, in disposing of arrears of correspondence, and in reading. St. Helena was reached at 4 a.m. on the 15th April. A "deputation of compliments" went on board. At 5 p.m. Hastings landed. He recorded the following in his diary:—

Received by ye Governor at ye landing-place. Supped with him. Put up at Mr. Greentree's. *16th.* Dined with ye Governor. Vansittart came in with Colonel Muir, Popham, C. Greene, etc. *17th* (*Sunday*). Rode before breakfast to Mr. Greentree's country house, and dined there. Passed ye morning in viewing ye island. At 3 p.m. set off to return by way of ye side path. *18th.* Dined and supped at ye Governor's. *19th.* At 9 rode with ye Governor to Longwood, and round by Mr. Bassett's to his house, dined there and returned at 6½. Supped with him. *21st.* At noon visited ye Governor, took leave of Mrs C., and went to ye wharf, ye Governor, &c., accompanying. At 5, weighed. At 5½, sailed.

The *Barrington* arrived at Plymouth on the 13th of June, 1785, four months and a quarter after leaving Calcutta, and Hastings posted up to London without delay. The following entries in his diary refer to his happy meeting with his wife, and his reception at Court, at the India House, and elsewhere:—

Monday, 13th June. At 9 a.m. left the *Barrington* with my fellow passengers, and landed at Plymouth at 10.30. Stayed and dined at Prince George's Hotel. Detained by the Customs House. At 4.20 left Plymouth, passed Ashburton, Ivybridge, Chudleigh, and slept at Exeter. A fine, beautiful, and highly cultivated country, but hilly. A cold wind from the sea.

Tuesday, 14th. Set off at 6, past Honiton (breakfast), Axminster, Bridport, Dorchester, Blandford, and Woodyeate's Inn. Arrived at 10.30. Shergold a good house. Slept there, very ill and headache.

Wednesday, 15th. At 5.30 proceeded. Baited at Salisbury, and dressed there. Andover, Overton, Basingstoke (dined), Cartford Bridge, Bagshot, and Staines. Arrived at 7, slept there; a most sultry day.

Thursday, 16th. At 5.30 proceeded. Baited at Hounslow, and at 8.45 arrived in London. Mrs. H. at Cheltenham. Saw Mr. and Mrs. Woodman. Visited Lord Thurlow and Lord Mansfield at Westminster Hall. Engaged to dine with Lord M. on Sunday. Left my name at Mr. Pitt's, Mr. Dundas's Lord Sidney's, and Mr. Devayeux's. Wrote to the latter, as Chairman, to announce my arrival. Letter from Mrs. H.; wrote to her express.

Friday, 17th. Sent back her servant at 8 with a letter in which I said I would set out to meet her in the afternoon. Received a note from Mr. Pitt desiring to see me at 3. Visited Lord Lansdowne, and attended

Mr. Pitt. At 6.45 set off to meet Mrs. H. Met at Maidenhead Bridge. Staid all night.

Saturday, 18th. Breakfasted. Visited Mrs. Johnstone (Mr. J. not at home) at Taplow. Returned with Mrs. H. to town. Engaged to call on Lord Sidney on Monday at 12, at the Secretary's Office, Whitehall, and to dine with Colonel Barré on Tuesday. Bills. Lord Thurlow's copy of my report.

Sunday, 19th. Dined at Canewood with the Archbishop of York, Lord Chancellor, Mr. Markham, and Major Scott. Came away about 8 with Archbishop.

Monday, 20th. At 12 attended Lord Sidney. Appointed to attend at St. James' on Wednesday, at 1.

Tuesday, 21st. Left my name at Mr. Smith's. Visited Lady Blunt and the Archbishop of York. Early with Lord Thurlow by appointment. Dined at Colonel Barré's with Lord Lansdowne, Sir J. Grey, Sir — Jarvis, Sir Elijah Impey.

THE INDIA HOUSE, LEADENHALL STREET, LONDON.

Wednesday, 22nd. At 1 went to Court. Introduced to King by Lords Sidney and Onslow . . . Lord Dudley, Lord Grantham, Lord Clarendon, Lord Gower, Marquis Carmarthen, Duke of Chandos, &c. Left my name at Lord Stormont's ; dined at home.

Thursday, 23rd. At 2 went with Mrs. H. to Court. Presented to the Queen, Princess Royal, Princess Augusta, and King. Afterwards visited Mrs. Schwellenberg. Dined with Archbishop of York.

Friday, 24th. Visited all the Directors. Saw Mr. Townson, Mr. Parry, Mr. Barens, and Sir Edward Hughes. Dined at home.

Saturday, 25th. Returned visits. Saw Lord Clarendon, Lord Dudley, and Lord Flood. Early at Lord Chancellor's. Dined at Sir Elijah Impey's, Parson's Green. Came away at 12.

Sunday, 26th. Not well. Mrs. H. headache. Breakfasted at 10. Visited my aunt at Kensington. Dined at home.

Monday, 27th. Mrs. H. still indisposed. Returned visits. Saw Lady Coote. Dined at home.

Tuesday, 28th. Breakfasted at Mr. Sullivan's. At 4.15 went by engagement to India House. Received in honour, and thanked by Court of Directors unanimously, and dined with them at the London Tavern. Visited Board of Control, invited; returned late, much inflamed.

In a letter to a friend he alluded to his having been summoned to the India House to receive the thanks of the Directors of the East India Company for his services; and added that the Chairman, in reading the resolution of the Court, "dwelt with a strong emphasis on the word 'unanimously.'" He was also, he said, received by the King and Queen "most graciously"; and his reception by the Board of Control "was more than polite to me." Shortly afterwards he dined at Twickenham, where Miss Fanny Burney first met him. "I was extremely pleased," she wrote to her father, "with the extraordinary plainness and simplicity of his manners, and the obliging openness and intelligence of his communications. He talked of India, when the subject was led to, with the most unreserved readiness, yet was never the hero of his own tale, but simply the narrator of such anecdotes or descriptions as were called for, or as fell in naturally with other topics." After meeting him a second time, she recorded in her diary that "I am quite charmed" with him; "and, indeed, from all that I can gather, and all I can observe, he appears to me to be one of the greatest men now living as a public character; while as a private one, his gentleness, candour, soft manners, and openness of disposition make him one of the most pleasing."

Hastings paid an early visit to Tunbridge Wells, where the community regarded him "with an uncommon degree of attention and respect. . . . I find myself everywhere and universally treated with evidences that I possess the good opinion of my country." Later on he took a furnished house in St. James's Place, and then in Wimpole Street, London, whence he made excursions to Cheltenham, Bath, and elsewhere. On one occasion he went to Churchill and Daylesford, and wandered among the scenes familiar to him in his childhood. He endeavoured to induce Mr. Knight, the owner of the Daylesford estate (grandson of the purchaser in 1715), to part with it for a sum considerably in excess of its market value, but for some time in vain; and he then, as he said, "bought a very pleasant little estate of 91 acres in Old Windsor, called Beaumont Lodge, a *modus agri non ita magnus, hortus ubi*, &c., exactly answering Horace's wish." Miss Burney noted in her diary that she passed an agreeable evening at the Lodge, "with that very intelligent and very informing man," whose "lively and very pleasing wife contributed largely to the evening's well-doing."

Mrs. Hastings.

From a sketch by Ozias Humphry, R.A.

CHAPTER IV

MRS. HASTINGS

IT has been stated on a former page that "Mr. and Mrs. Imhoff and child" were among Warren Hastings' fellow-passengers on board the *Duke of Grafton*, from London to Madras. Macaulay says that Imhoff "called himself a Baron," implying that he was nothing of the sort; and he added, on the authority of Gleig, that "he was in distressed circumstances, and was going out to Madras as a portrait-painter, in the hope of picking up some of the pagodas which were then lightly got, and as lightly spent by the English in India." Imhoff was probably in reduced circumstances, but he was a Baron for all that. It appears from a carefully compiled genealogical tree in the possession of Miss Winter, that he was seventeenth in direct descent from a Crusader of the name of Hoff, upon whom a German Emperor bestowed a coat of arms, and conferred the prefix of "Im," in recognition of an act of great gallantry in the field. He was the third son of Baron Christopher Imhoff, and a near kinsman of Baron Gustave Imhoff, who was appointed Governor-General of the Dutch East Indies in 1740, and in whose honour a large silver medal, bearing his image, with an appropriate superscription, was struck. This medal was bequeathed to Sir Charles Imhoff, from whom it has descended to Miss Winter. Baron Imhoff married Marie Anne von Chapuset, whose family (ennobled in Germany) is believed to have migrated from France to Germany after the revocation of the Edict of Nantes. Three children were born to them before they left Nuremberg for India; namely, a son named Ernest, who died in infancy; the above-named Charles, then aged two; and a daughter, named Amalie, who married General von Helwig, of the Prussian Army, and achieved some distinction as an authoress. It was Charles who accompanied his parents to India.

Hastings was a young widower, with much in him that offered a pleasing contrast to the characteristics of the Baron ; and the Baroness was very amiable and intelligent.[1] Macaulay remarks that "she had an agreeable person, a cultivated mind, and manners in the highest degree pleasing." This must be an accurate description, for otherwise she would not have enlisted, on her return to Europe, the regard of such severe moralists as King George the Third and Queen Charlotte, as well as of Fanny Burney and Hannah More. Macaulay says that "she despised her husband heartily" ; and Gleig argues that the "union was one of those against which Nature protests, and which are never contracted without entailing on the ill-fated pair long years of discomfort, if not of positive misery." There is a good deal of assumption in this, but her conduct warranted the criticism that the Baroness "was the wife of one whom she had never loved." The pair were ill-matched ; yet they may have made the best of their bargain for the sake of their children had they not encountered Warren Hastings. He is proved by his poetical effusions, and by his voluminous correspondence, to

[1] The sketch of Mrs. Hastings by Ozias Humphry, R.A., that was engraved for Gleig's *Memoirs of Warren Hastings*, published in 1841 by Bentleys, and which I have been courteously permitted by that firm to reproduce in photogravure for this volume, illustrates the truth of the observation in the *Dictionary of National Biography*, vol. 28, that "Humphry stands in the front rank of English miniaturists, and his works have always been admired for their simplicity, refinement, correct draughtsmanship, and harmonious colouring ; the same qualities appear in his crayon portraits." After achieving distinction as a miniature painter in London, Humphry went out to India, at the age of forty-three, to practise his profession at the courts of native princes, and he then became intimate with Hastings. He had a successful but a brief career in India, for his health broke down in 1788, and he was compelled to return to England. He resumed miniature painting in London, and was elected a Royal Academician in 1791 ; but as his sight then began to fail him, he relinquished the painting of miniatures, and devoted himself to crayon drawing, in which branch of art he speedily acquired such distinction that he was appointed Portrait Painter in Crayons to the King. In 1797 he became totally blind, and he died in 1810, aged sixty-eight.

have been a man of deep feeling. He never experienced a parent's love; but was brought up in a hard fashion, and was shipped off, while still a lad, to foreign parts, where his lot hitherto had been an anxious one. His first marriage was not fruitful of prolonged happiness; and he had been driven by impecuniosity, and the difficulty of obtaining employment in England, back to the East. He cherished a taste for classical literature, which beguiled him on his way, but he found greater distraction from the monotony of the voyage in the society of the Baroness.

Gleig observes in a professional manner that, "as if it had been God's will to try the strength of their principles to the utmost, Mr. Hastings was seized with a dangerous illness during the voyage, throughout the whole of which the Baroness nursed him with a sister's care, watching by his bedside, often when he knew it not, and administering to him all the medicines with her own hand." The Baron permitted this exhibition of solicitude; and he decided to land, and remain at the port to which the patient was bound in an influential capacity. But, soon after the ship reached Madras, either the Baron, with his wife's approval, or she with his, or both together, wrote to Germany, and filed a suit in the Court of Franconia for the dissolution of their marriage on the ground of incompatibility of temper. Gleig states that they "lived together with good repute a whole year in Madras." They preceded Hastings to Calcutta; and, shortly after his arrival there, he remarked in a letter, that she "has a good person, and has been very pretty, and wants only to be a greater mistress of the English language to prove that she has a great share of wit." It was not until 1775, or six years after the suit was filed, that the decree of divorce arrived in Calcutta. The Baron then returned to Germany, where, in the same year, he married a lady of noble birth, named Von Schad; and the Baroness's marriage with the Governor-General was celebrated with great festivity in Calcutta.

It has been assumed by some critics, who have not been animated by ill-will to Hastings, that his relations with the Baroness were not free from grave reproach; but, in the absence of reliable evidence on the subject, and in view to the characters of both parties as revealed after their marriage, it may be reasonably inferred that this conclusion is erroneous. Macaulay was a severe judge of Hastings, yet he declared that "his love was characteristic of the man. Like his hatred, like his ambition, like all his passions, it was calm, deep, earnest, patient of delay, unconquerable by time." Hastings was very ambitious, and it could not have seemed to him conducive to his advancement to engage, under the close observation of cadets and writers, in an intrigue with a married woman, first on a crowded East Indiaman, and then in the glare of publicity in a settlement where he occupied a prominent position, and which he desired to make the stepping-stone to higher things. He had a good character and good friends to lose. "I know too well," he remarked, in the letter to Sir George Colebroke, which is printed on a former page, "both the proneness which people in general have to misrepresent the actions of those in authority, and the too great readiness with people at home to credit implicitly such misrepresentation"; and it was, he said, his constant aim to show, "by the general tenour of my conduct," that "I have the good of the Company at heart, and I neglect no part of my duty." Self-control and self-respect were guiding principles of his life; and though, as events proved, he was capable of a romantic love that glowed without diminution for nearly fifty years, he cherished a high ideal of public duty and private responsibility which would have been outraged had he afforded ground for the moralist's censure. He made many friends, but he also made many enemies; and, almost from the time that he left Madras until the termination of his trial—a period of twenty-three years—he was the object of the inveterate hostility of able men, who sought to blacken his character in order to accomplish his ruin. But, with suggestive unanimity, his foes refrained from alleging that he had deserved reprobation by his intimacy with the Baroness; and it may be assumed, therefore, that they understood that that intimacy, however equivocal it may have seemed to some persons, was nothing worse than a platonic attachment which had not given occasion for local scandal. Sir Philip Francis, at any rate, would not have been deterred by any scruples from employing his genius for vituperation in holding up the moral weakness of Hastings to the scorn of the virtuous ; yet, with every temptation to gratify his rancorous hatred of his senior in Council, he remarked in a letter to his wife, after the marriage of Hastings, that "the lady is really an accomplished woman ; she behaves with perfect propriety in her new station, and deserves every mark of respect." Praise from Philip Francis was praise indeed.

Lady Impey and Madame Imhoff had, according to Francis, been "bosom friends for a long time" previous to the marriage of the latter with Hastings ; but, for a twelvemonth immediately preceding that event, they had not been on speaking terms, though the Chief Justice continued to show Madame Imhoff much friendliness. Doubtless each party to the quarrel considered that she was right to be angry, and that an apology was due from the other side. In those days, long ere "the hills" had been discovered, life in Calcutta during the greater part of the year must have been very monotonous and depressing for a lady ; and irritability of temper must have been induced by the high temperature, the want of useful employment, and the narrow ideas of such society as there was. Hastings gave an entertainment at Government House a week before his marriage, in view to bringing about a reconciliation between the two ladies ; but Lady Impey sent an excuse for her absence. Two days later Francis supped at the Chief Justice's, and "her Ladyship," he noted in his diary, "swears stoutly that Madame Imhoff shall pay her the first visit—an idea which I don't fail to encourage." Then, on the eve of the wedding, Madame Imhoff "sups at Lady Impey's by way of submission." Three weeks after the marriage Mrs. Hastings was indisposed, and Francis recorded that "Lady Impey sits up with Mrs. Hastings, *vulgo*, toadeating." The next day Francis supped "at the Governor's," and "Mrs. Hastings very handsomely acknowledges my constant attentions to her."

In 1780 Mrs. Hastings went for the benefit of her health to Chinsura, and the Governor-General soon desired her return to Calcutta. "I have all along wished it," he wrote to her, "though for reasons which I have mentioned, and for others which I have not, I opposed my own inclinations." He then sent her horse "Beauty" to her. "Poor fellow ! It will be a kindness to him as well as to yourself—and to me too—if you will be content to walk him till you are both a little stronger. . . . I am well. As I am persuaded that your health depends on yourself, I do beseech you to be well too." A week later he wrote: "I miss you most grievously," but "this letter will not add to your spirits, for it bears the symptoms of the total want of mine." Some days afterwards he urged her to rise early.

> The morning air—I mean the breeze which the rising sun sets in motion—will do you more good than all the rest of the day, and remember the Persian proverb which says, that the air of Paradise passes between a horse's ears to the rider that does not take too much of it, nor expose herself in the heat of the sun. I hear that you rode yesterday in the evening. I suppose you only mounted Beauty to try him; for that is not the time of day for such an exercise.

On the 14th July he remarked that the "only news of consequence is, that it is determined that I am to remain as long as I choose, but with the same associates." But on the morning of the 17th he wrote to her as follows:—

> I have desired Sir John Day to inform you that I have had a meeting this morning with Mr. Francis, who has received a wound in his side, but I hope not dangerous. I shall know the state of it presently, and will write to you again He is at Belvedere, and Drs. Campbell and Francis are both gone to attend him there. I am *well* and *unhurt*. But you must be content to *hear* this good from me. You cannot see me. I cannot leave Calcutta while Mr. Francis is in any danger. But I wish you to stay at Chinsura.

Francis made a good recovery; and as soon as he was in a position to do so, Hastings proceeded to Chinsura to meet his wife. He wrote:—

> If you set out on Friday, I will try to meet you. . . . Wrap yourself in shawls, and keep the wind as much as you can from you if this weather continues, when you come down. . . . May God bless you, and restore you safe, and in health to me, and as glad—or but half as glad—to see your husband, as he will be to regain possession of his Marian.

The health of Mrs. Hastings began to fail in 1783, after fourteen years' continuous residence in "the plains"; and, on the 10th January, 1784, she embarked at Calcutta for England. Hastings was then nearly fifty-two, and she thirty-seven years of age. Writing to his friend, Sir Elijah Impey, who had recently returned home, Hastings said: "I have made a sacrifice of my own judgment, my ease, and possibly the comfort and happiness of my whole life, to the opinions of others." He found some consolation in writing the numerous letters to "my beloved, my most amiable, my best Marian," which she preserved, and which are now in the British Museum.[1]

In the first of these he said: "Yesterday morning I held in my arms all that my heart holds dear; and now she is separated from me as if she had no longer existence! O! my Marian, I am wretched. . . . I love you more by far than life, for I would not live but in the hope of being once more united to you." This was from Culpee. On the following day he returned to Calcutta, and wrote that he had been relieved by much employment, "yet the instant that I am left to myself, and my ivory cot affords me no comfort, all my distresses rush back upon my thoughts, and present everything in the most gloomy prospect." He tried to indulge the imagination of seeing her; of hearing her conversation; of feeling her hand on his brow; but this "momentary illusion instantly disappears, and shows me through the void all the delights of that entertainment whose image I seek, and which my fancy cannot recover—the beloved face, the animated and varied expression of features, the look of benevolence unspeakable, the sweet music of her tongue, and a thousand imperceptible graces that embellished her words, and gave them the power of expression exceeding the strongest efforts of the understanding." In a later letter he alluded to his having been indebted to his first illness "for such a proof of your affection as is almost without example"; and added that, since that time he had not "perceived any alteration in that tender-

[1] These letters (and a large number of other papers connected with Hastings), after having passed through the hands of Southey, the younger Impey, and Gleig, were purchased by the British Museum in 1872, were referred to by Mr. Beveridge, in the *Calcutta Review*, in 1877, and were largely quoted from eleven years later by Dr. H. E. Busteed, C.I.E., in his charming *Echoes from Old Calcutta*. "They are," as Macaulay remarked with especial reference to those alluded to by Gleig, "exceedingly characteristic. They are tender, and full of indication of esteem and confidence"; and they show that Hastings loved his wife "with that love which is peculiar to men of strong minds, whose affection is not easily won or widely diffused." In this respect Hastings was a man after Macaulay's own heart, though Macaulay concentrated his own affection, not on a wife, but on a sister.

ness which I before experienced, and which constituted the great and only blessing of my life." He took himself to task for his neglect of her, and declared that " were I present with you, my constant attentions, and the evidences which my love would produce every hour, and every instant of its reality," would prevent the effect of that neglect " on a heart so generous as yours." His conscience reproached him with " a long catalogue of offences," and every trivial incident of the kind referred to " now appears with a black dye before me." But " it is not so in my remembrance of your behaviour, which I look back upon with love, respect, and admiration " ; and he begged her to recall " with what delight, my sweet Marian, you have known me frequently quit the scene of business, and run up to your apartment for the sake of deriving a few moments of relief from the looks, the smiles, and the sweet voice of my beloved."

I have copied the three following letters almost *in extenso* from the clearly written originals, as they afford an excellent idea of the tone of the whole collection :—

CALCUTTA, 21*st January*, 1784.

MY DEAREST MARIAN,—I have written three letters to you by Mrs. Sands, in the hope of her overtaking you at the Cape. I scarce wish you to receive them, for they were written under the influence of sorrow, discontent, and despondency, and something like the consciousness of infinite and incomparable folly in the recollection of the abundant pains which I have been taking to effect my own wretchedness. May the event prove it the reverse ! This resolution and its execution were very sudden, and I look back for the grounds of both, and scarce can trace them—none that justify one. I only recollect that in my enthusiasm to sacrifice every consideration that regarded myself to the preservation of your health, I thought only of the sacrifice, nor enquired of myself till it was too late whether it might not have been attained by easier means, and nearer our reach, or whether those which were chosen were not as likely to increase as to remedy the evil.

But I have already torn one sheet because I had half filled it with gloomy complaints. I will not afflict you with more, and it is unmanly.

The events of my life since our separation have been few and uninteresting. I left you early on the morning of the 10th, and passed a miserable day, with an aching heart and head. I saw the *Atlas* till half an hour past nine, and then lost sight of her for ever. I arrived in Calcutta on the afternoon of the 12th, having made my last stage in the Teelcherra. I have since had my mind so constantly occupied that it has had little time for reflexion, and I have avoided sleeping in the afternoon, so that, thank God,

I pass my nights in quiet, through weariness. I passed the three last days of the week at Allipoor, and shall continue to go there for the entertainment of my present guests, so long as they stay with me, on Saturdays and Sundays. When they leave me I bid adieu to Allipoor for ever, and I have actually advertised the sale of it in three lots, the old house and garden forming one, the new house and outhouses the second, and the paddock the third. Other schemes of retrenchment and economy I am forming, and they afford me a pleasure in the prospect which is connected with them. . . .

I do not expect the return of the pilot till the first week in February at the soonest, and shall reckon the delay of every day from the first as having proceeded from a necessity of detaining him to afford me better tidings than could have been written earlier by him. Yet I shall then hope to see your own handwriting, and, O God, grant it may give me the comfort of hearing that you were well, your health unimpaired, and your mind composed! Let me have but reason to believe that you will pass the voyage exempt from sickness, and I will forgive myself for having assented to part with you. Assented! It was my own act, and mine alone, and I felt a pride in urging it, because I owed to you every proof that I could give of my affection and disinterested regard for your safety and happiness, and what greater could I give, if these objects were promoted by it.

He then alluded to his approaching tour to Lucknow, and continued :—

I daily expect letters overland written after the receipt of mine by the *Surprize* Packet in which I declared my resolution of resigning my office, and desired that my successor might be appointed. I cannot foresee, but whatever it be, my resolution is fixed and unalterable, and it will be so concluded when it is known that you are gone before me. I have fulfilled every obligation which I owed to the Service, and done more than almost any other man against such inducements as I have had to restrain me would have done. But, my Marian, do not entertain hopes of improvement in our fortune. If your love for me is, as I am sure it is, superior to every other wish, you must be content to receive your husband again without other expectations, poor in cash, but rich in credit (at least he hopes so) and in affection unexampled. He is infinitely more concerned about his constitution than his wealth, trusting to the justice of his country for at least a competency, and to the good sense of his Marian for a sufficiency in whatever they may have for a subsistence. . . .

O my Marian, what an age is yet to pass before I can be again blessed with you, and what have I not to dread in so long an interval! May Heaven support and preserve you, and restore you to me in health and in affection all that my fondest hopes can require, and I will be contented, nor regret the many many days that I have lost in your absence; and if ever I part from you again, I shall deserve to lose you, and be wretched for ever. Let but a few months pass and I will begin to count the time which shall yet remain, and please myself with its diminution.

Continue, my sweet Marian, to love me, for in that hope and belief alone I live. Again, may the God of heaven bless and support you! Remember me affectionately to your dear Mrs. Motte. Adieu.

Your ever, ever affectionate,

W. HASTINGS.

BUXER, *8th March*, 1784.

The cold is still almost piercing in the mornings.

MY BELOVED MARIAN,—Hearing that the *Warren Hastings* was likely to be detained, and desirous of taking my chance of conveying by her a second copy of the paper which I sent to you in my despatch from Patna, I sent away one by the post from yesterday's encampment to Thompson, to be put by him into the packet. The letter which I wrote to accompany it, I in the hurry of closing the packet left out; but it was short, and of no consequence. Possibly this may arrive in time to go by the same despatch. The paper itself will show in what manner my mind was employed in the otherwise tedious hours of my journey; and I believe that I owe to this occupation of it that I suffered no fatigue or other inconvenience from so continued an exercise. How should I when my thoughts were all the time engrossed by the only object that I can dwell upon with delight, for a delight it is, though mixed with many very painful reflexions. It would hardly be understood by another, but you will know the truth of it, when I mention that I feel a higher gratification in brooding over the subject of the greatest unhappiness that has befallen me for years past than on such as in common estimation would be most pleasing to the mind. I must not let my thoughts wander, for I am at this instant surrounded by strangers, and others are gathering about me to whom I shall be compelled to give attention, and I must not lose this post, lest I should lose your ship.

I am in perfect health. Since I crossed the Soan, I have made the last parts of three marches on horseback. This morning I used Mr. Eton's chariot out of civility. Suliman and the Arab are with me, both in excellent order, and I use them in turns. I ride about eight miles in a morning, and find great benefit in it. In a word I flatter myself that this journey from which I dreaded the worst effects has effectually restored my constitution. You would be astonished to see me. . . .

I have been joined by Ally Ibrahim Cawn and Beneram Pundit, whom you know that I reckon among my first friends. To the first I am indebted for having raised my character and made it known to every quarter of India by his wise administration of the City of Benares. Poor Cleveland! Every tongue through Bengal and Behar is loud in his praises, and in expressions of regret for his loss. I hope to reach Benares in five days more, and probably this is the last letter that you can receive from me by the ships of this season. It will afford you the satisfaction of knowing that I am well, and I must add for confirmation of it, in better health than I have known for some years past. What a change! I crawled from the shore to Crofter's Bungalow at Sooksangur, my strength and breath failed me, and my knees shook under me. At this moment I think myself as stout as any one of the party. I ought to conclude here, for I can say nothing more acceptable, except that I love you more than my life, or even than my hopes of life hereafter.

Adieu, my Heart's beloved! May the God of Heaven bless and protect you! Amen.

WARREN HASTINGS.

ALLIPOOR, *Sunday the 5th of December*, 1784.

MY BELOVED MARIAN,—I am now again reading your most delightful though painful letter, and shall employ the afternoon in finishing the perusal of it. I have enclosed it in a case, and I keep it in my private box, which I always carry with me, both for privacy, and for the ready means of looking into it, when I can command the leisure and solitude which can fit me for it. These advantages I never possess. The afternoons indeed are always my own; but since my return to Calcutta I have never been able to sit up after dinner. This day and yesterday I am better and stouter than I have been, which I ascribe partly to the change of weather, and partly to the renewal of my morning rides and cold water. But what a wretch I am to talk of myself, when my Marian is before me! Yes, my lovely Marian, you are before me. Your delightful looks, your enchanting voice, even your touch—(O God! once more make them substantially mine!)—successively take possession of my senses as I read the animated picture of your mind, its sentiments and its sufferings. I can bear the description now. It racked my feelings, and made me almost feverish, when I first read it, because my passions were wholly occupied by their present sympathy, and I knew not what was to follow. I now know all, and bless many of the cruel symptoms which gave me pain when I read of them. All? No! not all. I only know that you departed from St. Helena on the 15th of May in perfect health, and in the full assurance of being in a state which might in its event make me most truly the happiest of all mankind. But in the unknown interval which has followed what may not have happened to make me the most wretched. A length yet remaining of agitation on the great ocean; a total change of climate approaching; perhaps tempest, I will not imagine worse; the fatigue of landing, of travelling seventy long miles in a condition of body requiring ease and repose even in the most healthy, the various agitations of mind, and consequent affections of the body on your arrival in London, reiterated with every dear connection, and with every friend that approaches to bid you welcome; how will your tender frame bear all this? Yet it has borne more, and I thank God that you will have arrived in London at a season when all the world is out of town, and will have found a house furnished and completely fitted for your reception. I will also believe—for my vast love for you has made me superstitious—that your virtues will secure to you a better destiny. I will believe that I am myself in the course of good fortune; for I can scarce trace my life for some years back, even to the greatest disappointments of it, but to be convinced that they led to some good which made me rejoice that they had befallen me. I will believe that I am now a blessed being, and most fervently pray that I may die, though instantly, in that belief, if the reverse of this has actually come to pass. . . . You will receive in detachments a very close and connected series of my adventures, wonderfully unimportant as they would appear to any reader but her to whom they are addressed, and as connected and faithful a display of the mind which wrote them. How will it grieve me if you should lose any of them!—except the first, for those, I remember, were peevish, desponding, and unmanly.

The next remark which strikes me in your letter, and for which I feel a sentiment greatly resembling that of thanksgiving, is the wonderful similitude between your thoughts and mine. While I read yours, I think I am reading my own, for their original impulse still remains unvaried through all its productive movements, though I cannot remember a single expression that I have written. A few, perhaps, only are retained in their original expression by being clothed with a poetical dress; but my poetry, mean as it may be, was never indebted to fancy, and derives its inspiration but from one source, which is the same as that which furnished the more expressive, but not more genuine, thoughts of your letter. I could give you extracts from yours which require but rhyme and measure to make them exactly my own. I will not repeat them. Yet I may be permitted to borrow one, and one only, which, I am sure, comes as nearly to my own feelings as it parted from you. "My mind often and often drew a picture of my state when *bereft of all that was dearer to her than life. The shade it cast was dark and strong*, but still *I could see at a distance a glimmering ray*, which, like the sun after a long absence, cheered and warmed my drooping spirits; but, alas! where are they? *What an obscure and dreary way have I yet to travel* till my eyes again behold that light which gives me life!" I am sure you will easily recollect the passage which corresponds with this, and in one part almost literally. My Marian, it was your genius which mixed itself with mine and dictated to me. I am sure that I felt it. At some time or other I will prove to you that there is not in all that production one idea or image which was not also your own, perhaps borrowed by sympathy from you. Let this be to you a demonstration of the warmth of my affection, as I trust to it for the proof—but do I want one?—of yours.

A letter from his wife, dated St. Helena, 15th May, reached the Governor-General at Benares on the 30th September, and gave him great delight. "I am, indeed," he wrote to her in reply, on the following day, "I am, indeed, a fortunate man, and am tempted to adopt the term even to superstition; and no wonder, for the belief has seized others long since, and universally." He congratulates himself on the fact that her letter "is written in the language of cheerfulness and of affection. . . . I am already happy; for as God is my witness that I prefer your happiness to my own, I feel the measure of my present joy full. I have food enough for my heart to feast on for more than a week to come. . . . I have but one wish remaining (yes, one more), viz., to be able to leave the stage of active life while my fortune is in the zenith of its prosperity, and while I have a constitution yet reparable. . . . May the God whose goodness I have so wonderfully experienced bless you with health, safety, and comfort, and me with the re-possession of my sweet Marian! Amen! Amen! Amen! I never loved you so much as I do at this instant." A week afterwards he added a postscript of a most tender nature, and said, in conclusion, "I shall hasten to Calcutta, and, if possible, leave it again before the end of this year. Adieu, my most beloved! Adieu!" Other love-letters have been written in Government House, Calcutta, including those which the lonely Earl of Minto addressed, during the course of his seven years' exile, to his beloved Countess in Scotland (who was to see him alive no more, as he died immediately after returning from India, when travelling from London to meet her at Minto Castle); but the *billets doux* of the first Governor-General of India are probably unique

Mrs. Hastings reached England after a long voyage,[1] and, a fortnight after her arrival, she was presented by Lady Weymouth to King George the Third and Queen Charlotte. Two more weeks passed, and she was again received by their Majesties; and, according to a letter that was written to Hastings by his agent, Major Scott, who escorted her on this occasion, she "met with still greater marks of attention, if possible." After talking some time to Mrs. Hastings, the amiable Queen turned to Major Scott, and said: "I am very glad to observe that Mrs. Hastings is so much recovered; she looks infinitely better than when I saw her a fortnight ago, and I hope this country will

[1] There is a list in the British Museum of "prohibited and other articles detained in the Baggage Warehouse, belonging to Mrs. Hastings, chargeable with duty." It includes silk dresses; silk handkerchiefs; gold and silver gauze curtains; squirrel skins; a tortoise-shell dressing box, inlaid with ivory and silver; a bedstead, plated with silver; part of an ivory bedstead, "gilt with gold"; an ivory armchair inlaid with gold, with velvet seat embroidered with gold, and an ivory stool; a second ivory armchair with a stool; two ivory armchairs and stands; and one smoking utensil of silver [a hookah?] weighing forty-eight ounces.

soon restore her to perfect health." In reply to his wife's letter describing her reception in England, Hastings wrote :—

The attentions shown to you on your arrival, though what I expected, make no small part of my rejoicing. Something might at the first have been yielded to you on my account ; more, surely, to your character, which had preceded you, and your character is marked with virtues, all original, and such as would naturally excite respect ; but I am certain that they who were your first visitors would have wished to repeat their visits early, and stimulate others with the same desire to see you.

KING GEORGE III. WHEN YOUNG.

QUEEN CHARLOTTE WHEN YOUNG.

He subsequently described her appearance in an "epigram borrowed from the French" :—

Flowers, Ribbands, Lappets, Feathers shaking,
And Cap that cost three weeks in making,
Pearls all in rows, and Pearls in drops,
And brilliant Pins set thick as hops,
Gay gown and Stomacher so fine,
And Petticoat of clouds divine,
With other silken things, and lac'd things !
Combin'd ye flutter forth, to shew
Your gaudy charms to public view :
Admiring swains with rapture eye
The Pageant, as it moves, and die :
And people call you Mrs. Hastings.

The friendliness of the Queen to a *divorcée* was regretted by Colonel Fairly and Captain Price, two of the King's equerries, and defended by Mrs. Schwellenberg, the Chief Keeper, and Miss Fanny Burney, the Assistant Keeper of the Queen's robes. After a heated discussion on the subject at Windsor, Miss Burney noted in her diary: "I felt so sorry that poor Mrs. Hastings, whom I believe to be a most injured woman, should be so ill-defended, even by her most zealous friend, that I compelled myself to the exertion of coming forward in her behalf myself." She accordingly represented to the equerries that in England "a divorce could only take place upon misconduct," whereas in Germany "a divorce from misconduct prohibited a second marriage, which could only be permitted where the divorce was the mere effect of disagreement from dissimilar tempers." The equerries said that they had never heard this before, and Colonel Fairly added, that "it ought to be made known, both for the sake of Mrs. Hastings, and because she has been received at Court, which gave everybody the greatest surprise, and me, in my ignorance, the greatest concern on account of the Queen." Mrs. Schwellenberg confirmed her colleague's arguments, little dreaming that, in consequence of her habitual petulance towards that observant little lady, a great historian would, nearly sixty years afterwards, heap a variety of contumelious epithets on her head, and, in one of his essays, hand her down to posterity as "an old hag from Germany," of "mean understanding," of "insolent manners," of "savage temper, exasperated by disease," a "hateful old maid," "rude," "peevish," "unable to conduct herself with common decency," an "execrable old woman," a "German crone," an "old fury," who "raged like a cat," and "raved like a maniac."

The Queen was so much interested in Mrs. Hastings that she recommended her son, Charles Imhoff, to the notice of the Prince of Waldeck, who thereupon had him trained as a soldier. Some years later Hastings endeavoured to obtain a staff appointment for Imhoff in Bengal; and, when the Marquis of Cornwallis was about to leave England to assume the office of Governor-General, Hastings begged him to make Imhoff his aide-de-camp, or to "nominate him to any other staff appointment which he can hold consistently with his present rank." He proceeded to say:—

Lieutenant-Colonel Imhoff is my son-in-law, and deservedly possesses as large a portion of my affection as I could feel for a son of my own blood. To no other person living would I allow the claim which has drawn from me this importunity. Of the requisites which might entitle him to your Lordship's protection, I beg leave to say that he has received the rudiments of his profession in the strict service of Germany, that he has been honoured with the express assurances or indications from every commanding officer to whose regiment he has been attached in this country of their approbation of his conduct ; and that he is a man of ingenuous manners, and of the strictest honour and integrity.

Hastings added in a postscript :—

The foreign service to which I have alluded as having occupied an early part of Colonel Imhoff's life was that of the Prince of Waldeck, who has bestowed upon him the most authentic testimony that could be afforded of Colonel Imhoff's merits, in a letter written to his mother by his Highness, in his own hand, and in another to the Queen, who had graciously recommended him to the Prince ; and he has since distinguished him by the most flattering personal kindnesses.

Lord Cornwallis was unable to comply with Hastings' request.

On the 16th January, 1797, Hastings wrote from Daylesford to Charles Imhoff, who was staying at the time at "Hastings House," in Park Lane :—

Though a letter received this morning from Charlotte gives me the pleasing expectation of seeing you in a very few days at this place, I cannot deny myself the pleasure of writing to you, to thank you for your New Year's wishes, which are (I can truly assure you) as welcome on the 16th as if they had been in form announced and received on the first of the month ; on which day I hope you and your dear Charlotte were sensible of the efficacy of those which were offered up most fervently.

Hastings expressed on the 10th May, 1797, to Charles Imhoff the anxiety that Mrs. Hastings felt respecting her daughter-in-law's health, and urged him to write at once in order "to satisfy her (and why should I not say *us*, for I too am interested, though not equally, in the knowledge ?) upon the point. I have used a term of qualification, which I might perhaps with truth revoke, and say that my interest in this point is equal to hers. In whatever regards you, my dear Charles, or your excellent and amiable wife, I have a concern of my own, and another besides attached to the pleasure, or pain, which it may give to another excellent and amiable wife." Mrs. Hastings was devoted to her son and daughter-in-law; and, notwithstanding a heavy loss, about the year 1796, by the failure of a Dutch firm in the City, she was in a position to make gifts to the former amounting to £40,000, and to settle £10,000 on the latter. "This," she wrote, "will enable him to live very comfortably with his beloved Charlotte, and my mind will be easy respecting my beloved children. Whatever my fate may be, let me see my children happy and comfortable."

On the 28th July, 1806, Mr. J. P. Ruhl, Clerk in Chancery to the Chapteral Order of St. Joachim, apprised Hastings of the election of his stepson to that Order, and that he was certain the Chapter would be happy to confer the same honour upon himself. Hastings acknowledged Mr. Ruhl's letter, and said:—

> I am yet more thankful for the intimation which you have been pleased to give me of the disposition which they, the Capitulars, entertained to confer the same degree upon me as they had done upon Colonel Imhoff. I am gratified in the extreme by this declaration, but I am mortified at the same time that I cannot avail myself of it. In my present undignified condition of life, after having passed many years of it in the public service, my acceptance of any title of honour from a foreign state might be liable to injurious constructions.

In another letter addressed to Mr. G. Hansen and Mr. J. P. Ruhl, the Commissioners of the Order, Hastings expressed his gratitude for the dignity that had been conferred "on a person whom you considered, as he is, most deservedly dear to me":—

> The obligation at this moment presses upon me with a stronger impulse, and I yield to it with pleasure, . . . having just received the information, long and anxiously expected, that the last sanction which was necessary to confirm the act of the Chapter of St. Joachim . . . has actually taken place, the King having been graciously pleased to grant unto Lieutenant-Colonel Imhoff his royal license and permission to receive and wear the ensigns of the illustrious Order of St. Joachim, and to order the same to be registered in the College of Arms.

King George the Third not only permitted Imhoff—who had now received a commission in the British army—to accept the insignia and rank of a Knight Commander of the Order of St. Joachim, but granted him at the same time leave to assume, in virtue of that foreign decoration, the titular distinction of a Knight in England. This was peculiarly gratifying to Hastings;

and he was so pleased by the manner in which Mr. Hansen and Mr. Ruhl had discharged their duties that he invited them to pay him a visit at Daylesford. He addressed the invitation to the former, who was residing on the Continent. He said :—

> You have inspired me with the desire of improving the valuable acquisition of your acquaintance. I am too far advanced in life to hope for an opportunity to seek it abroad ; but chance, business, or desire of revisiting the scenes of your early pleasures, and not the least endeared of your connections, may draw you once more to this country. In that case I should esteem it a happiness to be allowed the honour of receiving you as my guest. The lady of the house is already prepared, with sentiments of esteem and acknowledgments similar to my own, to offer you the most friendly welcome. Permit me, Sir, through you, to make the same tender to Mr. Ruhl.

CHAPTER V

HIS ARCH-ENEMY

As the private life of Warren Hastings was embittered for many a year by a phenomenal enmity that was at the root of his impeachment, it is necessary to refer at some length to the man who, in the effort to accomplish his destruction, was instrumental in conferring immortality upon, and in securing the sympathy of posterity for his would-be victim. That man was Philip Francis, the son of a clergyman at Dublin, where he was born in 1740. He accompanied his father to London in 1751; was placed at St. Paul's School, where, aided still by his father, he became a good classic. At the age of sixteen he entered the office of the Secretary of State as a junior clerk. He worked hard, was discreet, and made himself so useful that he was attached, in 1758, to the British expedition against Cherbourg, and, in 1760, to the British Embassy to Portugal. He then settled down once more to the routine work of a Government office in London, gave proof of talent, won the respect of his superiors, and slowly mounted the ladder of promotion, until, at length, he became Chief Clerk at the War Office. Meanwhile he had drifted into pamphleteering, and had learnt, it is believed, to make a ferocious use of the Press, notwithstanding that he is credited with the authorship of a letter to the *Public Advertiser*, in which the writer protested against the liberty of the Press being "prostituted to the meanest acrimony, scurrility, and contemptible ribaldry, to serve the infamous and pernicious purposes of envy, the child of ambition, and of detraction, the concomitant of envy." He is now generally regarded as the author of the *Letters of Junius*, which "exercised"—according to Lord Campbell in his *Life of Lord Mansfield*—"a tyranny of which we can form little conception, living in an age when the Press is more decorous, and we are able by law to repress its excesses." They were attributed from time to time to thirty-seven more or less notable men, including Francis and Burke, and at first the preponderance of opinion pointed to the latter. Francis was well aware that a discovery of the authorship would mean social ostracism and political ruin to the author, and he was not above the pretence of accepting the current suspicion that Burke was that author, in order, apparently, that he might the better divert suspicion from himself. Burke repudiated the authorship, and in November, 1771, he wrote to the Honourable Charles Townsend: "I have, I daresay, to nine-tenths of my acquaintance denied my being the author of *Junius*, or having any knowledge of the author, as often as the thing was mentioned, whether in jest or earnest, in style of disapprobation or compliment. I now give you my word and honour that I know not the author of that paper, and I authorise you to say so." But a lie often dies hard, and Burke may have suffered much from the difficulty he experienced in proving a negative.

Francis wrote in June, 1770, to his brother-in-law, Alexander Macrabie, who subsequently accompanied him to India in the capacity of Private Secretary, and for whom he entertained affection: "Junius is not known, and that circumstance is perhaps as curious as any of his writings. I have always suspected Burke, but whoever he is it is impossible he can ever discover himself. The offence he has given to His Majesty and . . . is more than any private man could support; he would soon be crushed." Francis's father never suspected the authorship of the letters, for he once enquired of his son: "Who is this devil, Junius, or rather legion of devils?" It need hardly be said that Francis did not satisfy his curiosity.

Mr. John Taylor, the author of *Junius Identified*, declared that "in all his researches he had not" met with one thought, one fact, one word which in the slightest degree impeded the course of the demonstration "that Francis was 'Junius.'" Joseph Parkes and Herman Merivale, in their *Memoirs of Sir Philip Francis*, endorsed this conclusion, and the latter said that he had not discovered, during his examination of the mass of

Francis's papers submitted to him, "a single record, or a single passage, which raises (by comparison of dates, sentiments, or other circumstances) the slightest improbability against the current supposition." Macaulay considered that the identification of Francis was established, and regarded him as a man who was "prone to malevolence," and also to the "error of mistaking his malevolence for public virtue." Leslie Stephen remarks that "it would be impossible to describe the character of Junius except in terms strikingly applicable to Francis"; and "there may have been two such men whose careers coincided during Francis's most vigorous period, but it seems more probable that there was only one." Malleson is convinced that "none but Francis could have been the parallel of Junius."

Francis's advancement was not proportionate to his expectations, and, while still comparatively young, he was a disappointed and a soured man. He was conscious of the possession of remarkable powers that he had diligently cultivated, but for which he could find no adequate employment in London. His official salary was small, and though it was supplemented by perquisites that, added to the precarious fruits of gambling, and of a little dabbling on the Stock Exchange, enabled him to make both ends meet, he lived in a very quiet way, in a house none too spacious for his large family. He had agreeable manners; he was witty, well informed, and good-looking. He had great self-control, and he bore himself at home and abroad so prudently that for a long time no relative or friend suspected that he was the most ruthless satirist of the age. He served under highly placed officials who were endowed with mediocre abilities, and by accommodating himself as a subordinate to their weaknesses, and by the exercise of great industry and ability in helping them in the discharge of their duties, he gained their confidence, and unobtrusively promoted their success. He found little sympathy among his associates for his advanced views about the rights of subjects and the responsibilities of Kings, Ministers, and Judges; but, however extravagant may have been some of his opinions, he was strongly imbued with public spirit. It was galling to a man of his talent to find the avenues to promotion in the public service blocked by members of the aristocracy and their friends. He was too cautious to wear his heart on his sleeve; but there is every reason to believe that he vented his spleen by anonymous contributions to the Press.

In 1773 he was First Clerk in the War Office, and imagining that he had been slighted by Lord Barrington, the War Secretary, he resigned, and revenged himself by letters in the papers, in which "all his dignity, all his power of keen, anatomising sarcasm, all his caustic elegance of language" deserted him, and he was guilty of assailing Lord Barrington with a "vulgar ferocity as discreditable," continues Merivale, "to the writer's intellectual power as to his self-respect and manliness of character." In one of his published letters Francis said: "Next to the Duke of Grafton, I verily believe that the blackest heart in the kingdom belongs to Lord Barrington." For all this Francis, being out of employ in the following year, and with poverty staring him in the face, begged Lord Barrington to use his influence to obtain for him the appointment of member of the new Council of India that was being constituted under Lord North's Act for the better government of that country. The appointment, though the large salary of £10,000 a year was attached to it, had been declined by Burke and others, and was almost going a-begging. Lord Barrington complied, and, according to an autobiographical fragment found among Francis's papers, "as soon as I had explained everything to him, he wrote the handsomest and strongest letter imaginable in my favour to Lord North. Other interests contributed, but I owe my success to Lord Barrington." This proves how well Francis succeeded in guarding the secret of his contributions to the Press. He kept up appearances so well that not only did Lord Barrington regard him with much respect, but even the King remarked in a letter to Lord North that "Mr. Francis is allowed to be a man of talents." On his return from India Francis became an intimate friend of Lord Barrington, and often accepted his hospitality. Lord Barrington died in 1793, little suspecting how unworthy Francis was of his esteem.

Francis thus sprang, at the age of thirty-four, from impecuniosity and insignificance in England to a position of great prominence and activity in India; and his views of life should have been modified by his unexpected good fortune. But he took out with him to India the same heart that had cherished so many evil feelings since his youth, and an inordinate self-consciousness. It was not surprising that he was prejudiced against Hastings from the first. There is some reason to suppose that this prejudice commenced during his visit to Lord Clive, at Walcot, in Shropshire, a few weeks after his appointment; for the mind of the hero of Plassey was at the time warped by the prejudices of which he himself was the object at Westminster. Apart from this, there was the fact that Francis arrived in Calcutta imbued with the not unusual contempt of home-trained men for public functionaries in India, who have acquired their knowledge of public affairs locally. Francis had not been on terms of private intimacy, but he had worked with many men of mark in England, and had acquired a varied knowledge of the administration of Departments. He was well read, especially in constitutional history and biography; he was an excellent Latin, Greek, and French scholar; and he had travelled in Portugal, France, Germany, and Italy. Hastings had been twenty years, in all, in India when Francis landed as one of the new Council that was to hold him in check. He was now constituted Governor-General, and he was in a mood to expect from everybody full recognition of the fact. He had risen from small beginnings by his own ability; but his experience was almost exclusively Indian, and he may have been in the habit of mistaking the cackle of Calcutta for "the murmur of the world." Existence from the susceptible days of youth to the prime of life in an atmosphere of Oriental obsequiousness is calculated to give an European an idea of his own importance and essentiality that is not usually shared by his countrymen on his return home. Hastings was a master of his own work, and he may have been tempted to regard with something like contempt the three locally inexperienced men who were thrust upon him as his counsellors. He did not, probably, feel the need of advice; and he could not but have doubted their competency to advise him. They soon showed that they wished to make up for their inexperience by being "wise in their own conceit," and by being meddlesome with, and suspicious of the expert at the helm. If Francis had been an amiable or a just man, he might have met Hastings in a conciliatory manner, and become his able ally; and Hastings then would not have been immortalised by Francis's impeachment. But there was little in common between the two men.

It has been said that Francis was associated in the new Council of the Governor-General with General Clavering,[1] Colonel Monson, and Mr. Barwell. The last-named gentleman, who was in Calcutta when he was appointed, was an experienced Civil Servant of the Company's who cherished a profound respect for Hastings, and was equipped with the knowledge necessary to his new position. But Clavering and Monson were gallant soldiers, and nothing more. The former had seen active service in the West Indies, and had exercised some influence over the supple minds of certain members of Parliament. Hence Lord North regarded him as a fit and proper person to send to India. The place suited the man; but whether the man suited the place, or whether the public service might suffer by the presence of the man in the place, was a matter that Lord North did not consider that his duty to his Sovereign and his country demanded that he should trouble himself about. Whatever may have been his professional merits, Clavering was a narrow-minded, ill-informed, and irascible gentleman, who was bound to be a nuisance in Council. Monson resembled him in attainments and temperament, but he had this advantage, that he had seen some service in Southern India. They were both as clay in the

---

[1] General Sir John Clavering, K.B., was the third son of Sir James Clavering, of Greencroft, Durham. He was born in 1722, and he married the Lady Diana, second daughter of the first Earl of Delawarr. He entered the Army in the Coldstream Guards; and in 1759 he served with marked distinction at the capture of Guadeloupe. He was then appointed Aide-de-camp to the King. In 1772 he became Colonel of the 52nd Foot, and in 1776 he was created a Knight of the Bath. He attained the rank of Lieutenant-General in 1770. In 1773 he was appointed to the command of the Bengal Army, with a seat in the new Council in Bengal, and a salary of £10,000 a year. In 1777 he died in Calcutta, aged fifty-five. He was "an honest, straightforward man, of passionate disposition, and mediocre abilities." (See *Dic. of National Biog.*)

hands of Francis during the weary voyage with him round the Cape; and they ranged themselves on his side long ere they arrived at the land where, as it proved, Monson [1] was to die in two, and Clavering in three years after they assumed office.

Francis embarked on the 1st April, 1774, in the *Ashburnham*, with General and Lady Diana Clavering, the three Misses Clavering, Colonel and Lady Anne Monson, Colonel Thornton, Mr. Macrabie, and seven others. The *Anson* sailed at the same time, carrying with her Sir Elijah Impey, Mr. Hyde, Mr. Chambers, and Mr. Lemaistre, the newly appointed judges of the Supreme Court of Calcutta, and Lady Impey. The *Anson* kept ahead all the way, and reached and left Madras before the arrival of the other vessel. "Nothing could exceed" the "marks of honour and respect" that were shewn—according to Macrabie—to Francis and his colleagues by the authorities of Fort St. George. Mr. Alexander Wynch was then Governor, but what Francis thought of him is not recorded. Letters of welcome to India from Hastings were received at Madras by some of the party. He assured Monson that he would "seek to cultivate both your friendship and confidence, as well from personal prepossession as from the conviction of the necessity of such a mutual understanding for the conduct of the great and difficult affairs in which we have been joined." Little dreaming, perhaps, that he was addressing the author of *Junius*, Hastings conveyed to

[1] Colonel the Hon. George Monson, third son of the first Lord Monson, was born in 1730, and, like Hastings, was educated at Westminster School, under Dr. Nicholls. He was appointed an Ensign in the 1st Foot Guards in 1760; was elected a member for Lincoln in 1754, and retained his seat in Parliament until 1768. In 1756 he was appointed a Groom of the Bedchamber of the Prince of Wales, and he retained that post when the Prince ascended the throne as George III. He exchanged from the Guards into Draper's Regiment, proceeded to India in 1758, and served with distinction as second in command at the siege and capture of Pondicherry in 1760. He also distinguished himself at the siege of Manilla in 1762. He returned to England in 1764, and in 1769 became full Colonel. In 1774 he was appointed a member of the Council in Bengal, and sailed to India accompanied by his wife, Lady Anne, daughter of Henry Vane, Earl of Darlington, and great-granddaughter of Charles II. He resigned his seat in Council on account of ill-health in 1776, and died the same month in Calcutta, aged forty-six. (See *Dic. of National Biog.*)

Francis his cordial congratulations on his appointment, and proceeded to say: "I received with particular pleasure a letter from General Clavering, wherein he unites with his own intentions an assurance of your disposition to co-operate in measures of public utility." This would seem to show that, while Clavering did, Francis did not write to Hastings during the nine months that intervened between the date of his appointment and that of his embarkation. "My hopes and wishes," Hastings proceeded to say, "are equally sanguine, to concur heartily in such measures as will most fully answer the intention of your appointment, and reflect honour on our councils. I shall impatiently expect your arrival here, both from the personal satisfaction that I propose to myself from it, and the desire of entering upon the several public measures which may be necessary for the discharge of the great trust confided to our joint direction."

Calcutta was reached on the 19th October, or in a little more than six months from England. Francis and his colleagues expected to have been received with more striking marks of distinction than Hastings prepared; but it was always maintained by Hastings that he did not fail in his duty, or in official courtesy on this occasion. He knew well enough that he would have to reckon with these new colleagues as possible adversaries in the future. He may have dissented from the idea that he needed their control; but he was too mature an official, and too alive to his own dignity, to put upon them a gratuitous affront on their reaching their destination. Most probably, therefore, the new arrivals had developed during their long voyage an overweening idea of their own importance, coupled with an inadequate recognition of Hastings' rights. They were prejudiced against him from the date of their appointment, and prejudice is easily nourished. Francis landed with the general conviction in his mind that Hastings was the representative of a pernicious system of administration, and the embodiment of official vices. He prejudged and precondemned him, in the evil fashion of Junius; and everything that Hastings did, or said, was attributed to low motives that should be habitually resisted.

It is not necessary to give a sketch of the incidents of Francis's conflict with Hastings. Suffice it to say that he systematically plotted his destruction, and cherished the hope of being his successor. He had not been in India five months before he alleged, in a letter to Lord North, the Prime Minister, that "without denying" the Governor-General "some little talents of the third or fourth order, we were as much deceived with regard to his abilities and judgment as to his other qualifications." There is no reason to suppose that at any moment Francis was inclined to think well of Hastings, yet he declared to Lord North that "I look back to my own prepossessions in his favour as to a sort of delirium, from which he himself has recovered me." He chuckled over what he regarded as the fact that "the honours which were intended" for Hastings had been delayed in consequence of the abatement of "the excessive admiration and esteem" which Lord North at one time professed for the Governor-General; and he soon wrote to a friend in London that, "I am now, I think, on the road to the government of Bengal, which I believe is the first situation in the world attainable by a subject. I will not baulk my future." He had leapt from the position of an ex-clerk of the War Office to that of a member of the Governor-General's Council; but his head was turned by his good fortune, and he failed to see the personal application of the remark which he intended as a sneer against Hastings, that "men suddenly raised to arbitrary power from low stations are seldom improved by it." High station did not improve him, for it increased his arrogance and malevolence while it fanned his ambition. Hastings had attained eminence by slow advancement up the official ladder, and the improvement on the way of his natural gifts; but he stopped Francis's way. The difficulties and dangers of Hastings' position were ample without their being supplemented by the remorseless enmity of Francis, and it is marvellous that he succeeded as well as he did in maintaining the honour of England, and promoting the prosperity of the Company. Yet Hastings, according to Francis, had "resided so long in Bengal that in many respects he may be considered as a native." He "has all the craft of a Bengalee," united with vanity and impatience of contradiction. He was capable of deceiving "any man unacquainted with his arts, or less proficient in hypocrisy than himself." His "first object is money," but he is not "strictly avaricious; rapacity, not avarice, is the general characteristic of our people in India."

Francis did not confine his hatred to Hastings, but it extended to all Hastings' friends or allies. As Junius, he is believed to have held up many notable men in England to public scorn as monuments of depravity; yet, in a private memorandum, he stated that "there are no such men in Europe as Hastings, George Vansittart, and Barwell." The last-named possessed, according to Francis, "all the bad qualities common to this climate and country, of which he is in every sense a native." He "is rapacious without industry, and ambitious without an exertion of his faculties, or steady application to affairs"; he "will do whatever can be done by bribery and intrigue"; his mind "is unequal to any serious constant occupation, except gaming, in which alone he is indefatigable." Francis accused Sir Eyre Coote of "settling the most infamous and atrocious measures in perfect conjunction with Hastings and Barwell," and "I will not content myself with saying I never knew, but upon my soul I never heard of so abandoned a scoundrel. It is a character to which your English ideas of dirt and meanness do not reach." Sir Hector Munro was another military man for whom Francis entertained the greatest contempt: "The character of the man is reprobated and abhorred by everybody who knew him," and he "has the blackest heart that ever was lodged in a human breast." It was sufficient for a man to thwart Francis to secure his scathing contempt and unscrupulous abuse. "I pass my life," he once wrote, "in an eternal combat with villainy, folly, and prostitution of every species." It must have been impossible —as Clavering and Monson, like Hastings and Barwell, soon found—to work harmoniously with a man intolerant of opposition, steeped in vanity, and prone to jump, on slight provocation, to the most cruel conclusions.

Francis did not take kindly to, or make the best of India. He never travelled a hundred miles from Calcutta, and the interest that he took in the natives was entirely theoretical. He regarded them as the helpless victims of the policy that he was called upon to reform, and he strove to obtain consideration for their rights as men, while he despised them in his heart. He could not, he said, "form a conception of more refined depravity" than was shewn by Bengalees in office; and he added, in a private memorandum, that "the united testimony of Moguls and Europeans is equally unfavourable to the inhabitants of the rest of the provinces." His "experience and observation" did not subsequently induce him to modify this sweeping judgment of a vast number of his fellow-creatures who were distinguished by domestic virtues, and by loyalty to those who promoted their welfare. At the same time he considered that the natives should be left to their own manners, customs, and devices as much as possible; and he advocated their employment in the government of their own country. He desired to make British power paramount; but he held, much as Russian officials in Central Asia now do, that the Government should merely "watch the administration of men in office," and "be content with a gross tribute," and that the moral improvement of the people was outside the range of practical politics in the East. He was opposed to conquest, and he had no sympathy with the arguments employed by Hastings, and ratified by the Court of Directors, to justify annexation.

Francis's salary was large, but it did not allow of such savings being made as he may have confidently expected when he was appointed. He was compelled by due regard for his official position to take a "large, but rather mean house" in Calcutta, rented at £500 a year, and to maintain an establishment of sixty servants, none of whom rendered efficient service. Later on he became, he said, "master of the finest house in Bengal, with a hundred servants, a country house, spacious gardens, horses and carriages." He was a great card player, and, by his own admission, he "won a fortune" in Calcutta at cards. "It is true," he wrote to a friend at home, "I have won a fortune, and intend to keep it. Your tenderness for the loser is admirable. If money be his blood, I feel no kind of remorse in opening his veins; the bloodsucker should bleed, and can very well afford it." On the 16th of September, 1776, he informed a friend that "on one blessed day of the present year of our Lord I had won about twenty thousand pounds at whist. It is reduced to about twelve, and I now never play but for trifles, and that only once a week." Barwell was the chief loser, his losses being estimated by Francis at £30,000, "of which Judge Lemaistre and Colonel Leslie had a share." Hastings may have conformed to the card-playing fashion of his time, but Francis did not mention having won money from, or lost money to him.

Francis "hated the thought," he said, "of dying of the spleen," in India, "like a rat in a hole," partly because "I know my death would give pleasure to people to whom my life has given none, and whose private wishes I am unwilling to gratify." He disliked Calcutta, but he enjoyed good health during his stay there. "With good management," he remarked on one occasion, "I am a match for the climate." But he suffered at times from depression of spirits, and a year after his arrival he wrote from Calcutta to Henry Strachey,[1] and said :—

As for myself, I lead too miserable a life to wish to continue here in bad company. The longer I live, and the more I observe, so much the more am I confirmed in thinking that no man, before or since my Lord Clive, has had the least idea of the constitution of a government in this country upon any great or even rational principles. I have worked double and treble tides. I hope I shall gain credit, for I assure you I see no prospect of profit. I persuade myself you will support my cause vigorously at the west end of the town. In the City I think I shall be a favourite. At the same time, I am not ambitious of popularity, much less do I desire to figure in the newspapers. It would mortify me beyond measure to have my merits canvassed in the *Public Advertiser* to my advantage.

Seven months later Francis wrote :—

I see no reason why Barwell should be alive, but that death does not think it worth while to kill him. He is a mere shadow. As for Hastings, I promise you he is more tough than any of us, and will never die a natural death.

Irritated at last beyond endurance by the systematic opposition of Francis, Hastings remarked on the 20th July, 1780, when replying to a minute of Francis : "I do not trust to his promise of candour, convinced that he is incapable of it. I judge of his public conduct by my experience of his private, which I have found devoid of truth and honour." He proceeded to explain

[1] Historical Manuscripts Commission, 6th Report.

that Francis had deliberately broken a solemn agreement formed between them. Hastings did not conceal from himself that Francis would be compelled by the custom of the age to demand "satisfaction." Francis was equal to the occasion. He met Hastings in the Revenue Board Office, and read to him a few words in which he said that he was preparing a formal answer to the accusation; but "no answer I can give to the matter of that paper can be adequate to the dishonour done me by the terms you have made use of. You have left me no alternative but to demand personal satisfaction of you for the affront you have offered me." Hastings replied that he "had expected the demand, and was ready to answer it." On the following day Hastings ordered his minute to be recorded; and Francis, in view of contingencies, employed himself in settling his affairs, "burning papers, etc., in case of the worst," which he found to be "dull work." On the morning of the 17th, at about 6 o'clock, Hastings, accompanied by Colonel Pearse as his second, and Francis, accompanied by Colonel Watson, met on the ground near Belvedere, and were placed at a distance of fourteen paces from one another. Francis thus described what followed :—

> My pistol missing fire, I changed it. We then fired together, and I was wounded and fell. I thought that my backbone was broke, and of course that I could not survive it. After the first confusion had subsided, and after I had suffered great inconvenience from being carried to a wrong place, I was at last conveyed to Major Foley's house on a bed. The surgeon arrived in about an hour and a half from the time I was wounded, and cut out the ball, and bled me twice in the course of the day. Mr. Hastings sends to know when he may visit me.

Francis desired Colonel Watson to "tell Mr. Hastings as civilly as possible that I am forced to decline his visit." On the 24th, or a week after the duel, Francis returned to Calcutta. On the 11th September he attended Council, and there was "great civility between H. and me." But it was a hollow truce; and four months after the duel, and while smarting under a sense of baffled hatred and official defeat, Francis left India, after a residence there of seven years. He probably buoyed himself up with the hope that the day would yet come when he would succeed in turning the tables on Hastings with a vengeance.

Francis went to Windsor, shortly after his arrival in England, to present to Queen Charlotte a parcel with which he had been entrusted by Lady Day, the wife of the Advocate-General of Madras. In a letter to Sir John Day he declared that it had not "fallen to my lot to see anything comparable to the gracefulness, affability, and dignity with which" the Queen "expressed herself to me and to everybody. In addition to all which I did not know there had been so many diamonds in the world as Her Majesty was covered with." He also said that he had had "a most gracious reception" from the King. But the Court of Directors offered him no greeting, or compliment on his return. "They know that I am alive," he said; "and as long as they know that, I think they will not quarrel with me." The recollection of this neglect assisted to embitter him against the whole system of administration in India. "The Court of Directors is devoted to Hastings," he wrote two months later, "and I am in great hopes will go to the devil with him." He endeavoured to distinguish between the East India Company and the Court of Directors. He owed much to the Company, he argued, but nothing to the Directors. All the same he seems to have shared the candid opinions of a friend of his, that a corporation like the East India Company, "composed of traders of various denominations, and instituted merely for mercantile purposes, *must* be a scoundrel from its very frame."

Mr. Barwell wrote on the 18th February, 1782, from London to Hastings at Calcutta: [1]—

It is with pleasure I inform you that Francis daily loses ground. The petulance and captiousness of his character have totally sunk him in the opinion of the Directors, and his manners have caused that disgust which breaks forth into reproach whenever his name is mentioned. Your friend, Mr. Sullivan, has, with infinite ability, defeated him in his attempt on the direction, and his impatience under it has completed the business. Just after Francis's arrival, he gave out how well he had been received, and how much distinguished by Lord North. Within six weeks of the promulgation of this puff, I had the satisfaction of detecting him; for upon questioning Mr. Brummell, his lordship's secretary, he laughed, and observed that Mr. Francis had been at Bushey once, and from that period to this had never

[1] Copied from the original letter in the Hastings collection by Mr. E. B. Impey, for his *Memoirs* of his father.

repeated his visit to Lord North. Lord Mansfield positively declined his first visit, and I do not find that any one of the King's Ministers hold any intercourse with him. Thus circumstanced he no longer exults, but, chagrined and mortified, complains in bitterness of spirit, and prophesies the loss of India under any government but his own.

Francis spared no trouble on his return home to bring about the ruin of Hastings, who had received a year's extension of office as a proof of the Company's satisfaction with him; and, so early as January, 1782, he wrote to a friend that "everything that could be done by one human creature to support a cause, has been done by me from the day of my arrival in England." He never disguised from himself the difficulty that attended the task which he had undertaken. Hastings had made many friends in the Houses of Parliament as well as in Leadenhall Street, and Francis could boast of comparatively few intimacies. But nothing daunted, and possessed as he was of wide experience and much craft, he soon established the right to be regarded as an important authority on Indian affairs, and made himself exceedingly useful to the politicians who professed to be animated by a desire to reform the administration of India. He is credited at the British Museum with the authorship of a political tract, entitled *A state of the British Authority in Bengal, under the Government of Mr. Hastings, exemplified in his conduct in the case of Mahomet Reza Khan, with a debate upon a letter from Mobarick al Dowlah, Nabob of Bengal, from authentic documents.* In a preface it is explained that this "appeal" is "not addressed to the passions, but to the people"; that it claims to be a "narration of facts"; and that "it exhibits one great example of that usurpation of the Company's servants, of that spirit of disobedience, I had almost said rebellion, which, while it threatens our affairs in India with instant ruin, holds forth a solecism in politics that is a mockery of every idea of Government and legal authority." The "debate" is that which took place in the Council at Calcutta on the 22nd and 23rd November, and the 15th and 20th December, 1779, and Francis's observations occupy the largest part of the tract.

Francis is also believed to have been the author of a *Short Account* of Hastings' conduct in 1775, in repudiating the action of Colonel Lauchlan Macleane, who, acting under the authority which Hastings had conditionally given to him and another gentleman, tendered Hastings' resignation to the Court of Directors, which the Court accepted. As a matter of fact, Hastings retracted his determination to yield to his enemies by resigning. "I am now resolved," he wrote to his friends, "to see the issue of my appeal, believing it impossible that men, whose actions are so frantic, can be permitted to remain in charge of so important a trust." There was certainly some misconception on the part of Hastings, or his representative, which was severely censured by the Court, though in the end Hastings was allowed to remain in office. The writer of the *Short Account* remarked in the preface that "it has been objected to the strictures which have lately appeared on the administration of Mr. Hastings that they are personal"; and he then proceeds to say:—

> For my own part, I covet not the praise of that cold philosophical justice, which, while it condemns the treason, suffers the traitor to escape. Such languid censure is, in my opinion, little better than the accomplice of crime. The most atrocious offenders will be the foremost to embrace a morality which terminates in abstract propositions, and contents itself with preaching rigid rules of piety and virtue, without presuming to interfere with practice, and without applying them as the measures of public approbation or contempt.

The writer then declared that, in the case of Hastings,—

> It is impossible to separate the person from the politics of the Governor. That gentleman, with the concurrence of one humble assessor, has, during the last five years, ruled the affairs of India by his absolute will, in violation of all the wise maxims of administration established by experience, and in contempt and defiance of the legal control and superintendence of his masters. In despotic states the character, nay, the caprices of the Tyrant must be studied in order to form a judgment of the principles of his Government.

The incident had been condoned by the Court of Directors, and must have been forgotten by the public when the *Short Account* appeared; and it is difficult to believe that any one but Francis could have thought it worth while to hark back so many years for the means of holding Hastings up to contempt.

But Francis perceived the risk of employing to any considerable extent in his designs against Hastings his aptitude for scurrilous pamphleteering, for he could not have long maintained his anonymity, as no one had cause to feel as he did. He paved the way for his entrance into Parliament by making himself useful to Burke, Fox, and others; and in 1783, on the introduction of the India Bill in the House of Commons, Burke acknowledged his indebtedness to him in the following words :—

> Consider the fate of those who have met with the applauses of the Directors. Colonel Monson, one of the best of men, had his days shortened by the applauses, destitute of the support, of the Company. General Clavering, whose panegyric was made in every despatch from England, whose hearse was bedewed with the tears, and hung round with the eulogies of the Court of Directors, burst an honest and indignant heart at the treachery of those who ruined him by their praises. Uncommon patience and temper supported Mr. Francis a while longer under the baneful influence of the commendation of the Court of Directors ; his health, however, gave way at length, and in utter despair he returned to Europe. At his return the doors of the India House were shut to this man who had been the object of their constant admiration. He has indeed escaped with life, but he has forfeited all expectation of credit, consequence, party, and following—this man, whose deep reach of thought, whose large legislative conception, and whose grand plans of policy make the most shining part of our reports, from whence we have all learned our lessons, if we have learned any good ones ; this man, from whose materials those gentlemen who have least acknowledged it have yet spoken as from a brief; this man, driven from his employment, discountenanced by the Directors, has had no other reward, and no other distinction but that inward "sunshine of the soul" which a good conscience can always bestow on itself. He has not yet had so much as a good word, but from a person too insignificant to make any other return for the means with which he has been furnished, for performing his share of a duty which is equally urgent on us all.

It must have been well known to most of the hearers of these remarks that Francis voluntarily resigned his appointment ; that, as the fruits of an actual service of only six years in India, he brought home a fortune that, by his own admission, yielded an income of £3,000 a year ; and that he was not welcomed by the Court of Directors chiefly on account of his malignant hostility against Hastings. For a time Burke deceived himself about the character and motives of the man who influenced his mind, but he failed to communicate his early estimate of Francis to many of his contemporaries, or to modify the calm verdict of history. It was an ill day for Burke's[1] reputation when he opened the "porches of his ears" to the "leprous distilment" of the reputed author of the *Letters of Junius.*

Francis was returned to Parliament in 1784, as member for Yarmouth, Isle of Wight, and seized an early opportunity to declare that he had not a "spark of personal animosity to Mr. Hastings. We are both, I believe, of a temper too warm to be capable of lasting resentments. Our contest is at an end, and the hostilities it produced expired with it. Assuredly I feel no enmity to him, and I readily acquit him of harbouring any against me." He professed too much, and claimed to be capable of a magnanimity that was foreign to his character. He had had many a struggle with Hastings in India, he had been defeated all along the line, and had finally been wounded in a duel that his uncompromising hostility provoked. To bring Hastings metaphorically to the block became the chief aim of his existence. But his bitter feeling against Hastings was well known in and out of the House of Commons, for it had become his master passion. When, therefore, it was proposed by Burke and his coadjutors in the preliminary proceedings to add the name of Francis to the Parliamentary Committee appointed to consider Hastings' reply to the articles of indictment, the sense of fair play in the majority of the members revolted, and the motion was rejected by nearly four votes to one. This well-merited rebuff greatly irritated the promoters of the prosecution, but they nursed their wrath for a while. Later on the selection of members to be managers of the trial took place, and Fox, unwarned by the former incident, moved the inclusion of the name of Francis. But the House threw out the motion by two votes to one. Thereupon Burke and the other managers addressed a letter to Francis, in which they humbly solicited his

[1] Burke entertained a sincere regard for Francis at one time. "Be assured," he once wrote to him at Calcutta, "that no person rejoices more sincerely than I do in hearing every circumstance of fortune and honour that attends you;" and he concluded by alluding to his own and his brother's "affection" for him. Later on, however, his opinion of Francis underwent a considerable change, and he ceased to regard him as a friend.

advice and assistance during the trial. They claimed that "an exact knowledge of the affairs of Bengal was requisite in every step of their proceedings, and that it was necessary that their information should come from sources not only competent but unsuspected." This no one could reasonably deny. But they went on to give Francis, who had systematically opposed Hast-

FRANCIS (*after Gillray*).

ings in Council, credit for an "exact obedience to the authority placed over him, an inflexible integrity in himself, and a firm resistance to corrupt practices in others." The House had issued its mandate to the managers of the trial. It had also pronounced on two occasions its deliberate opinion that, owing to notorious circumstances, Francis was not a fit and proper person to be a manager. Yet the managers did not scruple to bring the authority of the House into contempt by endeavouring to whitewash their ally, and declaring, in effect, that notwithstanding his formal and repeated rejection by the House, they would take it upon themselves to vest him with an authority, and concede him an influence which the House disapproved. They begged the whole question as to his impartiality, and plainly indicated that they would not hesitate about deriving inspiration from a tainted and discredited source.

FRANÇOIS PHILIPPEAUX,
Citoyen actif et sans culotte (after Humphry).

Party spirit ran high in those days, and prompted men of honour to lend themselves to a flagrant imposture that could have deceived no one. Francis may have been consoled by the letter for the want of confidence in him that the House displayed. He remained behind the scenes during the trial, prompting the actors ; and it was greatly, if not chiefly, owing to his inexhaustible aversion to Hastings, and his unremitting toil in the prosecution, that the proceedings were unconscionably protracted.

In one of the *Letters of Simpkin the Second to his dear*

brother in Wales, to which attention is drawn on a subsequent page, the author refers to Francis as a "hack in office in London who, by servility and flattery," became, according to his own description, the "fifth part of a potent King" in Bengal; and who, having striven in vain to effect the ruin of Hastings, had returned to England. The rhymster then proceeded :—

No sooner on shore had our Phill set his feet,
Than he drove, like a post boy, to Leadenhall Street;
In the flames of his malice, he burnt to disclose
A tale which had cost him some years to compose;
But he got a rebuff from the Court of Directors;
They were Hastings' friends; they were virtue's protectors;
They paid just regard to their honour and glory;
They read not Phill's papers, they heard not Phill's story.
Tho' like lightning to England from India he came,
In speed he was greatly surpass'd by his fame;
They knew how the measures of Hastings he crost,
How near his advice Coromandel had lost;
By the Court of Directors, it clearly was seen
That the man was a compound of envy and spleen.

Then away to the mongers of boroughs went he,
To try, if with some one he could not agree;
And find a fit corner—for once—to his use
For speech unrestrained, and for licenc'd abuse.
But when he discovered that loud declaration
Could produce no effect on a sensible nation,
His attention was turn'd to the Quixote-like Burke,
Who is fond of engaging in Quixote-like work.

The poet then describes Francis's negotiations with Burke, Fox, and Sheridan :—

Three years have elaps'd since the suit they began;
They may work many more, let them do all they can,
Before they will conquer this much injured man!

Burke declared that he could not proceed without Francis's aid as a manager, and thus :—

"Betray'd the base source whence thy charges all sprung,"
Said part of the House, which till then had believ'd
The story, now find themselves grossly deceiv'd.

How many good men now are griev'd to the heart
To think they were talk'd into taking a part;

But Fr——s triumphantly laughs in his sleeve,
To think he so long could the public deceive.
As he walk'd along Bond Street, he said to a friend,
"Tho' my foe be acquitted, 'twill answer my end;
Opprest with fatigue, and o'erburdened with cost,
His health will be broken, his fortune be lost."
Then he swore by the Lord, he would not cease pursuing
Till death and damnation had finish'd his ruin,
Tho' so generous an oath he confess'd gave him pain
To come from a bosom so kind and humane.

Mr. Fox retained his regard for Francis to the end of his life; and in January, 1806, when news was received of the death of

CHARLES JAMES FOX.

the Marquis of Cornwallis, Governor-General of India, at Gazeepoor, and when the new Ministry was formed in consequence of the premature death of Mr. Pitt, Hastings noted in his diary that among the appointments would probably be that of "Mr. Francis for India, urged by Mr. Fox." But Francis was now sixty-eight years old, and he was obviously disqualified by age —as Lord Cornwallis had been—for service in India. Fox was anxious to serve Francis; for, when almost the whole of his former allies in Parliament deserted him, Francis stood by his side, and he was among those personal friends who raised between them a fund that gave Fox £3,000 a year after he squandered all his own resources. But Fox knew Francis too intimately to thoroughly trust him ; and though he availed himself freely during the trial of Hastings of Francis's services as an informer and adviser, he could not overcome the apprehension that if Francis, at an advanced age, and with infirmities of disposition that age did not modify, were appointed Governor-General, he would set all official India by the ears, and provoke conflicts

FOX (*after Gillray*).

with the home Government. But he induced Lord Grenville to offer Francis the Governorship of the Cape of Good Hope, and the Order of the Bath. Francis declined the Governorship ; accepted the Knighthood of the Bath ; and aspired to, but did not obtain admission to the Privy Council. His ambition, however, was not satisfied, and he never forgave Fox for what he regarded as that statesman's ingratitude. The Prince Regent endeavoured to console him for his disappointment. "Francis," said he, "if you will accept the Cape, I'll send you on farther when I come into power." In 1812 the Prince desired him to state his "wishes and claims" in writing, and Francis complied by drawing up a memorial in which, after a brief allusion to his services in India and in Parliament, he remarked that the Prince[1] had always "designated me, and particularly to Mr. Fox, as the person whom he meant to appoint to the office of Governor-General, and that he had signified the same expressly to Lord Moira, who heartily concurred in it." Francis wrote to a friend that he would have "put a stop to great enormities in India," if Fox had found it to "coincide with his politics or his partialities to have permitted me to return to India in the office that was full as much my right as it was his to be Secretary of State." But Fox was right; and few persons at the time who were acquainted with Francis could have thought otherwise. It would have been an outrage on India to have appointed the "masked assassin" of Hastings to a position where he would have strained every nerve to undo, or discredit the good work that Hastings succeeded in accomplishing despite his inveterate hostility.

In 1813 Mr. John Taylor published his *Discovery of Junius*, in which he attributed the notorious letters to the Rev. Dr. Francis, who, he assumed, had the aid of his son; but on more mature reflection, and with the aid of other critics, he arrived at the conclusion, which he embodied in his *Junius Identified*, that Philip Francis alone was the culprit. The Duke of Gloucester lent an early copy of the second book to Hastings, at Cheltenham, when the latter visited him, and Hastings mentioned in his diary that he took it with him to

[1] The Prince raised expectations in Francis which he eventually disappointed. He acted in the same way to Hastings, and to many others. But though he professed regard for Hastings, he rarely commanded his presence at Carlton House, or at the Pavilion. With Francis, however, it was otherwise; for Francis was a man of the gay world, with political influence, and engaging social qualities, when he chose; and his company and conversation were welcome to the Prince. Francis told his wife that: "I would have made a great monarch of him, but personal vanity stood in the way, and, still more, want of moral integrity." The Prince was fickle in his attachments to those who contributed to his amusement, and in the end he turned the cold shoulder to Francis.

Daylesford; but he did not record his opinion about it. It is very probable that, with his bitter experience of Francis's character, he agreed with a learned judge of his day, who observed that, "If there is any dependence on the law of presumptive evidence, the case is made out."

It was some time before Francis opened the book. He "was extremely alarmed," says Lady Francis, "when he heard of the work, and refused for many months to read it, lest he might find something that might necessitate him to make some declaration." Gradually he gained courage, and proceeding to the shelter of the house of a friend in the north of England, where he was free from intrusion, he at length studied the indictment. "It was evident," continues his wife, "upon his return to his family, that he had been greatly agitated; past scenes, of which a long course of years had deadened the remembrance, had probably been recalled to his mind, and all the feelings and anxieties of the time long laid to rest had started up like spirits from their silent graves, and passed before him; his cheek burned, and his eye betrayed what was passing within him." He resented, and as far as possible evaded, the curiosity of his acquaintances which the book had excited, or revived; and as some of the members hinted at, or rallied him upon the authorship, he withdrew his name from Brooks's Club, which being close to his house had been one of his most favourite haunts since 1785, when he was "chosen" a member on the proposition of Fox.

Although, according to his widow, the "real man" was "little known" outside his home, Francis was a conspicuous person at the Club, and was held in much respect by the members. He had been a frequent guest at Carlton House, and at the Pavilion, Brighton, as well as at the town and country residences of notable persons; he readily adapted himself, when he liked, to his surroundings; and though obviously a cynic, whom it might be dangerous to affront, he did not indulge his cynicism in speech as he did on paper. He had a tall, erect, and slender figure; a well-shaped head; small and delicately moulded ears; and handsome features. His manners were refined; his culture was remarkable; his experience was extensive; and he was full of anecdote. His friends knew what a deprivation it would be to him in his declining years to be denied the congenial society of the Club, and they entreated him to recall his resignation. But he persisted in his intention, for "he knew," says Lady Francis, "that he could not continue his name without being tempted to go; and as at that time he never met with an acquaintance who did not mention the book to him, he felt that it was a necessary sacrifice." He accordingly took the step which was best calculated to convince the

SIR PHILIP FRANCIS.

members that the sacrifice was due to conscious guilt. Their conclusion, and that of other critics, must have been strengthened by the eloquent fact that, during the four years that elapsed between the appearance of the book and his death, Francis did not pursue the natural course, had he been innocent, of taking up the "pen of a ready writer," which was at his command to the last, to vindicate his reputation. He preferred to allow judgment to go by default. The curses of his early years came home to roost at last, and embittered the close of his life. He peremptorily refused to be interrogated about Junius; but he must have known that the deferential silence of his associates on the subject was no evidence of their rejection of the theory of his responsibility. He may have lived down some of the malignant hatreds of his youth ; but an essay on *The Characteristics of the Kings of England*, which was one of his latest literary efforts, shows that he was capable of extreme severity of judgment and unpardonable violence of language to the last. He did not lack the will to flay John Taylor alive. But he did not dare to gratify his intense rancour ; and Mr. Taylor survived him nearly half a century, and then died, in 1864, aged eighty-one, with the satisfaction of knowing that he had rendered a service to history.

Francis was remarkable, like Hastings, for what Merivale happily describes as "portentous industry"; and his activity with his pen "was something prodigious." He was a master of the art of producing minutes of exceptional ability—"quite able enough," in the opinion of Moore the poet, who read them with admiration of their literary merits, "to mark him as the author of *Junius*." From his twentieth year he had had no scruple about making digests of official correspondence that passed through his hands, for his private use ; and little did his official superiors imagine that letters marked "Private and Confidential," "Secret," or "Most Secret," which they rough-drafted or dictated, and which he fair-copied, were subjected to this process. Francis committed this breach of faith so systematically that at length his conscience may have ceased to hint to him that he was doing anything that was discreditable. But he was careful not to afford any subordinate of his own the opportunity of similarly abusing his confidence. He was singularly diligent in making, and careful in preserving copies of any letters of importance that he wrote ; and he left masses of manuscript that gave his executors no inconsiderable trouble. Like Hastings, he was in the habit of keeping letters that he received for future reference. But there was this marked difference between the two men, that whereas Hastings was incapable of taking a mean advantage of correspondence written in the confidence of private intimacy, Francis was an unsafe man to confide in, since, as an adversary, he had no scruple about his choice of weapons. Hastings was slow to think evil, and quick to think well of his associates, and the friendships that he formed were lasting; but Francis, sooner or later, broke with every friend whom he possessed outside the domestic circle. The objects that prompted the two men to preserve the correspondence which they received, and to keep copies of the letters which they wrote, were therefore not identical; but they both conferred an obligation on posterity by the extraordinary care that they took of their private papers.

Like Hastings, Francis enjoyed immunity from the usual infirmities of old age, owing in no small measure to his habitual moderation in eating and drinking, and to his precise habits of life. He did not share Hastings' innate love for rural surroundings, for he was essentially a man of the town, who shone in society, and loved movement around him. He gave the country a trial soon after his return from India; but he drifted back to London, and bought the large house known as 14, St. James's Square, which the East India United Service Club acquired in 1861, and still occupies. He reserved for his own use three rooms on the ground floor, and converted one into a library, which he supplied with a valuable collection of books. He lived here for several years, with occasional visits to the country seats of friends of note. Time passed on, but his "bodily strength seemed little abated, the power of his understanding remained almost as fresh as ever, his interest in the affairs of the world around him as great." At length, however, he laid down to die. "He had the happiness," says Lady Francis, "of his last prayers being listened to, and of never becoming a painful object to those who loved him." He passed quietly away early in the morning of December 23rd, 1818. "I thought," said Lady Francis, "he had awoke, and undrew the curtain, hung over him, and met his last breath; not a sigh, not a motion, not a change of countenance. Heart, pulse, and breath stopped at once without an effort. How blessed! how merciful!"

His will, written by himself, on one small folio sheet, contained a direction for his burial beside his daughter Elizabeth in Mortlake Church, close to East Sheen, where he once resided, and not far from Fulham, where he wooed and won her mother. He wished to be interred with the utmost simplicity. "Of all human follies," he said, in his characteristic way, in his will, "posthumous vanity seems to me the silliest," and "I therefore positively order that I may be buried as privately as possible, and at the least possible expense." His directions were obeyed. His daughter Elizabeth was interred in a vault under the vestry of the church which has given its chief feature to Mortlake for upwards of four centuries, instead of under the floor of the body of the church in accordance with the time-honoured, but dangerous practice which was in vogue until recent years. The vestry is a commonplace, square, two-floor building, of which a corner is shown on the left side of the accompanying illustration.

MORTLAKE CHURCH.

The upper storey is used as a schoolroom, and the basement bears few indications of being an integral part of a sacred edifice. The stone floor of the vestry is covered with planking, and the room is used by the choristers when robing and unrobing. There are a few old chests near the walls, in which the parochial records of many generations are preserved; and, at the west end of the room, there is a valuable oil painting, by Sachers of Antwerp (who died in 1641), of the dead Christ, that was formerly used as an altar piece. Above the recess in which the choristers' gowns are hung are two contiguous, plain, white marble tablets. The one to the left shows traces of greater age than that to the right, and it is obvious that the pillar which now bounds the right-hand side of the latter formerly adjoined the right-hand side of the adjacent tablet.

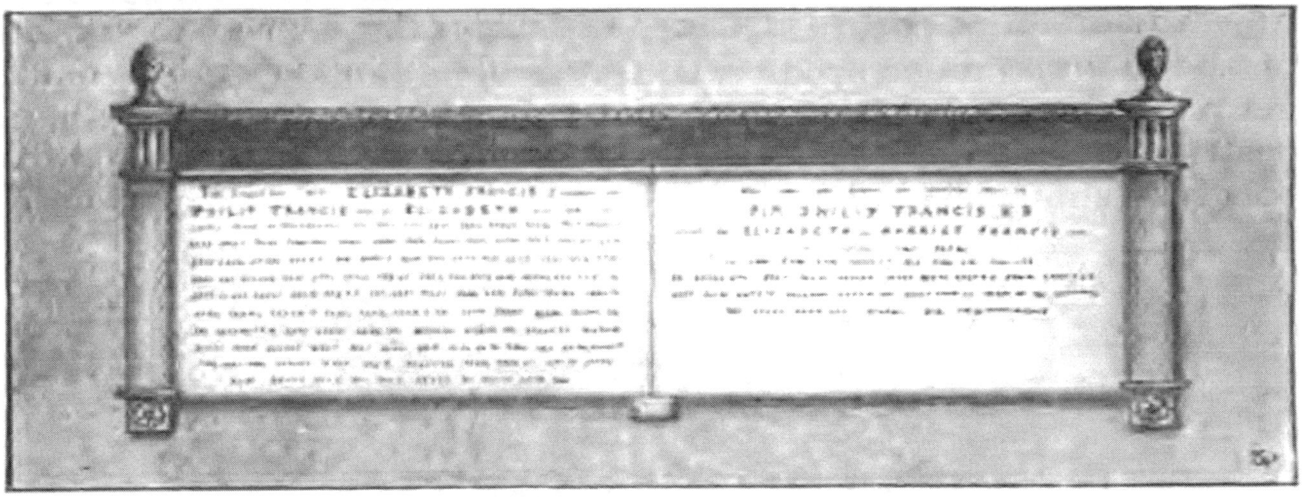

THE FRANCIS MEMORIAL TABLETS IN MORTLAKE CHURCH.

The left-hand tablet bears the following epitaph, which may be safely attributed to Francis :—

In Memory of ELIZABETH FRANCIS, daughter of
Philip Francis, Esq., and Elizabeth, his wife, who
departed this life 14th July, 1804, aged 40 years,
thus following to an untimely grave her beloved sister,
Harriet Francis, who died at Nice, on the 2nd Jan. 1803,
over whom she had watched with devoted affection during a
lingering consumption, and whose loss she had lamented but
nine months, when it was the will of Providence to afflict her
with the same disorder. Her sufferings were great, but she
preserved to her last minutes that fortitude of mind, and
tenderness of heart which had ever been the
most remarkable of her many virtues.

The inscription on the right-hand tablet is as follows :—

Here also lie interred the remains of
SIR PHILIP FRANCIS, K.B.
father of Elizabeth and Harriet Francis,
who departed this life
on the 22nd day of December, 1818, aged 78 years ;
in fulfilment of the earnest wish expressed in his Will
that he might be buried in the same grave with his dearest
and most lamented daughter, Elizabeth.

Francis was buried on the 31st December, 1818, and the vault was closed over his remains. But, five years later it was re-opened to receive those of his daughter Catherine, wife of George James Cholmondeley, of Cholmondeley in Cheshire, to whose memory a white marble tablet was placed to the left of the above-mentioned memorials. Thus Francis, who was a devoted father, whatever may have been his faults, rests beside two of his six children.

He will long be remembered as a man of industry, culture, administrative capacity, political foresight, and public spirit, who, in the gratification of a malignant disposition, misapplied great talents, and misused splendid opportunities. He was proud and arrogant in his relations with most people; yet he employed the strongest epithets at his command in denouncing pride and arrogance in others. Macaulay remarks that "no man is so merciless as he who, under a strong delusion, confounds his antipathies with his duties." No man was ever more smitten with this delusion than was Francis. But in an age of corruption Francis was not known to have been corrupt; and his protests against jobbery and venality in high places were prompted, in all probability, by none other than a sense of public duty that was in advance of his time. Yet his biographer, Merivale, was forced to the conclusion that he was "a political adventurer who was utterly unscrupulous in the use of means"; his "sincerity, even when he was sincere, was apt to assume the form of the most ignoble rancour"; and "no ties of friendship, or party, or connection seem to have restrained his virulence." Sir James Stephen concurred in this severe judgment, and held that Francis was capable not only of "ferocious cruelty," but was "as false and treacherous to his friends as he was persistent in his malignity against his enemies." History has abundantly avenged Hastings of his adversary.

CHAPTER VI

HIS TRIAL

A WEEK after Warren Hastings landed from the *Barrington* at Plymouth, Edmund Burke gave notice in the House of Commons that he "would at a future day make a motion respecting the conduct of a gentleman just returned from India." This was the small beginning of a great storm; for, two years and a half afterwards, Hastings, having been impeached by the Commons, was placed on his trial in Westminster Hall, before the Lords, to answer "charges of high crimes and misdemeanours exhibited by the knights, citizens, and burgesses in Parliament assembled, in the name of themselves and of all the Commons."

The memorable trial commenced on the 13th February, 1788. About 11 o'clock, the Lords came from their own House into the Court arranged in Westminster Hall, preceded by the Lord Chancellor's Gentlemen Attendants, two and two; the Clerk Assistant of the House of Lords, and the Clerk of the Parliaments; the Clerk of the Crown in Chancery; the Clerk of the Crown of King's Bench; the Masters in Chancery, two and two; the Judges, two and two; Serjeants Adair and Hill; the Yeomen Usher of the Black Rod; two Heralds; the Lords Barons, two and two; the Lords Bishops, two and two; the Lords Viscounts, two and two; the Lords Earls, two and two; the Lords Marquises, two and two; the Lords Dukes, two and two; the Mace Bearer; the Lord Chancellor, with his train borne; the Dukes of Cumberland and Gloucester; and the Duke of York and Prince of Wales, with their trains.

Each peer, as he passed the empty Throne that occupied the chief place of honour in the Court, made a profound obeisance. The Queen, wearing a dress of fawn-coloured satin, and a plain head-dress, "with a very slender sprinkling of diamonds," attended the trial, accompanied by the Princesses Elizabeth, Augusta, and Mary, and the Duchess of Gloucester. All the managers of the trial were in full dress, but the majority of the Commons wore their usual costume. The seats occupied by the Commons were covered with green cloth; the rest of the building was "one red." A body of Horse Guards, under the command of a field officer, attended daily; and three hundred Foot Guards, and a considerable number of constables kept the avenue clear. Two hundred members of each House of Parliament were present.

The following was the Committee for the Prosecution: Edmund Burke, Rt. Hon. C. J. Fox, R. B. Sheridan, Rt. Hon. T. Pelham, Rt. Hon. W. Wyndham, Sir Gilbert Elliot, Bart., Charles Grey, William Adam, Sir John Anstruther, M. A. Taylor, Viscount Maitland, Dudley Long, General J. Burgoyne, Hon. G. A. North, Hon. Andrew St. John, Hon. A. Fitzherbert, John Courtenay, J. Rogers and Sir James Erskine. For the Commons Dr. Scott and Mr. Lawrence, Messrs. Mansfield, Pigott, Burke, and Douglas, were counsel; Messrs. Wallis and Troward were attorneys; and Mr. Gurney was shorthand writer. For Mr. Hastings Messrs Law, Plumer, and Dallas were counsel; Mr. Shawe was attorney; and Mr. Hodgson was shorthand writer. Mr. Blanchard was shorthand writer for the Lords.

Hastings wished to be defended by Erskine, who distinguished himself during the trial of Lord George Gordon. But though Erskine admitted that he would have liked to cross swords with Burke, and to "smite him hip and thigh," he professed his inability to oppose Fox and Sheridan, who belonged, like Burke, to his own political party. Hastings then yielded to the recommendation of his former subordinate in India, Sir Thomas Rumbold, late Governor of Madras, to engage Edward Law, the latter's brother-in-law; and when a general retainer, with a fee for five hundred guineas, was offered to Law (who was in good practice on the Northern Circuit), he discerned the opportunity that the case would afford him for distinction, and accepted the position of leading counsel, with Thomas Plumer and Richard Dallas as juniors. He retired for a time, with masses of documents, to Windermere, to work up the case. An idea of the labour that devolved upon him may be gathered from the fact that the printed brief which was delivered eventually to counsel for the defence, with its index, extended to twenty-four folio volumes! A copy of it is preserved in the library of Sir Edward Strachey, at Sutton Court, Somersetshire.

Apart from the fees that stimulated his exertions, Mr. Law was probably influenced by a feeling of gratitude to Hastings for having given his patronage, when in India, to Thomas Law, the learned counsel's brother. Thomas Law was not slow in availing himself of the friendly offices of the Governor-General, and he acquired a large fortune in India, with which he returned to Europe, and then took with him to Washington, where he invested the greater part of it in the erection of houses near the Capitol, where he for some time resided. His building speculations were not successful, and it is said in the *Gentleman's Magazine* of July, 1807, that he lived "under the mortifying circumstance of daily witnessing whole rows of the shells of his houses gradually falling to pieces."

Edward Law, fourth son of Edmund Law, Bishop of Carlisle, was born in 1750; was educated firstly at the School of Bury St. Edmunds, then as scholar on the foundation at Charterhouse; became Captain of that School and Exhibitioner in 1767; matriculated at Peterhouse College, Cambridge, of which his father was then Master, in 1767; Third Wrangler and Senior Chancellor's Prizeman, 1771; graduated B.A. 1771, M.A. 1774; elected Fellow of his College, 1771; admitted a student of Lincoln's Inn, 1769; practised as a special pleader; and called to the Bar, 1780. In the defence of Hastings he acquitted himself with such ability, that he obtained a large increase of practice. He was elected a Bencher of the Inner Temple in 1787. He deserted the Whigs, and joined the Tories in 1793; was appointed Attorney-General of Lancaster, 1793; Attorney-General of England, and knighted in February, 1801; entered Parliament the following month as member for Newton, Isle of Wight; was appointed Chief Justice of the King's Bench, and raised to the peerage as Baron Ellenborough of Ellenborough, in the county of Cumberland, 1802; and died in 1818, leaving a fortune of £240,000. He was buried, by his own request, at the Charterhouse, near the grave of Sutton, the founder, who died during the reign of Queen Elizabeth. His eldest son, Edward, was appointed Governor-General of India, in 1841; and for the services that he rendered in that high position, he was created Earl of Ellenborough and Viscount Southam in 1844.

Hastings' second counsel, Thomas Plomer, or Plumer, was also greatly indebted to his association with the famous trial in Westminster Hall for his eventual advancement to a high position in the judicature.

LORD ELLENBOROUGH.

The son of Thomas Plumer, of Lilling Hall, in the county of York, and born in 1753, he was sent to Eton at the early age of eight years, and is said by Foss, in the *Judges of England*, to have gained both from the head-master and his schoolfellows "that character for classical ability and suavity of disposition, which afterwards distinguished him at University College, Oxford"; and the Rev. T. Maurice, in his *Memoirs*, represented him "as ardent, indefatigable in his studies, no difficulties can discourage, no pleasures allure him; but on he toils with unwearied application." He proceeded to Oxford in 1771; was elected Vinerian Scholar in 1777; and was chosen Fellow of his College in 1779. He was called to the Bar in 1778, and was made a Commissioner in the Bankruptcy Court in 1781. He was employed in the defence of Sir Thomas Rumbold, at the Bar of the House of Commons; and it was presumably on the recommendation of Sir Thomas that he was retained for the defence of Hastings. He performed his duties most conscientiously; and, shortly after the conclusion of the trial, he was made a King's Counsel. He was, a little later on, engaged in several important trials which brought him to further public notice. In 1805 he was appointed a Judge on the North Wales circuit. In 1806 he was promoted to be Solicitor-General;

SIR THOMAS PLUMER.

was then knighted, and entered Parliament as member for Downton. He retained the office of Solicitor-General for five years, when he succeeded Sir Vicary Gibbs as Attorney-General. In 1813 he was appointed Vice-Chancellor; and, five years later, he was raised to the Mastership of the Rolls, in which high position he remained until his death in 1824, at the age of seventy-one. He was a sound lawyer, but "his style," according to Foss, "was so heavy, and his speeches were of such length and elaboration, that he fatigued his hearers without interesting them." He was compared in the following epigram to Lord Eldon, who was notorious for his habitual procrastination :—

To cause delays in Lincoln's Inn
Two diff'rent methods tend ;
His Lordship's judgments ne'er begin,
His Honour's never end.

He was "impressive," as Lord Campbell says ; but his prolixity and tediousness made him unpopular with counsel, attorneys, and clients. He retained the suavity that had marked him at Eton to the end of his career, and he was respected for his erudition.

Robert Dallas, the third counsel for the defence of Hastings, was also remarkable for his polished manners. He was born in Kensington in 1756 ; became a member of Lincoln's Inn ; and acquired facility as a public speaker at a debating society held in Coachmakers' Hall. "With the gentlemanly address that distinguished him he was noted," according to Foss, "as one of the most elegant and accomplished orators in Westminster Hall." Having been brought to favourable notice by the zeal and ability which he displayed as one of the counsel for Lord George Gordon, when that harebrained nobleman was brought to trial on the charge of high treason, he was retained for the defence of Hastings, and thereby incurred the personal animosity of Burke, who, according to Lord Campbell, regarded Hastings' counsel as "venal wretches, who were accomplices in murder after the fact," though, in the opinion of Foss, "they never transgressed the strict line of their duty as advocates." Dallas was provoked on one occasion by Burke's virulence into making the following epigram (erroneously attributed for a long time to Law), which probably assisted to turn public opinion against the leader of the impeachment :—

Oft have we wonder'd that on Irish ground
No poisonous reptile has e'er yet been found ;
Revealed the secret stands of Nature's work,
She saved her venom to produce her Burke.

At the end of the Hastings trial Dallas was made a King's Counsel. In 1802 he entered Parliament as member for St. Michael's, Cornwall ; in 1804 he was appointed Chief Justice of Chester ; in 1813 he was created Solicitor-General, and knighted ;

six months later he was promoted to the bench of the Common Pleas; and in 1818 he became Lord Chief Justice. He resigned office in 1823, and died the following year, seven months after his former colleague, Sir Thomas Plumer.

There was an enormous demand for tickets of admission to the Hall, and it is said that as much as £50 was offered for a single ticket. Two caricatures, by Gillray, of the ticket were published. It will be seen from my sketches that in the left-hand plate Lord Thurlow is sitting on a stool of repentance, and that the trial scene is depicted at the foot of each picture. The heads of Burke, Fox, and Sheridan are introduced in the inner shield in each plate.

An interesting description of the commencement of the trial is contained in the following letter from Miss Mary Orlebar to her aunt, Mrs. Eliza Orlebar, dated Percy Street, 16th February, 1788, which was examined by the Historical Manuscripts Commission, and has been obligingly communicated to me by Mrs. Frederica Orlebar, of Merton, Buckhurst Hill, Essex:—

> Mr. Hill brought me a ticket for the opening of Mr. Hastings' trial, which was on the next day. We arrived at Westminster Hall about 10 o'clock, though not without having gone through some difficulties, notwithstanding the Guards kept excellent order; but, before we got to them, our back panel had met with the fate of many others; and on turning the corner into Palace Yard, we were very near being overturned, owing to Mr. Trotman's coachman having forgot that the coach, which was a borrowed one, had not a crank neck, and took too short a turn. The Prince of Wales and Duke of York passed us in magnificent carriages; they had the advantage of we plebeians, as they took the middle of the street, the Guards drawn up on one side, and our long string of coaches on the other. The Princes looked to great advantage in their robes. We had a very good seat in the Hall, after changing three times. I never saw so noble a sight; the Dukes, Peers, Bishops and Judges in their robes. On one side was the House of Commons; on the other the Peeresses. The Duchess of Gloucester and Mrs. Fitz Herbert were in the Royal Box, the Queen and four Princesses preferring to sit in the Duke of Newcastle's Gallery, to avoid the obligation of a numerous retinue. My eyes were much gratified, but not equally so my ears, as seven long charges were read over, of which not a word could I hear. Mr. Hastings has a very emaciated, though interesting countenance.

Among the curious descriptions of the English Court, and the times generally, between 1779 and 1846, that were given by

CARICATURE (*after Gillray*).

THE TICKET OF ADMISSION.

CARICATURE (*after Gillray*).

Miss Mary Frampton, of Moreton, Dorsetshire, in her "Diary," the following allusion to the trial appears :—

In 1788 the impeachment and trial of Warren Hastings were the subject of frequent conversation, and the attendance at his trial for the first few years was the object of every one's desire. I was fortunate and had a ticket for the Duke of Newcastle's gallery, where, besides the advantage of getting to your seat in Westminster Hall quietly, through a fine house, in the passage that communicated with that gallery, there was, for the first year or two, a handsome cold collation set out for those admitted by the Duke's ticket. My Aunt, Elizabeth Fanquier, attended with me one year,

LORD THURLOW (*after Gillray*).

and I heard Mr. Burke make his opening speech, and several of the other managers declaim against Mr. Hastings. Being very young, I was, of course, carried away by their eloquence to believe all the charges. Mr. Grey, afterwards Lord Grey, the Prime Minister, pleased me particularly by his person and manner. The *coup d'œil* was magnificent ; that fine building, Westminster Hall, full in every part, with gentlemen and ladies full dressed, and the peers in their robes. The Prince of Wales's bow to the Throne, on entering, and before taking his seat, was universally admired ; as was also the beauty of the then young Duke of Bedford, but he wanted the grace and noble air which the other possessed in the highest degree. The length of the trial put an end by degrees not only to the Duke of Newcastle's collations, which were omitted certainly after the second year, but to all interest respecting the parties concerned on either side, and empty benches and woolsacks, as well as empty galleries, succeeded to the crowding and pressure for places and tickets of admission.

At noon the Sergeant-at-Arms summoned "Warren Hastings, Esq., to come forth in Court, and save thee and thy bail, otherwise the recognisance of thee and thy bail will be forfeited." Thereupon Hastings appeared at the bar, and dropped upon his knees, but was at once requested by Lord Chancellor Thurlow to rise to his feet. He had complied with what he knew was required; but, in a letter to his former Private Secretary, Mr. Thompson, he said that the "ignominious ceremonial of kneeling before the House of Lords" was an "usage that

LORD THURLOW.

reflects more dishonour on that assembly for permitting its continuance than on those who are compelled to submit to it, and on whom it is inflicted as a punishment not only before conviction, but even before the accusations against them are read." The Chancellor, on the motion of a Peer, allowed the prisoner to have a chair. The accusations were then read, and Hastings replied: "My Lords, I am come to this high tribunal equally impressed with a confidence in my own integrity, and in the justice of the Court before which I stand." The Lord Chancellor then demanded who appeared in behalf of the Commons to substantiate the charges? Mr. Burke immediately rose, and made an obeisance to the Court: "He stood forth," he said, "at the command of the Commons of Great Britain, as the accuser of Warren Hastings."

As prosecutor-in-chief, Mr. Burke indulged, without let or hindrance, in excessive vituperation. He accused Hastings of "crimes which have their rise in the wicked dispositions of men—in avarice, rapacity, pride, cruelty, malignity of temper, haughtiness, insolence—in short, in everything that manifests a heart blackened to the very blackest—a heart dyed in blackness—a heart gangrened to the core. . . . We have brought

EDMUND BURKE.

before you the head, the chief, the captain-general of iniquity—one in whom all the fraud, all the tyranny of India are embodied, disciplined, and arrayed." He then proceeded to charge the prisoner "with having taken away the lands of orphans; with having alienated the fortunes of widows; with having wasted the country, and destroyed the inhabitants after cruelly harassing and distressing them. I charge him with having tortured their persons, and dishonoured their religion through his wicked agents, who were at the bottom and root of his villainy." He accused him of having "gorged his ravenous maw"; of never "dining without creating a famine"; of feeding on the "indigent, the decaying, and the ruined"; of resembling the "ravenous

Swan Electric Engraving Co.

A view of the Tryal of Warren Hastings Esquire, before the Court of Peers in Westminster Hall.

Drawn by E. Dayes and published Jan. 3rd 1789 by R. Pollard, Engraver, No. 15, Braynes Row, Spitalfields, London.

KEY TO THE TRIAL SCENE.

A Throne.
B Queen's Box.
C Prince of Wales, etc.
D Foreign Ministers.
E 1st Row, Duke of York's; 2nd, Royal Household; 3rd, Lord Chancellor's tickets.
F Attendants on the Royal Family.
G Peers' tickets.
H Duke of Newcastle's gallery.
I Board of Works.
J Lord Chamberlain of the Household.
K Deputy Great Chamberlain's tickets.
L Peers' tickets.
M Peeresses and their daughters.
N Marquises.
O Dukes.
P Prince of Wales and Duke of York.
Q Sir Isaac Heard, Knight, Garter Principal King of Arms on the right of the Throne and the Herald of Arms on the left.
R Peers Minor on each side of the Throne.
S Judges seated on Woolsacks.
T Lord Chancellor.
U Masters in Chancery.
V Archbishops of Canterbury and York.
W Bishops.
X Earls.
Y Viscounts.
Z Barons.
a Speaker of the House of Commons.
b House of Commons.
c Managers and Committee for the Prosecution.
d Mr. Burke opening the charges.
e Shorthand Writer for the Commons.
f Repeater of the Evidence.
g Witness or Evidence Box.
h Mr. Hastings.
i Prisoner's leading Counsel.
j Counsellors for the Prisoner.
k Prisoner's Shorthand Writer.
l Counsellors' Clerks.
m Counsellors for the Managers and their Clerks.
n Clerks of the India House.
o Shorthand Writer for the Lords.
p Usher of the Black Rod.
q Deputy Usher.
r Serjeant of Arms and Deputy.
s Mace Bearer to the Chancellor.

vulture who destroys and incapacitates nature in the destruction of its objects while devouring the carcases of the dead"; and of exhibiting a "cruelty beyond his corruption." He ridiculed him as a "swindling Mœcenas—swindling of glory, and obtaining honour under false pretences"; and declared that "his origin was low, obscure, and vulgar"; that he was "bred in vulgar and ignoble habits," yet was more proud than persons born under canopies of state, and swaddled in purple. He

BURKE (*after Gillray*).

alluded to "the damned and damnable proceedings of a judge in Hell"; and asserted that "such a judge was Warren Hastings." He regarded him as a "spider of Hell," as well as a "thief, tyrant, robber, cheat, swindler, sharper"; and he expressed his regret that "the English language does not afford terms adequate to the enormity of his offences." Finally, "I impeach him," said Burke, "in the name of the Commons' House of Parliament, whose trust he has betrayed. I impeach him in the name of the English nation, whose ancient honour he has sullied. I impeach him in the name of the people of India, whose rights he has trodden under foot, and whose country he has turned into a desert. Lastly, in the name of human nature itself, in the name of both sexes, in the name of every age, in the name of every rank, I impeach the common enemy and oppressor of all!"

As an oration Burke's speech was of extraordinary merit, and even Hastings was so enthralled by its eloquence that he said: "For half an hour I looked up at the orator in a reverie of wonder, and actually felt myself the most culpable man on earth. But I recurred to my own bosom, and there found a

RICHARD BRINSLEY SHERIDAN.

consciousness which consoled me under all I heard, and all I suffered."

Mr. Sheridan was another of the managers of the trial who was at a loss for epithets to convey an idea of his detestation of the conduct of the prisoner at the bar. "The administration of Mr. Hastings," he said, "formed a medley of meanness and outrage, of duplicity and depredation, of prodigality and oppression, of the most callous cruelty contrasted with the hollow affectation of liberality and good faith." This is the keynote of his speech, which was a marvellous example of oratory, however far it may have departed from truth and fair judgment. Burke listened to it with the utmost admiration. "That is the true style," he remarked to Fox while Sheridan was speaking, "something between poetry and prose, and better than either." On a later occasion Burke said that, in his opinion, the speech was "the most astonishing effort of eloquence, argument, and wit united of which there is any record or tradition." Pitt held a similar opinion, as he considered that the speech "surpassed all the eloquence of ancient and modern times, and possessed everything that genius or art could furnish to agitate and control the human mind." And Fox too declared that "all that he had ever heard, all that he had ever read, when compared with it dwindled into nothing, and vanished like a vapour before the sun." It was not to be expected that Hastings would join in this chorus of unstinted, not to say exaggerated praise. He could not but have acknowledged the exceptional brilliancy of Sheridan's oratory, but he did not forgive his reckless vituperation. The two met, many years after the trial, as the guests of the Prince Regent, in the Pavilion, at Brighton; and Sheridan, at the prompting of the Prince, advanced to Hastings, and said that: "The part which I took in events long gone by must not be regarded as any test of my private opinions, because I was then a public pleader, whose duty it is, under all circumstances, to make good if he can the charges which he is commissioned to bring forward." But Hastings drew back a step; looked Sheridan in the face; made a low bow; and remained silent. "Had he," Hastings subsequently said, "confessed as much twenty years ago, he might have done me some service."

Hastings replied with dignity to the allegations of his accusers. He declared that he had had the satisfaction of seeing all his measures terminate in their designed objects; that his political conduct had been invariably regulated by truth, justice, and good faith; and that he had resigned his charge in a state of established peace and security, with all the sources of its abundance unimpaired, and even improved. "I am arraigned," he said, "for desolating the provinces in India which are the most flourishing of all the States in India. It was I who made them so. I gave you all; and you have rewarded me with confiscation, disgrace, and a life of impeachment." He solemnly avowed that he "did in no instance intentionally sacrifice the interest of my country to any private views of personal advantage"; and "that according to my best skill and judgment I invariably promoted the essential interest of my employers, the happiness and prosperity of the people committed to my charge, and the welfare and honour of my country." But though Hastings maintained a calm demeanour in Court, he was greatly pained by the calumnies with which he was loaded. "I am charged," he said, in a letter to John Shore, "with cruelty, oppression, violation of treaties, and with the general guilt of having sacrificed every duty to the views of interest, ambition, or private vengeance. I am not sure that rapacity makes a part of the catalogue of my imputed crimes, because the instances which have been advanced in evidence to prove it apply only to acts done for the relief of the public necessities; and it is scarcely (I believe not at all) insinuated that I have practised it for any profit of my own."

The witnesses for the defence were so systematically browbeaten by the prosecution that the elder Mill was provoked into remarking that, in the courts of justice "the rule of humanity and decorum is most grossly and habitually violated by the advocate"; and he goes on to say that: "What excites the disgust and indignation of every honest spectator is the attempt so often made, and so often made successfully, to throw an honest witness into confusion and embarrassment, for the sake of destroying the weight of his testimony, and defeating the cause of truth—the torture unnecessarily and wantonly inflicted upon the feelings of an individual to show off a hireling lawyer, and prove to the attorneys his power of doing mischief."

In April, 1794, Burke reported the proceedings of the managers, and the progress of the trial, to the House of Commons; and, on the 20th June following, Pitt moved a vote of thanks to them "for their faithful discharge of the trust reposed in them." The motion having been carried by 50 votes to 21, the Speaker formally communicated the thanks of the House to the managers, and said that their exertions had "conferred honour, not on themselves only, but on the House whose credit was intimately connected with their own." But the managers, according to Mill, "brought a great deal of rhetoric, with papers and witnesses, to the trial, and seemed, unhappily, to think that rhetoric, papers, and witnesses were enough," for they brought "not much knowledge" and "not much dexterity," and "the intemperance of the tone and language of Mr. Burke operated strongly as a cause of odium." Dr. Horace Wilson, the Boden Professor of Sanskrit at Oxford, remarked in his edition of Mill, that "Burke's oratory was a tissue of falsehood," and "nothing had occurred to justify his exaggeration," to pardon his "unnatural appetite for disgusting details," or to excuse his "prejudiced disposition to listen alone to *ex parte* evidence, and an imprudent readiness to credit the exaggerated language of complaint." The investigation was not "instituted to ascertain truth, but to fix criminality upon Hastings." "Talents the most popular, and passions the most ungoverned, were let loose against him, and no reasonable man can believe that, if he had stood alone in his defence, his innocence would have shielded him from the combined assaults of Fox, Sheridan, and Burke."

Burke claimed to be a "sober and reflecting man," according to the powers that God had given him; but he lived long enough to know that public opinion, which had once been in his favour, gradually turned, and pronounced him in the wrong. He survived the conclusion of the trial but little more than two years; and though he maintained to the last that he had acted rightly, he made a "dying request" to a friend, "to erect a cenotaph most grateful to my shade," by clearing "my memory from the load which the East India Company, the King, Lords, and Commons, and, in a manner, the whole British nation (God forgive them), had been pleased to lay as a monument upon my ashes." With ill-regulated zeal he devoted nearly ten years of his life to the effort to prove Hastings to be a miscreant, and he succeeded in gaining for the object of his ruthless condemnation public sympathy as a martyr. Had it not been for the impeachment, which made him first notorious, and then famous, Hastings might have sunk into the obscurity in his native land that is the frequent destiny of men who have occupied exalted office in India. It was Burke who raised a cenotaph to Warren Hastings which does not lose its interest for the contemplative observer as the years roll by.

If it was hard for Hastings to listen to the opprobrious language employed by Burke, it was probably more difficult for him to hear without visible disgust the panegyrics which Mr. Grey, another manager, pronounced on his arch-enemy and former colleague, Philip Francis, who was gratifying his spleen by assisting the prosecution; and Miss Fanny Burney states that on one occasion he relieved his feelings by writing these impromptu lines :—

It hurts me not that Grey as Burke's assessor
Proclaims me Tyrant, Robber, and Oppressor,
Tho' for abuse alone meant;
For when he called himself the bosom friend,
The Friend of Philip Francis !—I contend
He made me full atonement.

The poet Cowper, an old schoolfellow at Westminster of the prisoner at the Bar, witnessed the trial, and urged his cousin, Lady Hesketh, to do so also, as it was "the trial of a man who has been greater and more feared than the Great Mogul himself." Lady Hesketh obtained a ticket of admission, went, and was much shocked by the severity of Burke's invective. In a letter to the poet, who had also been much scandalised by the virulence of the orator, she endeavoured to show that, from the days of Tully downwards, public prosecutors had been wont to adopt a violent attitude towards persons accused of offences against the State. "In order," she said, "to impress the minds of his hearers with a persuasion that he himself at least was convinced of the criminality of the prisoner, he must be vehement, energetic, rapid; must call him tyrant and traitor, and everything else that is odious; and all this to his face, because all this, bad as it is, is no more than he undertakes to prove in the sequel; and if he cannot prove it, he must himself appear in a light very little more desirable, and at the best to have trifled with the tribunal to which he has summoned him." Cowper thus expressed his opinion of the accused :—

Hastings! I knew thee young, and of a mind,
While young, humane, conversable, and kind;

Nor can I well believe thee—gentle *then*—
Now grown a villain, and the *worst* of men;
But rather some suspect, who have oppress'd
And worried thee, as not themselves the *best*.

In 1792, John Bell, of the British Library, Strand. Bookseller to the Prince of Wales, published *Letters from Simpkin the Second to his dear brother in Wales, containing an humble description of the trial of Warren Hastings, Esq.* The first of these Letters describes the procession of Burke into the Hall, with "his eloquent tribe":—

First, Edmund walks in at the head of the group,
That powerful chief of that powerful troop—
What awful solemnity's seen in his gait,
Whilst the nod of his head beats the time to his feet!—
Charles Fox is the second, and close on his right,
Whose waddle declares he will never go straight:
The ruby-fac'd Sheridan enters the third,
The opposer of Pitt, and the Treasury Board—
His attention, 'tis said, has so long been directed
To the National Debts that his own are neglected—
And in public affairs, when such management's shewn,
No wonder a man can't think of his own.
Next Adam comes in with a spit by his side,
And struts like a turkey-cock, swelling with pride;
Then Anstruther follows, that weather-cock elf,
Who shows how a man may desert from—himself—
To the Governor Hastings, his praise was profuse;
On Prisoner Hastings, he pours forth abuse—
Then follows young Grey, an exact imitator
Of the scurrilous Burke; a most promising prater;
Though all must lament that he's under such banners,
As evil community spoils our good manners.
Then Pelham, Fitzpatrick, and Windham come forth,
With Montague, Maitland, and Burgoyne and North,
Chick Taylor, and Erskine, are join'd in the votes,
And as Managers known by—a bag and dress coat;
Then Francis comes sneaking, with grief in his heart,
At not being indulg'd with a Manager's part—
Tho' he now and then steals in the Manager's box,
To suggest a shrewd question to Burke and Charles Fox.
The Commons, all those who from riding have leisure
In order come in, and go out at their pleasure.

In the concluding letter the author says that:—

When from engagements I'm free and at leisure
I visit the Hall as a matter of pleasure . . .
I could prove that a man, who his youth has expended
In serving his country, who bravely defended
Her possessions in times of most eminent danger
From ill-judging colleagues, and quarrelsome strangers
Should, when he can serve us in no other way,
Amuse and divert us—instead of a play.
The high-polish'd Athens, whene'er she beheld
A subject whose zeal in her service excell'd
His equals, with justice that subject expell'd.
And that mode of treatment was certainly wise
Howe'er it may seem in Humanity's eyes
. . . . There once was a time
I ingratitude held a detestable crime.
But since I've conversed with political heroes
Who are Tituses often, and frequently Neroes,
I am fully convinc'd that in ev'ry condition
We should study that only which serves our ambition
Or adds to our pleasure ; and hence I confess
I look on the whole as a contest of chess.

When Burke his game forward endeavours to bring
Law advances a pawn, and gives check to his King ;
Burke covers his King, Plomer instantly sees
An advantage—and lo ! Edmund's Queen is *en prise.*
Burke rallies his men, and prepares for the fight,
Dallas whispers a move, and Burke loses a Knight.
Burke speaks in a circle, it proves of no use,
It suggests the idea of playing at goose.
And hence inexhaustible pleasure I find,
While a thousand comparisons rise in my mind.

On the 23rd of April, 1795, or upwards of seven years after the proceedings commenced, and during which sixty of the two hundred peers who had walked in the procession on the first day, and many of the prosecutors in the House of Commons, had died, the Lords proceeded to judgment. Each peer in his robes was called upon by Lord Chancellor Loughborough, who was opposed to the prisoner, to reply to this question : "How says your Lordship? Is Warren Hastings, Esquire, guilty or not guilty of high crimes and misdemeanours, charged by the Commons in the first article of charge?" On this the Peer addressed, uncovered his head, and laying his hand upon his breast replied, "Not Guilty, upon my honour," or, "Guilty, upon my honour." The question was put sixteen times, corresponding with that number of charges. The first two charges alleged high crimes and misdemeanours in various political transactions; the next six charges imputed personal corruption; the ninth charge accused Hastings of granting an improper opium contract to Stephen Sullivan, a son of the Chairman of the Court of Directors; the tenth accused him of improperly borrowing money for the use of Mr. Sullivan; the eleventh accused him of granting an improper contract for bullocks to Charles Crofts; the twelfth accused him of granting a similar

LORD LOUGHBOROUGH.

contract to Sir Charles Blunt; the thirteenth accused him of making irregular and excessive allowances to Sir Eyre Coote; the fourteenth accused him of irregularly appointing James Auriol as agent for the purchase of supplies for Madras, etc., for 15 per cent. commission; the fifteenth accused him of irregularly appointing John Belli as agent for the purchase of stores and provisions for the Garrison of Fort William, with a commission of 30 per cent.; and the sixteenth laid to his charge the residue of the impeachment of the Commons.

According to the report that was published in the *Times* on the following day :—

To the first of these questions twenty-three Peers said Not Guilty, and six said Guilty. The second was determined as the first; and the third was twenty-three to one. The remainder lessened in the Minority, but some of them on the Majority; but the average, upon the whole, was about eleven to two in favour of Mr. Hastings. The six who voted in the Minority on the first and second questions were the Duke of Norfolk, Earl Carnarvon (who was the first Peer who said "Guilty"), Lords Suffolk, Radnor, Fitz-William, and the Lord Chancellor. Of the twenty-three who said Not Guilty, were the late Lord Chancellor (Lord Thurlow), the Duke of Bridgewater, Duke of Leeds, Duke of Gordon, Marquis Townshend, Earl Moira, Earl Mansfield, Earl Leicester, the Archbishop of York, Bishop of Bangor, Bishop of Rochester, Lord Fife, Lord Ferrers, Lord Auckland, and nine others.

The highest Minority on any of the charges was six, and the largest Majority twenty-three. The Duke of Norfolk and the Earl of Suffolk went away, after dividing against Mr. Hastings on the two first charges.

When the numbers were ascertained, Mr. Hastings was called in, and the Lord Chancellor informed him that the Peers had acquitted him of all the charges of High Crimes and Misdemeanours brought against him by the Commons, and that, on paying his fees, he was discharged. He immediately quitted the Bar, amidst the congratulations of his friends, and the Court adjourned to their own Chamber.

The number of Bishops who entered in the procession was nine; of these, three gave their votes; the others waived their privilege on this occasion. The Peers who were Managers also declined voting.

The Verdict of the Court, when pronounced, seemed to meet the general sympathy in the Hall, which was manifested by strong expressions of joy on every countenance.

Thus has ended this famous Impeachment, which, for length of time, has exceeded any trial in the history of the world, having entered into its ninth year of duration.

The female part of the Royal Family were expected to attend the Trial, but none of them were there. The Princess of Wales was to have gone, after receiving the Address (of congratulation on her marriage) from the Corporation of the City of London, at Carlton House; but the Trial was over before her Royal Highness's Court broke up. Many who went to see her were therefore much disappointed.

The *Times* offered no further comment. Hastings made, I find, the following brief note of the event in his diary:—

April 23rd, Thursday. I attended at 12. Was called in about 12.45, and ordered to withdraw. The Lords gave the verdict. I was called in and informed by the Chancellor that I was acquitted by a great majority, and discharged about ten minutes before two. At four I called upon Lord Thurlow. The following were my guests: General Calliaud, Sir F. Sykes, Sir E. Impey, Mr. Sumner, Mr. J. Sullivan, Colonel Poona, Mr. D. Anderson, Mr. Baber, Mr. Auriol, Mr. Gall, Mr. Thompson, Charles, Major Scott, Major Osborne, Sir J. D'Oyley, Mr. Lowe, Mr. Plumer, Mr. Dallas, Mr. Shawe, T. Woodman, Colonel Hastings, Mr. Payne—in all 22.

Hastings received from all sides hearty congratulations on his acquittal, and not the least interesting of these testimonies of goodwill is the following address from Officers of the Bengal Army, which is preserved by Miss Winter :—

SIR,—The Officers of the Bengal Army, bearing in their remembrance the wisdom, moderation, and justice of your administration in India, feel a very heartfelt satisfaction in congratulating you on your late honourable acquittal by the Peers of Great Britain from charges brought against you by the House of Commons, and supported by men of the first abilities in the nation. The energy and severity with which you have been for so many years prosecuted, the magnanimity and fortitude you have shown during your trial, and in declining to solicit support, even when all the power and abilities of your native country seemed combined against you, place you in a point of view the most envied, the most honourable, for your enemies have raised a monument to your fame, in which the justice of our country hath recorded the integrity of your mind, and the propriety and necessity of your public conduct. May the gratitude of the community you have so long, so ably, and so faithfully served be as conspicuous as your merits and disinterestedness have been publicly evinced. May your Sovereign, by conferring honours upon you, prove the value he has for such a subject, and by doing so increase the approbation and attachment of a free and a generous people. With us and with the natives of this country, your name must ever be revered, and, with Clive's, be handed down with honour, respect, and admiration to the latest posterity.

We have, &c.

1st October, 1795.

Hastings was now in his sixty-third year, and was almost ruined. His defence had cost him, or rendered him liable for £100,000, and his own means were exhausted, and his wife's accumulations out of her marriage settlement had been greatly reduced by the failure of a Dutch firm. But he was not broken in spirit as well as in fortune. The prosecution had failed ; and he considered that he could reasonably claim indemnification from the nation for the expense to which he had been put in the vindication of his character as a public servant, since he had been assailed by the elected representatives of the public in Parliament at the expense of the State. He thereupon memorialised the House of Commons, submitted that he was entitled to compensation, and prayed for a grant for that purpose. He forwarded the petition through a friend to Mr. Pitt, the Prime Minister, who, after a few days, returned it with a short note stating that, "under all the circumstances, he did not conceive that he should be justified in submitting the petition of the late Governor-General of India to the consideration of the Sovereign." In effect, therefore, Pitt refused to accept the arbitrament of the tribunal which he had been instrumental in creating. It was owing to the unexpected support which he, the all-powerful Prime Minister of twenty-eight years of age, gave to the manœuvres of Fox, Burke, and Sheridan, that the

WILLIAM PITT.

Opposition succeeded in bringing about the impeachment, and it was repugnant to him to do anything tantamount to the reversal of his own vote. As Chancellor of the Exchequer he had no hesitation in debiting the country with the enormous cost of the prosecution ; but he sternly refused to bestir himself to obtain for Hastings compensation from the country for the ruinous cost of his defence. What King George the Third called Pitt's "long obstinate upper lip" was never more stiff than when the name of Hastings was mentioned in his hearing. His pride forbade him to forgive the defeat that Hastings had inflicted ; and though Hastings was honourably acquitted, Pitt was willing to mulct him in the whole of his fortune, and to leave him, notwithstanding his eminent services, to starve. There was a littleness in this, to say the least of it, that was unworthy of so great a man.

There was a special reason why Pitt might have been to Hastings' alleged faults a little blind, and to his actual merits a little kind; for Hastings was accused and acquitted of faults of which a Pitt was accused and condemned. The second William Pitt was the younger son and intellectual heir of the great

PITT (*after Gillray*).

statesman who made the family name revered throughout Europe; but that statesman was indebted for his good start in public life to the social and parliamentary influence which was acquired for the family by his grandfather, Thomas Pitt, Governor of Madras from 1698 to 1709, who was dismissed the Company's service in the latter year, at a moment's notice, for irregular practices. Thomas Pitt returned forthwith to England with his ill-gotten wealth, including a diamond, still named after himself, which he eventually sold for three millions of livres to the Regent Orleans for addition to the Crown Jewels of France. He was not impeached, nor in any way molested ; and having bought houses, lands, and rotten boroughs, he entered Parliament as member for Old Sarum (as his son and grandson did in succession after him), lived long, and died in the odour of opulence.

Hastings appealed to the Court of Directors of the East India Company, and, being requested to state the amount of his property, he explained his financial position, and then said : "I possess the estate of Daylesford in Worcestershire, which cost me, including the original purchase, and what I have expended upon the house, gardens, and lands, about £60,000. The estate is 650 acres, and may be valued at £500 clear yearly rent. . . . In 1789 I purchased the principal part of the estate, and about two years since the remainder ; it was the spot in which I had passed much of my infancy, and I feel for it an affection of which an alien could not be susceptible, because I see in it attractions which that stage of my life imprinted on my mind, and my memory still retains. It had been the property of my family during many centuries, and had not been more than seventy-five years out of their possession."

According to the rough draft of a letter, dated 13th February, 1798, in Hastings' handwriting, at the British Museum, the Proprietors of the East India Company resolved in June, 1795, to grant "me the sum of £71,080 as an indemnification for the legal expenses incurred by my impeachment, and an annuity of £5,000 from the 1st January, 1795, during the term of their present charter, as a reward for my services." But the Board of Control, influenced by Pitt, refused to sanction these proposals. The Court of Directors then entered into an importunate correspondence with the Board, and eventually a compromise was reluctantly agreed to by the latter. Thereupon

The Court of Directors were pleased to grant me, as a reward, an annuity of £4,000 for a period of twenty-eight years and a half, to commence from the 24th of June, 1785, the day of my arrival in England ; and a loan of £50,000 without any interest, for the purpose of relieving me from my then present embarrassments. The first of these grants received the express confirmation of H.M.'s Ministers ; and I have no doubt that the last, which did not require their formal sanction, yet passed with their approbation. The Court of Directors in a subsequent arrangement made to ensure the future payment of the loan, received from me a mortgage of my estate of Daylesford, estimated at £14,000, and ordered that one half of my annuity should be withheld for payment of the remainder. This, of course, reduced my annuity to £2,000, and I was under the necessity of mortgaging £1,000 of that sum for payment of the interest of debts which still remained undischarged, notwithstanding their large and seasonable aid. . . . With respect to my expenses, if, in any part of them, I have exceeded the bounds of discretion, it has been in such as are now become the great objects of taxation, my allotment of assessed taxes amounting (if my computation of them is accurate) to £803.

After Hastings had repaid £16,000 of the loan the balance was remitted, and at a General Court of Proprietors held at the India House on the 25th May, 1814, the resolution of the Directors, continuing his pension of £4,000 per annum for life, was approved. The liberality which was shewn by the Court of Directors to Hastings during the twenty-three years following his acquittal, reflected honour both on the Company and on the distinguished recipient of its uncovenanted favours.

CHAPTER VII

CARICATURES

THE debates in Parliament which culminated in the impeachment, turned the attention of Gillray, Sayer, and inferior caricaturists to Hastings; and, during the year 1788, a number of cartoons were published which reflected the predominant opinion about him at that period, and illustrated the manner in which an under-trial prisoner of State was liable to be treated, "when George the Third was King," by those whose avocation it was to "apply the grotesque to purposes of satire." Most of the pictures involved an outrageous contempt of Court, and gross personal libels; while some of them were flagrantly disloyal; but no one was prosecuted for their production. The artists assumed that, allowing for oratorical exaggeration, and the unscrupulousness of party feeling, there was a good deal to justify the chief managers of the trial in describing Hastings as a monster of iniquity; yet they invariably represented him as a man with a benign expression of countenance, refined features, and a dignified bearing, while they usually depicted Fox as an unshaven, vulgar, and sensual-looking man, with large hands, who was prone to violence of gesture when declaiming. It was known that the King and Queen sympathised with Hastings; it was suspected, on scanty evidence, that they had, on his return home, accepted from him some costly tokens of his respect; and it was believed that they were avaricious; so the caricaturists pilloried them unmercifully. The Chancellor, Lord Thurlow, who was the staunch friend of Hastings, was also handled roughly by the artists, who generally depicted him as a man with a strong face somewhat resembling that of the late Chancellor, Lord Herschell. Hastings scorned to take notice of the cartoons, though they were calculated to excite prejudice and hatred against him; and, within a year, public opinion began to veer round in his favour, and the caricaturists, having done their worst, then left him severely alone. As a certain historical value attaches to these works of art, I will enumerate the more important of them that are preserved in the British Museum.

In a picture, dated February, 1788, published by Rich, of Fleet Street, Hastings is represented in a cart, as the "Governor

"H-ST-NGS! HO! RARE H-ST-GS!"

of Rue-peas." The cart, which is full of pea-pods, is drawn by a pony, led by Thurlow, who cries: "Fine Begum Hastings! a lack a peck!" Hastings exclaims: "Truth must come out, there's no denial"; and Burke, who is a spectator, replies: "You'll have a fair trial." Beneath the picture are the following lines:—

He who acts upright in his station
Dreads not the censure of the nation,
For Truth o'er all will yet prevail
While Justice holds her equal scale.
Be candid then to every party,
And prove your mind is true and hearty:

Time will determine what is right,
And banish envy, malice and spite.

In a badly executed caricature, without date, published by Dicksee, 195, Strand, Hastings is depicted devouring the body of an Indian woman, and trampling on five other bodies of natives of India. It is entitled "The prodigious monster arrived from the East."

A small caricature, dated 8th February, published by

CUPPED.

Doughty, 19, Holborn, and entitled "Court Cards, the best to deal with!" shows Hastings in Oriental costume, with the King on the one hand, as King of Clubs, and Thurlow, on the other hand, as the Knave of that suit.

On the 12th February, a picture, entitled "H—st—ngs! ho! rare H—st—gs!" appeared, in which Hastings is shown trundling the King and Thurlow in a wheelbarrow, to illustrate the maxim that "What a man buys he may sell," which is quoted from Blackstone.

In the same month Holland published a cartoon showing Hastings being cupped by Pitt, who says: "Courage, my dear friend, you will feel wonderful benefit from this bleeding!" Hastings replies: "I trust entirely to your skill for my recovery."

On the 1st March Doughty published a cartoon, entitled "Such things may be: a tale for future times." Hastings, in a cart, with his hands bound behind him, is seen under a gallows; Fox, as the executioner, is placing the noose over his head; Burke, as the chaplain, stands close by; North holds

"BLOOD ON THUNDER."

the head of the horse in the shafts, and Sheridan eagerly pushes the cart from behind to secure a "drop" for the culprit. Hastings exclaims: "Walpole said, every man had his price; but, alas! I never could find out any of your prices." Burke mutters: "A poor atonement this for millions!" To which Fox replies: "A poor atonement do you call it, Ned? Egad, it would have been a devil of a job for me if my F——r had made such an atonement for unaccounted methods." North enquires of Sheridan: "Don't you remember, Sheri, that my Right Honourable friend often threatened to bring me to this, or the block?" Sheridan replies: "Psha! Fred, you know that was only to frighten you from your station; and drive on, or our friend Edmund will stand here preaching all the day!"

On the same day Forres, of 3, Piccadilly, published a cartoon, entitled "Blood on Thunder; fording the Red Sea." Hastings, holding in each arm a bag labelled £4,000,000, is being borne on the shoulders of Thurlow, through a sea of blood, on the surface of which float the heads and bodies of his victims, and some instruments of punishment.

On the 18th March Doughty published a large picture, entitled "The struggle of a Bengal Butcher and his Imp-pie." Hastings is shown in the centre in Oriental dress, being dragged to the right by Thurlow and Satan, and to the left by Burke, Fox, Sheridan, and two others. Before him is a tray, on which small imps are dancing. Burke exclaims: "For the sake of injured millions I and my worthy friends and colleagues demand these wretches as victims to public Justice!" Thurlow replies: "And for the sake of consigned millions I, with the assistance of my old friend and colleague here, am resolved to protect these worthy gentlemen!"

On the 28th March, 1788, Forres published a cartoon by Gillray, entitled "A dish of Mutton Chops"; in which Hastings, Thurlow, and Pitt are represented at dinner, feeding ravenously off the calf-like head of the King. Pitt is carving the tongue; Hastings is extracting an eye; and Thurlow is helping himself with two spoons to the brains. The trencher, on which the head rests, bears the inscription, "Mal-y-pense," and a Royal crown.

On the 10th April Berry, of Oxford Street, published a caricature, representing Hastings in Oriental dress, proceeding in state to pay a visit to a friendly Prince. He is smoking a hookah, borne by an attendant, the fumes of which are labelled "Articles of Impeachment," and he exclaims: "Old care in a whiff of tobacco I'll smoke." Thurlow holds a state umbrella over his head. There is a gibbet in the corner, marked "For the Governor"; near to which Fox and Burke, as two dogs, are lurking. Fox says to Burke: "Edmund! I'll finish the law." And Burke replies: "I'll bring the culprit to justice."

On the 27th April, a large picture by Gillray, entitled "The Westminster Hunt," appeared.

Thurlow is represented as a jockey, riding a donkey with the King's head, and whipping back the hounds. North having been ridden over is insensible; one of the forelegs of the donkey is trampling on Burke; Francis, Fox, and Sheridan are in pursuit of a hyæna, with the head of Hastings, and a tail marked "diamonds and rupees." Hastings is reaching the shelter of St.

"THE WESTMINSTER HUNT."

James's Palace, and is passing between the sentries Rose and Pitt. Thurlow shouts, "Back! back!"

On the 1st May there was published a caricature, bearing the initials "J. S." and purporting to be the work of Sayer, but attributed notwithstanding to the pencil of Gillray. It is entitled "The Princess's Bow, alias the Bow Begum."

It represents the Begum of Oudh (whose alleged wrongs at the hands of Hastings furnished Burke with the materials for some of his most bitter denunciations) seated, receiving the abject homage of Burke, Fox, and Sheridan; while Francis, secreted beneath the seat, says: "I am at the bottom of this." There is a picture above the seat, entitled "*Parturiunt montes*, *nascitur ridiculus mus,*" showing a mouse emerging from a hole at the foot of a mountain.

Six days after the publication of the above caricature there appeared a parody of it, undoubtedly by Gillray, entitled "The Bow to the Throne, alias the Begging Bow."

In this picture Hastings, in Oriental costume, occupies a throne, and holds out bags of pagodas and rupees to Lord Chancellor Thurlow and Pitt respectively, who are eagerly grasping at the gifts. Hastings says: "Dear gentlemen! This

"THE PRINCESS'S BOW, ALIAS THE BOW BEGUM."

is too little; your modesty really distresses me!" Before the footstool the Queen is shown, on her knees, kissing the toe of one of Hastings' shoes, and clutching a bag, inscribed "£200,000," in her right hand. She holds a box tightly under her left arm. This box—according to Wright and Evans's account of Gillray's caricatures (Bohn, 1851)—is "supposed to contain the celebrated diamond sent by the Nabob of Benares"; but the short word commencing with "B" and ending with "E" points rather to "Bute." The King, also on his knees, is helping himself freely to the coin of which the throne is full. He exclaims: "I am at the bottom of it!" The picture behind Hastings shows a monster bag, labelled "£4,000,000," with two arms outstretched, and hands from which showers of coin fall on three worshippers on their knees before it. Beneath the picture on the frame are the words, "Out of it came not a little tiny mouse, but a mountain of delight." Behind Thurlow and Pitt are the hats and hands of various claimants for Hast-

"THE BOW TO THE THRONE, ALIAS THE BEGGING BOW."

ings' generosity, as well as the Garter and Star, and the badge of the Bath suspended from a broad ribbon.

In a large picture by Gillray, entitled "Market Day," dated 2nd May, 1788, the alleged venality of the House of Lords is illustrated. Thurlow, with a purse in his right hand and the mace in his left, is standing like a drover, before a group of cattle having the heads of peers, whom he is supposed to have bought. In the background some of the cattle are upsetting a watch-box on which Burke, Fox, and Sheridan are perched. Pitt and Dundas are in a balcony above, "at the sign of the Crown," smoking long pipes, and holding pots of beer, regardless of the scene below. Hastings, mounted on a sorry steed, is carrying away a calf with the head of the King, that has its legs tied.

A large picture, entitled "The Political Banditti assaulting the Saviour of India," attributed to Gillray, was published on the 11th May, by William Holland, 66, Drury Lane. Hastings is represented riding a camel, and being assaulted by Burke, North, and Fox. Burke is armed with a blunderbuss, which he has

"THE POLITICAL BANDITTI ASSAULTING THE SAVIOUR OF INDIA."

just discharged at Hastings. Suspended from his shoulders is a pouch, labelled "Charges"; and he is partly clad in armour. Hastings, wearing the typical costume of an opulent Oriental, is armed with a shield, labelled "Shield of Honour" above the Royal Crown, and on this shield he is receiving the bullets discharged from Burke's blunderbuss. He has an undisturbed and benevolent expression of countenance, as though he is quite prepared to meet the "charges." Two large bags, labelled respectively "Saved to the Company," and "Eastern Gems for the British Crown," with a roll inscribed "Territories acquired by W. Hastings," are suspended from the camel's neck, and on the back of the animal are two other bags labelled "Lacks of Rupees added to the Revenue," and "Rupees ditto," respectively. North is detaching the bag labelled "Lacks of Rupees added to the Revenue." He wears a helmet and breastplate, and is armed with a notched scimitar, on the scabbard of which the words "American Subjugation" are inscribed. Fox is in the act of making a stab with a dagger at Hastings' back. His countenance is distorted by passion, and his attitude is indicative of intense excitement that offers a great contrast to the placid demeanour which is conceded to Hastings in all the caricatures under notice.

A cartoon, entitled "State Jugglers," was published on the 16th May by Forres. Hastings is shown on a platform between Thurlow and Pitt. From his mouth are issuing streams of coins, for which the crowd beneath are scrambling. Flames of fire are being ejected from Thurlow's mouth, and ribbons from the mouth of Pitt. Fox, on the shoulders of Burke, is in the background, stretching out his hat to catch some of the coins. The King and Queen are on a see-saw overhead. Beneath the sketch are the following lines:—

> Who wrought such wonders as might make
> Egyptian sorcerers forsake
> Their baffled mockeries, and own
> The palm of magic is ours alone.

In a large cartoon, called "The Trial," dated 17th May, and purporting to be by "H. H.," Thurlow is represented on the judgment seat. To his right is Fox, as Shylock, with a knife in his hand, exclaiming: "My deeds upon my head, I crave the law!" Behind Fox are Burke, Sheridan, and others. To the left of Thurlow is Law, as an advocate, pointing with his right hand to Hastings behind him, and holding a heavy purse of rupees in his left. Hastings wears Oriental costume, and exclaims: "He seeks my life, his reason will I know."

In a picture, entitled "Opposition Coaches," about three feet long and ten inches broad, published 20th May, 1788, by Forres, and bearing no signature, but which is evidently the work of Gillray, two four-in-hand coaches are shown starting from a sign-post in the middle of the picture. The post bears two indicating hands—one, pointing to the left, being inscribed, "To the Slough of Despond"; and the other, pointing to the right, being inscribed, "To the Temple of Honour," respectively. The Parliamentary coach on the left hand, proceeding to the left, is descending a hill into the slough. It is "Licensed by Act of

THE ROYAL COACH.

Parliament, Pro Bono Publico," according to the inscription on the panels. Burke is driving. Immediately behind him is Fox, armed with a blunderbuss, and showing great alarm. There are four persons inside the coach. The horses have human heads. In a basket behind the coach are scrolls labelled "Magna Charta," "Bill of Rights," and "Impeachment of W. Hastings." The Royal coach on the right hand, proceeding to the right, is being driven furiously by Thurlow up a steep hill, and the four horses have the heads of Dundas, Arden, Grenville, and Sidney respectively. (I am compelled by the exigencies of space to dispense with the leaders in my sketch.) On the roof of the coach the Queen is seated, holding in her right hand a basket containing a goose, and in her left another basket containing "golden eggs." Hastings occupies the seat of honour within the coach, and opposite to him is a stout lady wearing a crown, intended doubtless for Mrs. Hastings. The King sits behind in the rumble, armed with a gun. Under the Parliamentary coach the words "O Liberty! O Virtue! O my Country!" are inscribed; while beneath the other coach, which has the Royal arms on the panels, superscribed "Licensed by Royal Authority," these lines appear :—

The very stones look up to see
Such very gorgeous Harlotry
Shaming an honest Nation.

Public interest in the trial began to flag before the expiration of 1788, and, as has been said, the caricaturists then began to leave Hastings alone. Later on the violence of the prosecution prompted sympathy for the accused, and suggested the idea that Burke had gone mad on the subject. On the 8th May, 1789, Aitken, of Castle Street, Leicester Square, published a cartoon, entitled "Cooling the Brain, or the little Major shaving the shaver."

In this picture Burke is represented as a lunatic chained to the ground, being shaved by Major Scott, Hastings' Parliamentary agent. Hastings carrying a sack, labelled "£4,000,000," is being welcomed to St. James's, and Burke exclaims: "Ha! miscreant, plunderer, murderer of Nuncomar, where wilt thou hide thy head now?" The following lines are appended to the sketch :—

Madness! thou chaos of the brain
What art, that pleasure giv'st a pain,
Tyranny of Fancy's reign,
Mechanic Fancy that can build
Vast labyrinths and mazes wild
With rude, disjointed, shapeless measure,
Fill'd with horror, fill'd with pleasure,
Shapes of horror that would even
Cast doubt of mercy upon Heaven.

On the 8th May, 1795, or a few days after Hastings had been

acquitted, a cartoon was published illustrative of "The Last Scene of the Managers' Farce," which "lies in an old Hall, formerly a Court of Law." The bust of Hastings, surmounting a pedestal, occupies the centre of a theatrical stage, with bright light radiating from it. The pedestal bears the inscription: "*Virtus repulsæ nescia sordidæ incontameninatis fidget honoribus.*" Dense fumes are passing away. Above the fumes the

"COOLING THE BRAIN, OR THE LITTLE MAJOR SHAVING THE SHAVER."

figures of Lord Loughborough and Lord Thurlow are shown, and the former exclaims: "Black, upon my honour!" while the latter replies: "Not black, upon my honour!" On the right hand is a stage-box, occupied by Fox, holding a magnifying glass, and other Managers. On the side of the box is the track of a snail, marked "1787–1795." Near the box is a cauldron that contains, according to the explanatory notes at the foot of the picture, "ingredients mixed up by" the Managers "to blacken a character out of their reach." Burke, the principal performer, having "out-Heroded Herod, retires from the stage in a passion at seeing the farce likely to be damned," and makes "an exit *in fumo*" by a trap-door to Hades—a "Court below to which the Managers retire upon quitting the stage." Francis is shewn as the prompter, peeping from behind the stage. He filled "no character in the farce, but was very useful behind the scenes."

CHAPTER VIII

PARK LANE AND DAYLESFORD

IN the second year of his trial Warren Hastings sold his estate at Windsor for £4,300, and he bought, ostensibly on behalf of Mrs. Hastings, for £8,000, from John, Viscount Bateman, the lease of a large house overlooking Hyde Park, London, then known as No. 1, Park Lane, which that peer had taken for ninety-one years from Lord Grosvenor of Eaton, in 1773. He remained in this house during the remaining six years of his trial, and during his negotiation for the purchase of the Daylesford estate. In 1797 he determined to retire permanently to Worcestershire; and he sold the house, for Mrs. Hastings, to Neil, Earl of Rosebery, great-grandfather of the late Prime Minister, with the fixtures and effects, for £11,249. Messrs. Christie Sharp & Harper, who acted as house-agents, described the house as a "noble, spacious, and singularly elegant mansion," that was furnished "in a superior style of taste and elegance, forming a most complete *rus in urbe*"; and had "stabling for eight horses, three coach-houses, and numerous attached and detached offices."

Shortly before Hastings relinquished possession of the house he had eleven paintings of scenes in India, by the "late ingenious artist Hodges"—to quote from the catalogue — removed to Christie's rooms in Pall Mall, where they were sold by auction. They were illustrative of scenes or buildings in Calçutta, Benares, Agra, Lucknow, Bangalpoor, Tilliagarry, Chunasghar, Sungulterry, Ranjamahal, and Gwalior respectively; and though they were sold one by one, they realized in all no more than £125. As they were souvenirs by no mean artist of places that Hastings had visited, or been associated with during the most notable period of his life, and as there was a large amount of wall space available for pictures at Daylesford House, it is surprising that he allowed them to be sold outright, instead of sending them down to Worcestershire to add to the attractions of his new home. He was caused much annoyance by the miserable results of the sale, and, in a letter from Daylesford to Mr. Richard Johnson, his banker,[1] he said that few things had "given me so much vexation as the disgraceful sale of my pictures. I would rather have burnt them." He was not prepared to assert that the auctioneer was wholly to blame, but "my newspaper never contained an advertisement of the sale"; and though he was in town, he was never informed of "the necessity of giving the auctioneer authority to buy in the pictures till it was impossible for it to reach him." He was "particularly vexed at the mean price at which Shuja Dowlah's portrait sold, because I never intended to part with it, and do not know how it came to be joined to the rest." He had intended to "cut it down to a kit-cat." He asked Mr. Johnson to endeavour to repurchase it for him, "for a sum not much exceeding that at which it was knocked down." Warned by the fate of his pictures, he was determined that—

My stud shall not come to the same shameful end. I have thoughts of advertising them for private sale, and fixing, and publishing their prices,

---

[1] According to the *Handbook of London Bankers*, Messrs. Edwards, Smith, Templer, Middleton, Johnson & Wedgwood, to which firm the above-mentioned gentleman belonged, were established bankers in 1794, at 18, Stratford Place, Oxford Street, London. In the following year Mr. Smith's name did not appear among the partners of the firm. In 1805 the style of the firm became Davison, Noel, Templer, Middleton, Johnson & Wedgwood, carrying on business at 34, Pall Mall. In 1807 the name of Johnson disappeared from the firm, and the business was carried on by the other partners until 1816, when this banking house ceased to exist, and many of the customers were recommended to transfer their accounts to Messrs. Coutts & Co., who still have possession of their ledgers, etc. Their premises were taken by Messrs. Hopkinson, who occupied them until 1819, when they were acquired by Messrs. Ransom & Co. Both Mr. and Mrs. Hastings transferred their accounts to Messrs. Coutts & Co. on the failure of Messrs. Davison & Co. On the death of Mr. Hastings the balance of his account was, in accordance with his will, carried to the credit of his wife, who in the following October transferred the amount from Messrs. Coutts & Co. to Messrs. Gosling & Co.

which shall not be varied. If I do this, I will send the rest of my four-year-olds to be included in the same advertisement, and to stand in the same stables for a fixed time. In my agricultural experiments I have been successful almost to a prodigy, and wish I had confined my experiments to that line. Yet it is a pity. I could have produced a pure breed of Arabian horses, and provided for the perpetual increase of it in this country, if I had met with encouragement. But I fear I have had both ignorance, poverty, and taxes to defeat my purpose.

A deed was drawn up which set forth that the purchase money of the house was "the only proper money of the separate estate" of Mrs. Hastings, and had by her been "really and bona fide paid" out of her "sole and separate estate," with "the privity, consent, and approbation" of her husband. It was then stated that, of the sum received from Lord Rosebery, £1,249 was paid into the "own proper hands" of Mrs. Hastings, and £10,000 was settled on her son, Sir Charles Imhoff, and his wife on their marriage. Mrs. Hastings wrote to Mr. Johnson, the banker, to thank him for all the trouble he had taken about "my house in Park Lane," and remarked, "What trouble his Lordship has given us! By the Lord! I would not sell another house to him if I had one to dispose of, and he wish to be purchaser."

Mr. George Nesbit Thompson, Hastings' former Secretary in India, wrote from Panton Lodge to Hastings on the 13th March, 1797, and said :—

Before I can venture to rejoice in Mrs. Hastings' disposal of her house, I must know that the sacrifice has cost her no pain. Sincerely, however, and without any hesitation, do I pray that, as it does her honour, so it may not impair her future happiness. Circumstanced as you have been, Wealth could not have elevated you. Comparative Poverty does. Riches and Honours are the ordinary rewards of ordinary virtues. There is no truth better established than that persecution and want have been the usual meed of transcendent merit from the days of Palamedes to these.

Lord Rosebery was not wealthy, and Hastings was caused some anxiety about his being allowed to take possession of the house before he had paid a deposit, and signed an agreement. "Your letter"—he wrote from Daylesford, on the 27th March, to Mr. Johnson—"has done what the impeachment could not. It has broke my rest. If you have given his Lordship possession, or suffered him to take it, without receiving his agreement, nothing but a long suit in Chancery can force him to pay the price of the house and furniture, unless he considers his honour a sufficient pledge. I shall not recover the tranquillity of my mind till I hear from you, if then. Yours affectionately." But two days later he informed Mr. Johnson that "all is well," for he had written to Lord Rosebery "requesting that he will pay, or cause to be paid to Messrs. Edwards, Temple & Co., whom I have constituted my Attorneys, the remaining sums when they shall become due, for the price of my late house in Park Lane, and the appraisement of the furniture appertaining to it, and to take their receipts for the same as a full acquittal." In this letter Hastings refers to "my late house," although, according to the deed above mentioned, the property formed part of the "sole and separate estate" of his wife. She had no fortune when she married him; and it is probable that he gave her the "only proper money" of her "separate estate" on the eve of his trial, as security against the contingency of a conviction that might have been followed by the confiscation of everything belonging to him.

In 1808 Lord Rosebery[1] sold the house to the 11th Duke of Somerset; who bequeathed it to his son, the 12th Duke; who left it, on his death in 1886, to his daughter, Lady Hermione Graham; who died in 1888, and bequeathed it to her husband, Sir Richard Graham; by whom it was sold, in 1890, to Mr. George Murray Smith, of Messrs. Smith & Elder, the publishers, the present occupant.

[1] Shortly after he entered into possession of the house Lord Rosebery enquired what rates and taxes Hastings had been in the habit of paying during his occupancy of it; and Hastings stated that he was charged as follows:—Duty on windows, commutation tax, duty on houses, servants, horses, and carriages, at 10 per cent., £45; land tax, £18; parochial rates for St. George's, Hanover Square, £40 5*s.*; parochial rates for Marylebone, £1 12*s.* 6*d.*: total, £104 17*s.* 6*d.* It is interesting to compare these rates and taxes in 1797 with those that are charged on the same house in 1894; and Mr. Murray Smith informs me that he pays:—Parochial rates, £256 6*s.* 5*d.*; inhabited house duty, £48 15*s.*; and income tax, £37 18*s.* 4*d.*: total, £342 19*s.* 9*d.* The ground rent is now £300, and the house is rated for parochial purposes at £1,084 per annum. The property is assessed at £1,300 per annum for income tax.

The house is now known as 40, Park Lane. It is next to the Oxford Street end of the Lane, and commands a fine view of the northern portion of Hyde Park. It is not remarkable for its architectural features, and it is, probably, a great deal larger now than it was a century since; but, even allowing for the additions that have been made to it by successive occupants, it must have been an important residence, in the best part of

THE PORCH, 40, PARK LANE.

town, in Hastings' time; and, as he was able to occupy it during the long ordeal of his trial, and to keep up appearances, and dispense a generous hospitality as it was his invariable practice to do, he must have had the command of no inconsiderable income while he lived there, notwithstanding the frightful expense of his defence. There is a handsome porch to the house, through which Thurlow, Law, Plumer, Dallas, and many other friends of Hastings must have repeatedly passed.

The purchase of Daylesford entailed a longer negotiation, Hastings said, "than would have served for the acquisition of a province." His importunity at length prevailed, and Mr. Knight accepted £11,424, and an annuity of £100 a year for himself and his wife for the estate. Hastings then pulled down the dilapidated mansion, and erected the present edifice on its site; and he spared no expense in laying out the grounds. Thus it was that the estate represented in the end an investment of as much as £60,000. "From first to last," says Mr. Gleig, "it was a conspicuous trait in Hastings' character that he never put the smallest value upon money." Even the drain of the protracted trial on his resources did not hinder him from continuing his lavish expenditure on the beautification of his property. It was a passion with him to build and to plant, and had it not been for the liberality of the Court of Directors, that passion would have led him into the Bankruptcy Court. The fact that the estate realized, about seventy years after he acquired it, only half the sum that he spent upon it, notwithstanding the rise in the value of landed property in the interval, proves that he spent too much on the gratification of the dream of his life.

In order to form some ornamental rock-work in his grounds, and to make an island in his lake, Hastings caused a number of large stones to be removed from the summit of a hill in Adlestrop parish, where they had lain from time immemorial. Once upon a time, according to a local tradition, an old woman, named Alice, was driving her geese to pasture upon this hill, when she was met by a "weird sister," who demanded alms, and, upon being refused, transformed the geese into so many stones, which consequently obtained the name of the Grey Geese of Adlestrop Hill. "A clerk of Oxenford," who paid a visit to Hastings at Daylesford, wrote a ballad, in 1808, in honour of the Grey Geese, and contributed it to the *Gentleman's Magazine.* Having related how the old woman was treated by the witch, the poet proceeded to say, that she was offered some consolation for the loss of her geese by the following prediction :—

DAYLESFORD HOUSE.

But pitying fate at length shall abate
  The rigour of this decree,
By the aid of a sage in a far distant age :
  And he comes from the East country.
A Pundit his art to this seer shall impart,
  Where'er he shall wave his wand,
The hills shall retire, and the valleys aspire,
  And the waters usurp the land.
Then Alice thy flock their charm shall unlock,
  And pace with majestic stride
From Adlestrop heath to Daylesford beneath,
  To lave in their native tide,
And one shall go peep like an isle o'er the deep,
  Another delighted wade,
At the call of the wizard to moisten his gizzard,
  By the side of a fair cascade.
This sage to a dame shall be wedded, whose name
  Praise, honour, and love shall command,
By poets renown'd, and by courtesy crown'd
  The queen of that fairy-land !

In 1807 an anonymous bard published a poem, entitled *Daylesford*, which he dedicated to Hastings. He described the meadows, lawns, mimic isle, and "breezy copse" of the estate, and exclaimed : "How dear to Meditation is the scene!" Then, as the *Gentleman's Magazine* remarked, with his mind dwelling more or less consciously on the "Man of Ross," he proclaimed the beneficence of Hastings :—

For who yon smiling hamlet can survey,
The rising farm now rescued from decay,
The churchway path repair'd, the warm-clad poor,
The garden fence that skirts the cottage door,
Who can unmov'd survey, what breast so dark
But at the sight would catch a kindred spark ?
Till rous'd, and bursting into kindled fire,
It glows, it burns to be what it admires.

The house which Hastings erected is built of the pale grey stone of the neighbourhood, on an eminence, in an undulating and well-wooded park of about 600 acres, which is entered by three lodges. The style of architecture is unpretentious, but it is favourable to internal comfort. At the chief entrance is a portico that leads to a large hall with a tesselated pavement, whence access is obtained to a library of considerable size, fitted with carved marble mantelpiece, decorated cornice, etc., and to a dining-room, 37 feet by 21, with a bay window opening on to a lawn, and fitted with massive marble mantelpiece, gilded cornice, etc. By a corridor, or picture gallery, 50 feet long, with polished oak floor, the reception rooms are approached. These rooms, which have a southerly aspect, include a drawing-room, 40 feet by 25, well decorated, with windows opening on to a stone balcony overlooking the garden, lake, and park; a smaller drawing-room, 26 feet by 22, with a particularly handsome marble mantelpiece, showing Mahomedan female figures in a zenana, and a ceiling painted with emblematical subjects; a morning room, also 26 feet by 22, opening on to the terrace; a circular vestibule, with a roof supported by Ionic columns; a billiard-room, 26 feet by 22, and a smoking-room nearly as large. The next floor is reached by a fine oak staircase, and a wide corridor. Here are five large bedrooms, of which four were decorated in Hastings' time in white, buff, pink, and green respectively. There is also a circular boudoir, decorated in white and gold, like the chief bedroom, with a lofty dome roof, supported by Ionic columns, and three windows commanding beautiful views over hill and dale. A stone staircase leads to the upper floor, on which are five rooms for bachelors, and six for servants. The offices on the ground floor include a large kitchen, a scullery, a pantry, a plate closet, a butler's room, a housekeeper's room, a still room, a store room, a servants' hall, and five other rooms for servants; wine and beer cellars; and an enclosed court surrounded by a dairy, a bake-house, a game larder, a fuel house, a carpenter's shop, a laundry, a drying closet, and five bedrooms for men servants, surmounted by a clock tower. The stabling includes a large enclosed courtyard with six carriage houses, a 6-stall stable, a 4-stall stable, a 3-stall stable, twelve loose boxes for hunters, two harness rooms, and rooms above for coachmen and grooms. The highly cultivated kitchen garden is surrounded by a wall covered with fruit trees, and contains houses for growing grapes, pines, melons, peaches, cucumbers, and mushrooms. There is also an outer garden. The pleasure grounds were laid out by a notable landscape gardener, and are very beautiful, with their extensive lawns of velvet-like grass, their beds of flowers, and their clumps of fine trees. The plantations are exceedingly attractive. They contain a great variety of indigenous trees, including some grand elms and beeches, and many exotic trees that Warren Hastings introduced and acclimatised. There are also several charming lakes, that are believed to be full of fish, and alongside one of these is a romantic footpath that leads to the village. By the carriage road the house is nearly a

DAYLESFORD HOUSE, FROM THE LAKE.

mile from the lodge close to the village. At the two farms on the estate Hastings unsuccessfully endeavoured to cross English sheep and goats with breeds from India.

Furniture, like apparel, "oft proclaims the man." This must have been peculiarly the case in the days antecedent to those in which upholsterers are prepared at short notice to supply the want of good taste in a customer. Hastings was remarkably attached to his home; and its surroundings and embellishments testified to his innate love of the beautiful in Nature and Art.

The cruel ordeal through which he passed at Westminster Hall did not, as it might well have done, render all things associated with India distasteful to him. He was proudly conscious that he had deserved well of his country, however ill the representatives of that country had acknowledged his services; and, having fought a good fight against great odds and much prejudice, it was an abiding source of gratification to him to recall the incidents of the best years of his life, which he had given, in the society of his wife Marian, to India. Consequently, his "halls, so large, were hung around" not with trophies of the chase, for he was no sportsman (though Francis, as has been stated, realized to his cost that he could shoot straight), but with paintings, drawings, and illuminated parchments that recalled to his mind scenes and studies of the far East, and suggested topics of conversation with the guests whom he loved to have around his table. He never forgot that he had filled an eminent office under the Company and Crown; and he regarded it as to some extent incumbent upon him to adopt a style of living in keeping with the position which had once been his.

It was in his drawing-room that this feeling was most manifest to visitors. The four long windows of this apartment were hung with pale blue satin curtains, with deep white satin borders, painted in flowers, and ornamented with silver lace and spangles. The furniture was for the most part made of ivory. There were two sofas of solid ivory, of Oriental design, superbly carved and richly gilded, the elbows finished with tigers' heads, and the back and seat covered *en suite* with the curtains. There were nine solid ivory elbow chairs, corresponding in style and finish with the sofas; and a solid ivory table, beautifully carved and gilded, fitted with drawers with silver locks and handles, and covered with fine green cloth, edged with silver lace. There were also two solid ivory ottomans, gilt, and covered *en suite* with the sofas; and a pair of carved ivory Oriental official staffs, ornamented with silver-gilt bands and wires, and mounted in ebonised and gilt frames and silk mounts, to form fire-screens. There were two Oriental fly-flaps, the handles carved out of the finest jade, mounted and inlaid with gold, and set with rubies and emeralds. A superb suite of Persian chain mail, inlaid with gold, was arranged near a variety of Oriental weapons; specimens of old Derby, old Dresden, and Sèvres china were displayed on side tables, and in ornamental cabinets, together with alabaster vases, ivory caskets, and specimens of Indian silver filigree work resembling the finest lace. There were also eight ebonised and gilt chairs, covered with blue silk, and banded with spangles; a Brussels carpet fitted to the room; and other accessories.

The other rooms were furnished in a comfortable manner without anything very distinctive about them, except the pictures on the walls; but, in the boudoir of Mrs. Hastings, there were, among other things, six solid ivory chairs, delicately painted and gilt; and a richly gilt square foot ottoman, covered in crimson velvet, and embroidered in silver-gilt lace. Hastings was very partial to furniture made of ivory. It has been said that in one of his earliest letters to his wife, after her departure from India, he alluded to his own "ivory cot." In one dated Calcutta, 14th November, 1784, he stated that "he had hastened his return from Benares, *via* Buxar, Patna, and Bugulpoor." "The Begum," he continued, "sent me more than one message expressive of her disappointment at my passing the city, as she had prepared an elegant display of your couches and chairs for my entertainment. These are since arrived, with a letter for you, recommended most earnestly to my care. There are two couches, eight chairs, and two footstools, all of the former patterns, except two of the chairs, which are of buffalo horn, most delicately formed, and more to my taste than the others, not designed for fat folks or romps." Then, in one of his first letters from London to Mr. Thompson, he said:—

> Remember, too, to inquire for, and to secure my ivory cot. Mrs. Hastings desires me to inform you that the Begum's ivory chairs are of very great value, not of little, as you seem to estimate them. She requests that you will present her respects to the Begum (and mine, pray), and desire that she will not order any velvet, or other worked seat to the chairs, as they will make the whole seizable by the Custom House officers; she also begs that they may be sent by a ship that will swim.

Two ivory chairs, quaintly carved and gilded, each with five legs, were presented by Hastings to Queen Charlotte, and were subsequently acquired by the Duke of Buckingham and Chandos for Stowe, where they were sold at the famous auction in August, 1848. Some of the other articles of solid ivory that once occupied places of honour at Daylesford have found their way back to India, and now adorn the palace of the Maharajah of Dharbunga.

Hastings possessed numerous portraits of notable persons who sat to distinguished artists for him, including the Duke of Gloucester, the Duke of Bridgewater, the Marquis Townsend, the Earl of Warwick, the Earl of Fife, the Earl of Coventry, the Earl of Dorchester, Lord Thurlow, Sir Thomas Plumer,

IVORY CHAIRS, FORMERLY THE PROPERTY OF WARREN HASTINGS.

etc. He also owned good examples of Teniers, Matsys, Ruysdael, Corregio, Rembrandt, and other old masters; as well as numerous specimens of the skill of Hodges and Zoffani, which he had cordially encouraged when those two artists visited him at Government House, Calcutta. Several of Hodges' Indian landscapes are still preserved at Daylesford; and among them the most notable are views of Calcutta from Fort William; of Alipore, near Calcutta; of Benares; of the Taj Mahal, at Agra; of Gazapoor on the Ganges; of Cuttera; of Shekoabad; of the Himalayas, etc. A picture by this Royal Academician, representing a boat in a squall on the Ganges, which illustrates an incident in Mrs. Hastings' life, when she was hastening to Calcutta to attend her husband in an illness, was removed from Daylesford after Sir Charles Imhoff's death, and is now owned by Miss Winter; as also is a life-size portrait of Mrs. Hastings, that was taken in Calcutta by Zoffani. In a letter dated London, 29th March, 1787, Hastings complained to his friend, Mr. Thompson, in Calcutta, that: "Not one of my pictures has been sent after me, none of my Tibbet pictures, not one but Mrs. Hastings', of Zoffani's, and that packed so negligently that it arrived almost spoiled." Mrs. Hastings did not think that this portrait did her justice, and she caused it to be hung in a remote part of Daylesford House. The figure is well painted; but is more suggestive of a Siddons in a *rôle* in a tragedy, than of the lady whose beauty and amiability fascinated the "great Proconsul" for nearly half a century.

Hastings was rich in prints, miniatures, enamels, etc., and his collection of Persian drawings was especially remarkable. His library was extensive, and included numerous folio and quarto volumes of high repute, as well as octavo and smaller books, periodical publications, magazines, reviews, Parliamentary blue-books, plays, romances (bound and unbound), atlases, and music. Many of the books were presentation copies; others contained his autograph; and the majority were handsomely bound in old calf, or morocco. Numerous works bearing on India and the East were interspersed with rare editions of the ancient classics, narratives of voyages, antiquarian researches, treatises on natural history, biographies, sermons, histories, geographies, poems, essays, debates, tracts, pamphlets, operas, sonatas, and glees. There were two copies of a book containing a summary of the debates in the House of Lords on the evidence in the trial of Hastings, with a proof portrait of Lord Thurlow, the Chancellor. This work was privately printed in 1797, at the expense, and under the superintendence of Hastings, to "vindicate," according to the preface, "his character from the malicious, vindictive, and foul aspersions so unjustly cast upon it by his enemies; also to convince such as have not sufficient time to wade through all the details of a trial which lasted twenty years, of his innocence." He presented it to a few private friends. There were several other reports and memorials of his trial among his books.

It has been stated that upwards of a thousand years ago the dale's ford, or Daylesford, was given by Ethelbald, King of the Mercians, to Begia, "a servant of God," for the endowment of a monastery. This retreat for those who were weary of such pomps and vanities of this wicked world as were to be had in those simple days, was built near the ancient village of Adlestrop, and a small church occupied the most honoured part of the establishment. Little is known of the monks who lived in this remote locality. Doubtless, they performed certain ceremonies; had their relaxations; and did what they could to ameliorate the hard conditions of the lives of the peasants around them. Their bell tolled the knell of many a parting day, and the carrying of many a rude forefather of the hamlet to his long home near the church. It also tolled for themselves on their departure from this transitory life. Decades accumulated into centuries, and the monastery fell on the evil days of disestablishment. Then, in all probability, the villagers helped themselves to such building materials as it offered to the first comer. But the church occupied ground consecrated to holy uses; and the villagers stayed their hands when they approached it on predatory thoughts intent. There is a tradition in the neighbourhood that a good deal of the material employed in the erection of the first Daylesford Manor House was pilfered from the monastery, and it is also said that a curse permanently rested on the house on that account. But the little church escaped the effacement that overtook the buildings around and about it. The Saxons were followed by the Danes, who, in their turn, were supplanted by the Normans. The Royal Houses of Plantagenet, Lancaster, York, Tudor, Stuart, and Hanover succeeded severally to the throne, and the church continued to weather all dynastic and meteorological storms. Divine service was performed with small hindrance from generation to generation. Many of the quaintly expressed prayers that still form part of the liturgy of the Church of England were composed, and were in use in parish churches throughout the land before the Norman Conquest. They must, therefore, have been read a countless number of times in this building, first by Roman Catholic, and then by Protestant ministers ; and the beauty of their imagery, the poetry of their language, and their adaptability to the spiritual needs of all classes and ages, at all times, and in all places, may have often afforded comfort to, and strengthened hope in those good folk at Daylesford who reverently responded to them in the days of old.

As a child, Warren Hastings may have been frequently driven over from Churchill to Daylesford on Sundays to attend service in his grandfather's church ; but, from the year 1740, when he was taken to London, until 1764, when he returned for the first time from India, he did not see Daylesford again. Most probably he visited the place during the four years that he then remained in England. He came home "for good and all" in 1785, and became Lord of the Manor, and patron of the living, in 1788. Twenty-eight years more passed, and then, at the age of rather more than eighty-three, he resolved to pull down the old church, which was in decay, and to re-erect it, as far as possible, with the same materials, supplemented by such new woodwork and masonry as might be needed. He informed the Rev. J. Owen, the Rector of Daylesford, of his intention, and the latter agreed to perform the Sunday services in the church of Oddington until the reconstruction was completed. The following entries in Hastings' diary show how the work proceeded, and the methodical interest that he took in it:—

8th July, 1816: The workmen began to remove the pews (mine, of course, to remain so), desk, and pulpit, and to unslate the roof. The woodwork deposited in the stable. *9th:* The rafters all removed, and lastly the belfry taken down. *10th*, *11th*, and *12th:* Demolition. Part cleared to the foundation, which was found to be free stone all round, and the walls 12 ft. 6 in. high, and 2 ft. 3 in. thick. The wall, composed of irregular stones, was laid in plain earth. The Gothic porch down. Bell 19 in. diameter at bottom, and 15 in. deep in the inside. *13th:* Laid four of the groin stones for the foundation, the fifth to be re-laid. *15th:* Bank removed. *16th:* First courses well advanced. *20th:* The church much impeded by yesterday's rain, but otherwise going on well, and the timber frame much advanced. *23rd:* The wall is above the window sills. The ladies went to see the church. *25th:* I wrote to countermand the Gothic, and directed Roman instead. At 12½ the walls were 7 and 7½ ft. *27th:* The south-west window in the way of being done to-day. *29th:* At 2 I visited the church. Lead laid over the arch.

31*st:* The north-west and north-east windows finished. 1*st August:* The masons employed in raising the scaffolding. 5*th:* The principal parts of the belfry brought home. The projection of the north-west wall finished.

7*th:* Letter from Mr. Rowe proposing a tablet of 29½ by 25½, which I answered thus : 'Sir,—I have attentively considered your drawing in every point of view, and particularly with relation to the situation in which the proposed tablet is to be placed. The tablet you recommend is, I think, considerably larger than will be necessary, nor do I quite like the proportions of it. I request, therefore, that the tablet which you are to prepare for me may be precisely 28 in. and one-third by 20 in. Within that space I am persuaded that you will be able to engrave the whole of the inscription in capitals large and distinct enough for the situation which is to receive it. I particularly request that all the words and the lines may be kept distinct from each other, and I approve the method you have taken to separate and

DAYLESFORD CHURCH, AS REBUILT BY WARREN HASTINGS.

mark the Scriptural quotation from the rest of the inscription. You will be pleased, according to your own suggestion, to provide that the tablet shall stand half-an-inch from the wall, and have two hitch blocks for its support. I am, etc.'

10*th August:* The principal rafters, and many of the smaller, and the wall tablets are fixed, and the water tablets and the pediment finished. 13*th:* The base stone of the belfry well laid and bedded. 17*th:* The arch of the tower in three pieces, and the bell placed. 19*th:* The turret finished. The remaining rafters laid, and the chancel partly demolished, begun to-day. 24*th:* Half the slating done, and 3 ft. of walling to the chancel. 26*th:* The slating of one side finished. 4*th September:* The two front windows up and covered ; the arches waiting for the others ; the floor about half laid ; the cornice arranged on the ground. 7*th:* At eleven the opposite walls were completed, and the end wall far advanced ; the flooring laid. *8th:* The tablet arrived. *10th:* All timbers and masonry of the chancel finished, and slating two courses done. *11th:* The slating of the south-east side of the chancel completed. *14th:* The ridge laid, and the roof finished ; the rubbish removed, and the floors swept. *23rd:* Plastering finished ; labourers unemployed. *31st:* The tablet put up and fixed, and well done. *12th November:* Eight stained windows arrived. *15th:* The painted window fixed. *27th:* Pews complete. *29th:* Gibbs brought the tablet of E.H. and began the excavation of the gravestone ; ordered to be inserted above in the wall at the height of 6 ft. I gave directions to Gibbs to erect a gravestone in the churchyard, with this local inscription : 'The Rev. Penyston Hastings, B.A., Rector of this church, was buried here the 1st of October, 1752.'

8th December: This day, just five months from the demolition of the church, Divine service was performed by the Rev. J. Owen, curate, with a prayer and sermon for the occasion, most appropriate and impressive. A full congregation. No sensible damp or offensive smell. Mrs. Hastings prevented from going by the remains of a very severe indisposition. Sir Charles and Lady Imhoff and all our servants, with two unavoidable exceptions, present. Of these none have on this day (Monday) suffered any symptoms of indisposition from the recency of the masonry. *Sunday, 15th:* We all went to church. *17th:* My eighty-fourth birthday. *5th January:* Gibbs fixed the stone over my grandfather's grave.

The tablet referred to bears the following inscription :—

This Church derives its foundation from a grant of Ethelbald, King of the Mercians, who reigned between the years of our Lord 716 and 757. Sanctified by the prayers, rites, and oblations of its successive parochial members through a period exceeding 1,000 years, it was rebuilt with such of the same material as constituted its primitive structure, and had escaped the mouldering hand of Time, with its identity unchanged ; and the uniformity of its Saxon architecture, which had suffered some encroachment upon it from the license of incidental reparations, was restored in the year of our Lord 1816.

"For a thousand years in Thy sight are but as yesterday when it is past, and a watch in the night," Psl. XC. 4.

CHAPTER IX

AMUSEMENTS AND EXCURSIONS

THERE was a vein of romance in Warren Hastings which found expression, not only in his love letters to his wife, but also in his poetical effusions. He was always fond of Latin and English poetry, and though, in the opinion of some persons who never made a rhyme, he demeaned himself by straying from the region of prose where he excelled, it may be conceded by less austere critics that, moderate though their literary merit may be, his poems show a depth of feeling, a love of nature, and a sense of humour that do him honour. In the intervals of official business in India he sometimes sought distraction for his thoughts by poetical composition ; and, long after his return home he copied some of his poems, in his own neat handwriting, into a volume, bound in crimson morocco and gold, that he presented to his wife, and which is now treasured by her grand-niece, Miss Winter. The collection opens with the following sonnet by way of dedication :—

This Book replete with many a varied lay,
  Which stream, though diverse, from one common source,
  To thee, my Marian, seeks its destin'd course ;
Thy right ; which I in grateful tribute pay.
For 'twas from thee alone its glowing ray
  My genius drew, that with resistless force
  Impell'd me first to sing ; else mute, or hoarse,
Nor daring in the Muses' walks to stray :

There, frequent as the Summer's insects, rove,
  'Mid the gay scenes where Youth and Beauty shine ;
Those who the sweets of transient Passion prove :
  But rare, whose path is one unvaried line
Of wedded courtship, and domestic love ;
  For rare the merit of a heart like thine.

Ye, who the common suff'rings feel
Of love, yet wish your pains to heal,

To distant plains and objects rove ;
For absence is the cure of love.
But why should I, ill judging, roam
With risk of such a change at home ?
Nor Time, nor Space, though both combine,
Can cure a heart of love like mine.

Wilt thou, my Marian, when we meet,
With equal joy thy lover greet ?
Wilt thou his transports share, and prove
That absence is no cure for love ?

The book contains a copy of his ode entitled "Rooroo and Promodbora—a Hindoo Tale, borrowed from Mr. Wilkins's Translation of the Mahâ-bhaurut, and sent from Patna to England in the year 1784." He tells the tale, and proceeds to apply the moral :—

And now, my Marian, from its shackles free,
My wearied fancy turns for ease to thee ;
To thee, my compass through life's varied stream,
My constant object, and unfailing theme.
Torn from the bosom of my soul's repose,
And self-devoted to surrounding woes,
Oft o'er my solitary thoughts I brood—
(For passing crowds to me are solitude)—
Catch thy lov'd image, on thy beauties dwell,
Improv'd by graces which no tongue can tell,
The look, which I have seen, by love endear'd,
The voice to love attun'd, which I have heard.
Or rapt in thoughts of higher worth, adore
Thy virtues, drawn by mem'ry's faithful store ;
Or court, as now obsequious at her shrine,
The Muse, unkind on ev'ry theme but thine.
Nor foreign deem from such a frame of mind
This tale, to meet thy gracious ear design'd.
To me, and to my state, alike belong
The subject, and the moral, of my song.

'Tis true, no serpent of envenom'd breath
Hath stung my love, ere yet a bride, to death ;
And, O ! may Heav'n for many years to come,
Preserve her life from Nature's final doom !
Yet is she lost to me, in substance dead,
With half the travers'd globe between us spread :
Dreadful transition ! in one moment's cost
My soul's whole wealth I saw, and held, and lost.

Then Fate and Silence clos'd life's blissful scene,
Its being past, as it had never been.
The sad remembrance only now remains,
And by contrasting aggravates my pains.
Hope still attendant and delusive stands,
And points, but coldly points, to distant lands ;
Gilds their faint summits with her flatt'ring ray ;
But deserts, rocks, and seas obstruct the way ;
And age, and sickness, and the clouds that teem
With unknown thunders, through the prospect gleam.

Ah me ! no Gods, nor Angels now descend,
The sons of men in pity to befriend !
My sufferings else might some kind Spirit move
To give me back on terms the wife I love :
And more than half my life would I resign,
For health, her purchase, and herself, for mine.
Borne by the Pow'rs of Air, or she should rise,
Or I rejoin her through the distant skies.
No more my thoughts in solitude should mourn
My sweet companion from my presence torn ;
Nor rigid duty force me to remain,
And see her sails diminish on the main.
To her my destin'd hours, though few, I'd give,
And while I liv'd, a life of bliss I'd live.

While Hastings was at sea, on board the *Barrington*, on his way home, he addressed the following imitation of Horace, Book II., ode xvi., *Otium Divos*, etc., to John Shore, afterwards Lord Teignmouth, who eventually succeeded him as Governor-General. He made an exceedingly neat copy of it in his diary ; and, many years afterwards, transcribed it into the presentation volume above referred to :—

For Ease the harass'd seaman prays,
When equinoctial tempests raise
  The Cape's surrounding wave ;
When hanging o'er the reef he hears
The cracking mast, and sees, or fears,
  Beneath, his wat'ry grave.

For Ease the starv'd Mahratta spoils,
And hardier Sic erratic toils,
  And both their Ease forego :
For Ease, which neither gold can buy,
Nor robes, nor gems, which oft belie
  The cover'd heart, bestow.

For neither wealth, nor titles join'd
Can heal the foul, or suff'ring mind,
  Lo ! where their owner lies !
Perch'd on his couch Distemper breathes,
And Care, like smoke, in turbid wreaths
  Round the gay ceiling flies.

He who enjoys, nor covets more
The lands his father own'd before
  Is of true bliss possess'd ;
Let but his mind unfetter'd tread
Far as the paths of knowledge lead,
  And wise as well as blest.

No fears his peace of mind annoy,
Lest printed lies his fame destroy
  Which laboured years have won ;
Nor pack'd Committees break his rest,
Nor Av'rice sends him forth in quest
  Of climes beneath the sun.

Short is our span ; then why engage
In schemes for which Man's transient age
  Was ne'er by Fate design'd ;
Why slight the gifts of Nature's hand ?
What wand'rer from his native land
  E'er left himself behind ?

The restless thought and wayward will
And discontent attend him still
  Nor quit him while he lives :
At sea Care follows on the wind,
At land it mounts the pad behind,
  Or with the post-boy drives.

He who would happy live to-day
Should laugh the present ills away,
  Nor think of woes to come :
For come they will, or soon or late,
Since mix'd at best is Man's estate,
  By Heav'n's eternal doom.

To ripen'd age Clive liv'd renown'd,
With lacs enrich'd, with honours crown'd
  His valour's well-earn'd meed.
Too long, alas ! he liv'd, to hate
His envied lot, and died too late
  From life's oppression freed.

An early death was Elliot's doom,
I saw his op'ning virtues bloom,
And manly sense unfold
Too soon to fade! I bade the stone
Record his name 'mid hordes unknown
Unknowing what it told.

To thee, perhaps, the Fates may give
(I hope they may) in wealth to live,
Flocks, herds, and fruitful fields;
The vacant hours with mirth to shine,
With these the Muse, already thine,
Her present bounties yields.

For me, O Shore, I only claim,
To merit, not to seek for fame,
The good and just to please;
A state above the fear of want,
Domestic love, Heav'n's choicest grant,
Health, leisure, peace, and ease.

His transcript of these lines in the presentation volume is followed by a copy, also in his handwriting, of what Hastings calls a "beautiful and harmonious poem," by Mrs. Burrell. These are the introductory verses:—

No wonder that the skilful pen
Of one amongst the best of men
His noble soul displays!
He in whose bosom Virtue dwells,
Can best describe the thoughts he feels,
When Virtue claims his praise.

Hastings, to thee applause is due,
Whose anxious care, whose utmost view,
Was still the public good.
Wealth, Power, and all their tempting train
Strove to engage thy mind in vain,
Thy mind with worth indued.

No thorns can from thy pillow spring,
Nor Conscience feel a poignant sting
From retrospective scenes.
Thy Mem'ry, when she backward treads,
From thy disinterested deeds
A secret pleasure gleans.

Thou ne'er hast with tyrannic hand
Spread desolation through the land,
  Nor taught the poor to weep.
Thy breast no keen remorse can know,
Nor pangs that from dishonour flow,
  Nor care that murders sleep.

To bless has been thy glorious aim,
The worthy, not the great, could claim
  A patronage from thee.
No ostentatious love of pow'r
Has ever gain'd dominion o'er
  A mind from error free.

Those who amass unbounded store
May in their prosp'rous state be poor
  In virtue and in fame;
But thou, of higher wealth possest,
Hast brought this treasure from the East:
  An uncorrupted name.

Hastings addressed an ode of eighteen stanzas to Mrs. Burrell, in reply to the foregoing, and prefaced his transcript by saying, that: "As there are some passages in this composition which may seem to allude to a series of events which were neither known nor suspected by the author at the time in which it was written, it may, therefore, be proper to premise that it was written and finished some time within the month of January, 1786. On the 17th of the following month the charge of impeachment against him was opened in the House of Commons." The first four verses are as follows:—

Sweet is the sound of praise; as sweet
As the seraphic airs that greet
  The dying martyr's ear;
If seated in the conscious breast
Truth strike accordant, and attest
  The worth applauded there.

Be praise to latest ages heard,
Be wealth and honors the reward
  Of deeds of virtue done;
That feebler minds the blazon'd name
May see, and emulate its fame,
  So profitably won.

For ruin shall that Land await,
Whose Genius, heedless of its fate,
Like Fortune on her throne,
Its trusted gifts at random throws,
Or partial to its trait'rous foes,
Is kind to them alone.

But not for interests like these
The moral man shall aim to please
The world's uncertain will ;
And these denied, the spark divine,
That lights the frame within, shall shine
With equal lustre still.

The remainder of the poem is devoted to allusions to his trial, and to a correct forecast of the vindication of his conduct by posterity.

In October, 1806, the octogenarian Earl of Coventry sent Hastings a copy of the following verses, of which he was the author :—

"O RARE LONDON!"

Led by curiosity and fame,
A stranger to this town I came,
To see the lions and St. Paul's,
The parties, masquerades, and balls,
Banquets so costly and so fine,
That some have thought, without a mine
The charges could not be defrayed.
But all is for the good of trade,
And so, indeed, I grant it might
If bills were payable at sight.

More wondrous things than these I saw,
A Chancellor at odds with law ;
A mitre, too, without decision,
'Twixt Papal and reformed religion.
I saw a man who made it clear
Without horse, foot, or volunteer,
And all such usual reliance
England might bid to France defiance.
I saw a youth just come from school,
Teaching arithmetic by rule,
He knew that two and two make four,
That taking ten from just five score,

The sum of ninety would remain,
With which you might begin again.

I saw a man for parts renown'd,
On whom Dame Fortune lately frown'd,
Though now she plenteous fare affords,
Reduc'd to dine on his own words :
A brewer, too, to forego "entire,"
To vent his patriotic ire.
He proved that fraud and peculation
Would be the ruin of the nation.
"Grains" of allowance for his trade
I must suppose he would have made.
Alas, how prone is man to spy
The mote that's in another's eye!
But above all my chief surprise is
(A thing unknown at our Assizes),
That when a man has been acquitted,
It should to others be permitted
To persevere in ill report,
And doubt the justice of the Court.

Hastings appreciated the delicate allusion to himself in the last six lines; and, in acknowledging the Earl's courtesy, he said that, "being impressed by the spirit and ease of the model before" him, he had presumed to make the following addition to the poem :—

I saw a greater wonder still
('Twas at a place they call Spring Hill),
A man whom time, affliction, pain,
Have join'd their powers to bend, in vain ;
To whom reflective conscience shows
A life improving to its close ;
Like summer's suns, in day's decline,
That with more vivid colours shine :
With talents grac'd, with wisdom more,
And wit that blooms at eighty-four.

The Earl died three years afterwards, aged eighty-seven.

In March, 1810, Hastings availed himself of "the frank of a basket to Mrs. Motte," to send his friend, Halhed, the following lines, which were, he explained, "composed of shreds and patches between Portman Square and Daylesford" :—

From the days of Job Charnock, scarce known on record,
To the triumphs of Plassey's redoubtable Lord,
   The Company traffick'd unheeded :

WARREN HASTINGS (*after Masquerier*).

She sent her ships forth, the wide ocean to roam,
With rich cargoes well freighted, and brought richer home ;
   And in all she adventur'd succeeded.

By oppression provok'd, she to arms had recourse,
And soon made her oppressors submit to her force ;
From defensive proceeded offender :
And her courage attemper'd with wisdom conspir'd
To aggrandize her pow'r, till at length she acquir'd
Of an empire entire the surrender.

Now the sages in schools of diplomacy bred,
Civil doctors, divines, and state-moralists said—
(And the senate confirm'd their opinion ;)
That for her, a mere trader (for what was she more ?),
Or her factors and clerks, from her counting-house door,
To pretend to the rights of dominion ;

That to give up the pen in exchange for the gun ;
To hold rule over nations—no matter how won ;—
To make treaties ; assume legislature ;
Nay worse, of finance to distribute the drains,
To elicit their currents, and pocket the grains ;
Was to gospel repugnant and nature.

So they stripped off her robe ; but the loss to atone,
His Majesty gave her a cloak of his own ;
Lent her armies and fleets for protectors ;
To diminish her cares, and to lighten their weight,
For her guardians appointed the Lords of the State,
And a Board to direct her Directors.

Thus equipp'd, and embrac'd by the beams of the throne,
As once Semele, wrapp'd in Jove's attributes, shone,
Now as meek and resigned as a martyr,
With the guilt of imputed offences defil'd,
By rapacity pilfer'd, by malice revil'd,
She gave up the ghost, and her charter.

Though ignoble her birth, yet in death she may boast,
That her orb in the colors of glory was lost,
Like the sun, when he sets in Orion ;
This reflection of comfort at least to produce—
That her greatness arose from the quill of a goose,
And was crush'd by the paw of a lion.

The following lines[1] were entered by Hastings into his diary shortly before the close of his life :—

[1] Quoted by Dr. J. Grant in an article, entitled "Warren Hastings in Slippers," which appeared in the *Calcutta Review* of March, 1856.

"ET QUÆ TANTA FUIT ROMAM TIBI CAUSA VIDENDI?"

As the lone traveller, from Alpine skies
Looks down upon the storm he cannot feel ;
Through the spread clouds that far beneath him rise,
Sees the dim flash, and hears the tardy peal,
Yet warn'd by time which not unheeded flies,
Quits his calm sunshine, and illusive weal,
Braves (for he must) the tempest ere it dies,
While quickened steps his latent fears reveal :
So I, with mind of self-dependence vain,
My lot of life in ease and comfort laid,
And smiles of love with smiles of love repaid
Look down with pity mingled with disdain
On care-bound mortals ; till of want afraid,
I stoop, like them, to care, and court the chain.

Hastings was exceedingly hospitable at Daylesford, and, as a host, he preached temperance by his own life-long practice of the virtue. Like Herodotus, as described by Faber, he was, in his retirement, a "mild old man." He was neighbourly both to his equals, and to the poor at his gates. He was habitually cheerful, and he was the cause of cheerfulness in all around him. He was a lively and well-informed conversationalist with all ranks and all ages. His ample library, his taste for Oriental literature, and his love of poetry, served to shield him from *ennui* during inclement weather. He was an horticulturist and an acclimatisor ; and his flower, fruit, and vegetable gardens, his stables, his flocks, his herds, his menagerie, his farm, and his fish-ponds afforded his enquiring and intelligent mind constant delight. He loved trees, and, on the 30th November, 1810, when he was in his seventy-eighth year, he wrote an elegy on some beeches in his park, which were blown down by a storm. Having described the tempest and its effects, he says in the poem which is in his handwriting before me :—

Pride of my lands ! long shall remembrance dwell
On your lost worth. Pride of my lands, farewell !
I lov'd to see your stately columns rise,
And lift your plumy tenants to the skies ;
To hear the blackbird's short but mellow lay,
And the sweet thrush that hymns the closing day :
And all the happy warblers of the grove.
Join in one chorus of accordant love.

Pleas'd I beheld my flock at noontide laid
Beneath your cool and hospitable shade;
Nor less the opposing screen, that shew'd, withdrawn,
The bursting prospect of the varied lawn.
The joy I daily felt, by habit prov'd
A purer int'rest, and its source I lov'd;
And you, perhaps, as love the growth it made
Of love, the gen'rous sentiment repaid.

He then touches upon the uses to which the wood of these lamented trees would be applied, in the making of fences, frames, beds, and cabinets; and concludes with reflections on the political storm that was (under Napoleon) threatening England when he wrote.

He took some interest in science; and in 1801 he was elected a Fellow of the Royal Society. It is stated in the *Journal Book* of the Society that, on the 19th of March, a "certificate was read recommending for election Warren Hastings of Berkeley Square, late Governor-General of India, as a gentleman of great and extensive knowledge in various branches of science, and likely to become an useful and valuable member." It was signed by Lord Morton, Messrs. R. J. Sullivan, P. Russell, and J. Bruce, and it was "ordered to be hung up in the public meeting room." The election took place on the 25th June, and, on the 5th November (at which date Sir Joseph Banks was President of the Society), "Warren Hastings, Esq., elected at the last meeting, attended; he paid his admission fee, compounded for annual contributions, signed the Obligation in the Charter Book, and was admitted a Fellow of the Society." There is no record of his having made any communication to the Society.

He left among his papers, which are now in the British Museum, "A comparative account of the cost and charges of the Flail and Thrashing Machine"; a pen-and-ink sketch, and minute measurements of a "picota," by which rude apparatus water is raised in India from a well, or pond, by a lever; a memorandum on the effect attributed to the barberry bush of debilitating ears of corn, and conducing to blight; a paper showing that the leaves of trees and plants are essential to their strength, to the growth of buds, and the maturing of fruit; a project for constructing and regulating a stove for tropical fruits, accompanied by a neatly executed geometrical drawing; some directions for the cultivation of chillies and beringauls; instructions for dibbling; a diary of the readings of the thermometer, and a record of the weather at Daylesford; recipes for dressing a curry and boiling rice; an estimate,[1] in tabular form, of the produce of wheat, barley, and oats in the parish of Daylesford, with remarks; etc.

Hastings had no taste for sport in any form. He discharged a pistol two or three times before his memorable duel with Francis, who admitted that he had never had even this very slight acquaintance with fire-arms; but he never dreamt of finding pleasure by taking the life of either large or small game when he was in India; and he did not preserve in order to shoot game at Daylesford. Nor did he care for horse-racing or gambling. But on one occasion he was induced to take part in a lottery. This was in March, 1809, when "Mr. Towney bought a lottery ticket in partnership with me for twenty guineas, No. 1808. I paid him half by draft, and we gave the ticket in custody to Lady Imhoff, superscribed 'The property of W. H. and C. P. Esqres.,' in his handwriting." The lottery referred

[1] It appears from this paper that, on the 1st October, 1801, the inhabitants of the parish of Daylesford were 98 in number, and included "Mr. and Mrs. Hastings and their domestics," 21; "their other servants and their families living out of the house," 8; Mrs. Bowles and her family, 7; "Mrs. Hart and her household," 2; Mrs. Dadge and her family, 3; and other inhabitants, 57. The population, he said, "had progressively risen from fifty-one, the number of which it consisted in 1788, when my household was first added to it, to sixty-eight, the number of which it consisted in the autumn of last year exclusive of that addition. . . . The quantity of wheat consumed in my family from the 31st October, 1799, to the 1st of November, 1800, was 150 Winchester bushels." He had 49 acres under wheat in 1801, which produced 109 quarters; 26 acres under barley, which produced 56 quarters; and 16 acres under oats, which produced 50 quarters. The wheat crop showed a deficiency as compared with the yield in 1800. "I have reverted," he remarked, "to the notice of the last year's produce, to show with what ease a case of deficiency, in this instance as great perhaps as any that is likely to occur in the course of some years to come, may be remedied by the accommodation of the appetite, not only to such a diet as will satisfy nature, but to such as even the fastidiousness of unconstrained luxury may relish." This end could be attained, in his opinion, by the employment of equal quantities of wheat and barley in the making of bread.

to was a State one, and the chief prize was a large sum of money. As no further mention of the ticket was made by Hastings in his diary, it must be concluded that he and his partner drew a blank.

From the restless standpoint of the concluding decade of the nineteenth century it may seem strange that Warren Hastings, after he settled down at Daylesford, rarely sought amusement, with change of air, scene, and society, except in the metropolis, to which he bent his steps twice or thrice a year. The means of communication a century ago left much to be desired; yet, if there were no railways to bring the ends of the land together, there were stage-coaches that plied regularly between the large towns, and the public roads were available for equestrians, and for private conveyances. But Hastings seldom diverged from the direct route to and from London; and though he became a valetudinarian in his latter years—as is so frequently the case with retired Anglo-Indians, when they realize the fact that they are shelved, and superfluous in their native land—he was little disposed to travel at home, much less abroad, in search of health or recreation. He paid flying visits to Cheltenham, Oxford, and a few other places, and he spent, as will be seen, a couple of days at Brighton; but it was habitual with him to be content with ringing the changes on a corner of Worcestershire and the west end of London. In respect to making himself acquainted, by personal and comparative observation, with the physical features, the historic edifices, the local populations, the manners and customs of England, he was, it must be confessed, unenterprising. He was not, perhaps, more so than the average country gentleman of his time, who usually cherished an aversion to the trouble and expense of straying beyond the beaten path to his county town; but Hastings had been far afield in his youth and prime, and he was no average man of the stay-at-home type. Circumstances compelled him, irrespective of personal inclination, to make many and long journeys in Northern India, and he might thus have acquired a taste for travelling for its own sake that may have survived his return to Europe, and assisted to reconcile him to the uncongenial inactivity of a pensioner's lot.

Such, however, was not the case. He was a good, but not an ardent horseman; his personal wants were few; his physical activity was remarkable; his manners were genial; he was fond of, and was appreciated by good society; and he was not tied down to any spot by the inexorable demands of sport. Yet he never visited Wales or Ireland; he did not penetrate into Scotland beyond Edinburgh; he saw little of the Midlands; and he was a stranger to counties so accessible to Worcestershire as Devon and Cornwall. The quiet life at Daylesford, agreeably diversified as it was by the exercise of hospitality, and by occasional contact with men and women of light and leading in town, met his requirements, and was conducive to his longevity; but his sympathies were narrowed by his disinclination to see the world beyond Adlestrop and St. James's.

In the autumn of 1805 he visited the Isle of Thanet, accompanied by Mrs. Hastings and Miss Dalling, a daughter of Lady Dalling. He left London on the 26th October, and drove with his own horses to Rochester; proceeded thence with hired horses to Sittingbourne, where "we were all accommodated." The party arrived at an hotel at Margate the following afternoon, and "slept at an adjacent house, the hotel being full." The next day Mrs. Hastings and Miss Dalling went to Ramsgate "in quest of a house." On the 1st October "we took possession of No. 38, Churchfield Place." On the 12th "we all went to the play, bespoke by Mrs. H." On the 14th they left Ramsgate about noon, "baited at Deal, and arrived in the evening at Dover. The York Hotel, where we stopped, was full, and the landlord insidiously conducted us to the London Hotel—the Ship, a good inn, having vacant accommodation."

15th. We saw Dover Castle, and the famous cliff. Sir William and Captain Dalling and Mr. Sullivan dined with us.

16th. We proceeded to Canterbury, where we stopped by the pressing invitation of Captain Hughes at his house; dined and slept there. The Marquis of Douglas dined with us. Captain Hughes accompanied Miss Dalling and me to the Cathedral.

17th. We set out after 11, and, contrary to our intention of stopping at Rochester, we went on to town, reached Lady Dalling's unexpected at 10, having travelled five hours in the dark.

Hastings and his wife spent New Year's Day, 1806, at

Brighton. He stated in his journal that they left London about 1 p.m., and arrived at Brighton about 4. On the Marine Parade they "were stopped and graciously accosted by the Prince of Wales." They received an invitation to pass the evening at the Pavilion—the palace in an Oriental style of architecture and decoration that the Prince had erected for his marine residence. They went there at 9, and the Prince "sat with us an hour and a half, and invited us to dinner to-morrow." On the morrow "we dined at the Pavilion, the Prince leading Mrs. H. and Mrs. T. H." The next day Hastings wrote his name in the Prince's visiting book, and "at half-past 11 we departed from Mrs. Barton's. We slept at Ryegate." The following morning they started early, and "reached Park Street, No. 112, a little past 1."

Hastings made a tour to Edinburgh and the English lakes in the same year, and he jotted down his experiences in his diary :—

August 4th. We left Daylesford at 8.40 a.m. for Scotland, and this day reached Lichfield, where we slept at the George, good. Miles 62.

5th. Derby. King's Head, good. Here our postillion drove against Colonel I.'s chaise, and broke the left wheel. We deviated to Kiddleston Hall, and saw Kiddleston House. 27 miles.

6th. Sheffield. Tontina, very good. 86 miles.

7th. Northallerton. Golden Lion, good. 75½ miles.

8th. Newcastle, very good. 48½ miles.

9th. Proceeded at 10, and continued till 8.50 p.m., the last two hours through a heavy storm of rain, with some hail, and frequent flashes of lightning. Slept at Berwick. 63½ miles.

10th. St. Germain's, where we arrived after 3. 44½ miles. Here we found Mr. and Mrs. Anderson, their eldest son and daughter, Mrs. Sands and her son, John Anderson and his son, who departed in the evening.

11th. Mr. Anderson and Charles (Imhoff) went to Edinburgh to see the examination of Warren Hastings Anderson, my godson, whom they brought with them to dinner.

There is no entry for the six following days, which were probably spent in Edinburgh. The diary then proceeds :—

17th. We went to church. Dr. Hamilton.

19th. Charles and Mrs. Imhoff left.

22nd. Mr. Anderson and I went together to a dinner made for us at Oman's Hotel, by the gentlemen of the Edinburgh India Club, to which Lord Morton and Charles were also invited. We left them at half-past 8, and returned to St. Germain's.

A friend in Edinburgh has hunted up for me the following paragraph, which appeared in the *Edinburgh Evening Courant*, and also in the *Edinburgh Advertiser* of the 23rd August, 1806:—

The Edinburgh East India Club and a number of gentlemen from India gave an elegant entertainment to Warren Hastings, Esq., late Governor-General of India, on Friday last, at Oman's tavern. The occasion was particularly gratifying to the feelings of a very numerous meeting, many of whom, from a long residence in India, had the best opportunity of knowing this distinguished character, and appreciating the services he had rendered his country during his government of British India. After the health of Mr. Hastings and many loyal and patriotic toasts, the following sentiment from the President was drunk with universal applause: "Prosperity to our settlements in India, and may the virtue and talents which preserved them be ever remembered with gratitude." The evening concluded with that spirit of conviviality which has ever distinguished this respectable society.

The Club, which was founded in 1797, ceased to exist many years ago.

Hastings made these further entries in his diary:—

25th. We all went to Tyningham; going early saw much of the garden and plantations.

27th. We returned late in the morning to St. Germain's. Colonel and Mrs. I. left us to make the tour of the lower Highlands.

28th. We dined at Mr. Liston's, and returned to McGregor's hotel at Edinburgh.

29th. Mr. Anderson and I visited Mrs. Rowland and Mrs. Kerr; we afterwards met at dinner at Mr. Sands's in Edinburgh.

30th. We visited Reg'n Office, &c., with Mr. Wachop, and all dined at Mr. Samuel Anderson's.

31st. We went to the Presbyterian church, but heard nothing.

Sept. 1st. Mr. Anderson, Mrs. H. and I dined at Dalmahoy with Lord and Lady Morton.

2nd. We walked round the Park; returned to Edinburgh; visited Mr. Wachop; proceeded to St. Germain's, where we arrived at 5.

7th. Lord Morton arrived, and staid. Mr. and Mrs. S. Anderson and Mr. H.

8th. All departed about noon, with Miss Swinton.

10th. We set out (Mr. and Mrs. Anderson and ourselves, 8) for Wilton Lodge, at 10 a.m. We arrived at Wilton at 1. While we were here we visited the castle of Branxholme. Wilton Lodge is the most beautiful place we have seen. The Vale of Teviot well cultivated. Very recent improvements. Farmhouses all new; hedges none of ten years' growth.

13th. We left Wilton Lodge. Messrs. Anderson, Mrs. Anderson, and Miss Anne accompanying us at 7¾; at Moss Park baited, 13 miles; Longholme, 11 miles. At three miles past Longholme we took leave of our friends. Longtown, 11. Carlisle, Bush Inn, 9. Total of this day 44 miles.

Thus ended Hastings' first and last visit to Scotland.

14th. We all went to the Cathedral, and at 2 proceeded over a dreary country, without a tree, at 5.20 Penrith, the Crown, 18 miles.

15th. Visited Ulleswater, Aira force, and Patterdale.

16th. At 9 40 we left Penrith, and at 1.25 arrived at Keswick, 18 miles, Royal Oak. We took boat, and saw Lodore.

17th. About 9 we started, the ladies in a chaise, Charles, I, Hutton, and Thomas riding, on the Lorton road. The ladies rode about three miles to Scalo Hill, and one more on the way to the boat, which carried us to the head of the lake of Cummoc, stopping first at the inn of Scalo Hill. We landed and walked to Buttermere, 1 mile. We returned by the vale of Newlands, the ladies having rode 13 miles, walked 2, and been rowed 4, total 19 miles ; carriage added 25, and scarce fatigued.

18th. At near noon we started, the rain, which had fallen all night, having just ceased. Borrowdale, Bowdarstone, Rossthwaite ; crossed the Derwent, riding about 300 paces along the rapid stream, and ascended a steep hill to Watterlath, and home, about 16 miles.

19th. Charles rode up Skiddaw. We went together to Vicktor's Island, and on our return I fell over some fir trees lying across the path. I called on Mr. Edmonstone, a surgeon, purposing to be bled, to which he objected. Mary, Mrs. I.'s maid, following Patrick and Nancy up Skiddaw, missed them, and did not return till dark.

22nd. At 11 we departed. Ambleside, 15 ; Kendal, 14.

23rd. Burton ; Lancaster ; Garstang ; Preston,—Black Bull,—good ; 43½ miles.

24th. Wigan ; Warrington ; Knutsford ; Congleton ; Newcastle ; 66½ miles

25th. Stone ; Wolseleybridge ; Lichfield ; Birmingham ; Hockley House ; Stratford,—Lion ; 70 miles. A beautiful day and pleasant roads. John rode a blind mare from Wolseleybridge, which fell with him. He was blooded at Lichfield, and not much hurt.

26th. We breakfasted, and proceeded and reached home about noon, having travelled altogether 900 miles.

The defeat of the Emperor Napoleon early in 1814, his abdication of the throne of France, and his exile to Elba restored peace to Europe, and Louis XVIII. thereupon emerged from his retreat at Hartwell, near Stanmore, Middlesex, and was escorted thence, with much ceremony, by the Prince Regent to London. The Royal party made a triumphal entry into the metropolis, and the King was lodged at Grillon's Hotel, in Albemarle Street. On the 23rd April the Prince Regent proceeded to Dover to receive the King, who on the following day embarked for France. On the 8th May the Emperor Alexander I. of Russia—he was not then known in England as the Czar—and King Frederick William II. of Prussia, arrived at Dover from Boulogne, in the *Impregnable*, accompanied by the Prince Royal of Prussia (afterwards King Frederick William III.); Prince William (afterwards the Emperor William I.); other Princes; Marshal Blucher, etc. The Prince Regent had caused rooms to be prepared for the Emperor in St. James's Palace; but his Majesty drove up unexpectedly from Dover to the Pulteney Hotel in Albemarle Street, where his sister, the Duchess of Oldenburg, had been staying for five weeks, and remained there. The King of Prussia arrived in London on the following day, and went to Clarence House, St. James's Park. The Prince of Orange, the Prince of Oldenburg, and the Prince of Mecklenburg also arrived.

On the 12th June, Hastings left London with Mr. E. B. Impey for Oxford, and "baited at Tetterworth." On the following morning, after breakfast, they continued their journey to Oxford, and Hastings was welcomed there by Mr. Theophilus Leigh Cooke, of Magdalen College, whose guest he was during his stay at the University City. There was an excited demand for horses and conveyances, and Hastings took the precaution to "engage the same horses and postillions for the time of my stay" as had brought him from Tetterworth. In the afternoon he attended the levée—or "lever" as he wrote it in his diary in the old-fashioned way—of Lord Grenville, the Chancellor of the University. "We dined (Mr. C. and I) at his brother George's of Corpus." On the 14th the Prince Regent and his Imperial and Royal visitors drove from London to Oxford, where degrees were to be conferred on the most distinguished of the nation's guests. Hastings noted in his journal:—

14*th*. A procession of all the gownsmen, and of the Mayor and Aldermen, met the Prince Regent at the bridge, and conducted him to the Divinity School. I joined them on the way. Then the Chancellor read the Address of the University to the Prince, who read his answer. I joined the procession about 10, and returned to the College about 1. I dined by invitation, ratified by H.R.H. in Redcliffe Library. Present all the Royal Guests, the Duchess of Oldenburg, etc. The city illuminated. At the dinner Lord Grenville presided. I walked home about 12, Dr. Hughes, of Exeter, accompanying me.

15*th*. At 9 I went to the Divinity School, where the Princes, the Duchess of Oldenburg, &c., were assembled. All proceeded to the theatre. I was assisted through the throng to the lowest bench, when a gentlemen insisted on resigning his place to me. The Prince Regent came in a Doctor's robe. The Emperor and King were elected by diploma, and robed. On departing I was greeted by the gownsmen. The Dean of Christ Church invited me to dinner in Christ Church Hall, to which afterwards I received a card of invitation "by the gracious permission of H.R.H. the Prince Regent," as yesterday. I came home between 12 and 1; dressed; and past 2 went to the Prince's lever; was introduced by Sir T. Tyrrwhit before it began, and *most* graciously received. Invited by the Bishop of Oxford into his apartments, after which to Dr. Barnes's, where I staid till 5½, when I went to the Deanery. The Prince, &c., assembled there, and proceeded to the Hall for dinner. At 9½ the Royal guests departed, the rest following. I walked home.

He returned to Portugal Street, London, on the 16th, with Mr. E. B. Impey, and he was one of the guests at the banquet that was given by the Lord Mayor and Corporation of the City of London to the Prince Regent and the Allied Sovereigns. The Corporation realized the importance of the occasion. The Lord Mayor, William Domville (bearing the sword of state), the Sheriffs and twenty Aldermen (including Sir Richard Carr Glyn, Bart., Sir James Shaw, Bart., Sir Claudius Hunter, Bart., Sir Charles Flower, Bart., Sir William Lewis, Knt., and Sir John Eames, Knt.), all in their robes of office, mounted on chargers lent them by officers of the Royal Horse Guards, rode two and two, suitably escorted, through the crowded and decorated streets of the City to Temple Bar, where they alighted, and respectfully received the Prince Regent. They then remounted their horses, and preceded the Prince to the Guildhall, where, at 5 o'clock, they offered him a hearty welcome. He made a brief reply, and concluded by stating that, in honour of this auspicious occasion, and in conformity with usage, he had ordered Letters Patent to be prepared for granting the dignity of Baronet to the Lord Mayor. The civic functionaries then received the Imperial, Royal, and other guests as they reached the Guildhall. The banquet was announced at about 7 o'clock. The company included the Prince Regent, the Emperor of Russia, the King of Prussia, all the English and

Prussian Royal Princes, the Prince of Wurtemberg, the Prince of Bavaria, the Prince of Orange, the Duke and Duchess of Oldenburg, the Duke of Coburg, the Duke of Saxe Weimar, Prince Blucher, numerous British peers, and members of the House of Commons, Warren Hastings and others. Hastings recorded in his journal:—

> *18th.* I went by invitation to the grand dinner at Guildhall. At 4, I entered the line of procession at St. James's. After some time the Prince Regent passed on the left, and a new procession followed of the foreign Princes and other privileged persons. I reached Guildhall not much after 6. The Prince Regent himself presented me to the Emperor, and to the King of Prussia, in terms of most flattering commendation, and as the most injured man, &c. He had made me some compensation, but not enough. This was pronounced aloud to the Emperor in English; to the King in French, and short. He afterwards presented me to the Duchess of Oldenburg, who recognised me. I met with great attentions, and from many who were unknown to me. The whole scene was magnificent beyond example. The Prince, &c., departed at 11. I waited about an hour and a half more, and came home past 2, not worse, though my seat at dinner was in a draft of air. Lord Sidmouth promised a place for Mrs. Hastings to see it, if the Prince Regent should go to the Parliament in State, while the Sovereigns remain.

On the following day, Sunday, Hastings said: "I wrote my name at Carlton House with difficulty in a book of the King of Prussia, and left my name for the same purpose in those of the Emperor and of the Duchess of Oldenburg." He did not attend the grand review in Hyde Park, on the 20th, for the purpose of proclaiming the treaty of peace with France, at which the Prince Regent and the Allied Sovereigns were present, nor did he witness the Naval Review at Portsmouth on the 25th. The Emperor and King left London for Dover, *en route* to the Continent, on the 27th; and, on the following day, the Duke of Gloucester, who had taken an active part in all the brilliant functions in their honour, called on Hastings, and probably gave him an animated account of what he had seen and heard during the memorable epoch. On the 7th July, at 7 a.m., Hastings went with Sir John Sinclair to the Thanksgiving-for-Peace Service at St. Paul's Cathedral. The Prince Regent arrived at 11½. "We returned after 4."

A few days previously Sir John Malcolm—or Malcomb as Hastings wrote the name in his journal—who eventually became Governor of Bombay, called on Hastings to enquire "whether it would be convenient to me to receive a deputation from the Gentlemen of India proposing an invitation to the Duke of Wellington, and myself to preside at a dinner given him, and proposing Monday next at 12, to which I assented." The "Indian Committee" duly called, "and I accompanied them to the Duke of Wellington, when they invited him to a dinner, announcing me as their Chairman, and he fixed on Monday, the 11th July, for the dinner." Hastings was far from

THE DUKE OF WELLINGTON.

well on that day, his "spasms having returned with violence and continuance"; but "I went before 7 to the dinner given by the Gentlemen from India to the Duke of Wellington, of which I was nominated Chairman. I prefaced his health by an appropriate address." He copied his speech into his journal. He said :—

My Lord Duke,—The gentlemen of this assembly, who formerly held occupations in the various departments of the East India Company's service in India, have solicited the honour of your Grace's presence on this day's festival, to congratulate your Grace on your happy return to the bosom of your country, and to testify in this manner their admiration of your good and eminent services. In offering this tribute they are animated by the same sense of gratitude which glows in every British heart; but they claim to feel it, if not in a superior degree, in a peculiar manner, from having been, some of them, the associates of your early warfare, many near witnesses of it, and all possessing a common interest in the train of victories by which you supported and extended the power of the British Empire in India, thus uniting at the same time a brother's glory and your own. They have seen the same spirit displayed in the plains of Berar as hath since shone on the heights of Vittoria; but the course of your later achievements has been distinguished by a much more elevated character, in which you have appeared as the delegated champion of the most sacred relations of human society.

He then glanced at the defeat of Napoleon's "wanton and perfidious aggression," and declared that it was the Duke, "who, himself led by an unseen hand, conducted all the movements of this awful scheme of over-ruling justice." In conclusion he said, addressing the company: "This was the consummated work of our most noble guest, under the auspices of that Being, who, whatever means He may employ for the chastisement of offending nations, invariably makes choice of the best moral characters as His fittest instruments for the dispensation of His blessings and His mercies to mankind."

He noted in his journal that the *Pilot* remarked that:—"The Chairman's speech, from his feeble voice, could only be heard by those who were near the chair; but it was received with much satisfaction, and the health was drunk with long, loud, and repeated shouts of applause." There were two other toasts which were received with all honours, viz., "Mr. Hastings and the Government of India," and "The Marquis of Wellesley, and thanks to him for his distinguished services in India." He "came home at one, after a very spare repast, not much heated or fatigued."

On the 14th of July, Hastings and his wife went to the Queen's drawing-room, and "both (Mrs. H. particularly) were received most graciously by the Queen and Princess Sophia of Gloucester. The Duchess of Wellington announced herself to me, referring to my presiding at the dinner on Monday." The next day he "left his name" with Sir T. Picton, Lord Hill, and the Duchess of Wellington, and called on the Duke of Gloucester. The Prince's fête having been fixed for the 21st, Hastings and his wife agreed to stay till the day following in order to attend it. On the 16th he dined with the Court of

Directors at the City of London Tavern, and he responded to the flattering toast of "Mr. Hastings and the Government of India." He attended the Prince Regent's fête, on the 21st, with Mrs. Hastings, and merely noted in his diary: "We went at 10 to the Prince Regent's fête, and returned home at 6 in the morning." He was an octogenarian, and it is not surprising that on the 22nd, "he slept a great part of the day."

BISHAM ABBEY.

On the 23rd he left London with Mrs. Hastings for a visit to his friend Mr. Henry Vansittart at Bisham Abbey, the picturesque old house near Clievden, on the Thames.

On the 24th, "we all went to church."

On the 25th, "we took leave at 9, and arrived at home at 5½. A burning journey. Our house repaired, cleaned, and painted and the bath finished."

CHAPTER X

BELATED RECOGNITION OF HIS SERVICES

LORD THURLOW said to Major Scott, shortly before Hastings left Calcutta, that "it would be base and dishonourable in Ministers not to advise his Majesty to confer some mark of Royal favour" upon so eminent a man; and he expressed the hope that Hastings would receive an English peerage and the ribbon of the Bath; but Mr. Pitt, though he assured the Major that he regarded Hastings as "a very great, and, indeed, a wonderful man," did not see how he could with propriety advise his Majesty to confer a peerage pending the refutation of the allegations that had been made against him in Parliament. Those allegations were refuted. Hastings then expected that he would receive the distinction which had been so long withheld; and it is believed that he determined to select Daylesford as his title, and to continue to use "*Mens æqua in arduis*" as his motto. He had no child on whom would devolve any hereditary honour bestowed upon himself; but he was not indifferent to the fact, that as peerages were conferred on his successors, it was invidious to exclude him from the benefit of what came to be regarded as the proper recognition of services in the office of Governor-General of India. It was remarked by Lord Cornwallis, when he received the Garter, to his son, Lord Brome, who was then at Eton, that "the reasonable object of ambition to a man is to have his name transmitted to posterity for eminent services rendered to his country and mankind," yet "no one enquires whether Hampden, Marlborough, Pelham, or Wolfe were Knights of the Garter." And the Prince Regent once facetiously asked his guests at a party at the Pavilion, when Francis was present: "What think you of Lord Shakespeare, Lord Milton, and Duke Dryden?" But, without setting an inordinate value on rank,

Hastings must have felt that, if his wish were gratified by his being created a peer, the crowning atonement would have been made to him for many undeserved wrongs.

It was Hastings' lot to see his immediate successor, Earl Cornwallis, created a Marquis, in the peerage of Great Britain, and Knight of the Garter, for his services as Governor-General. Then came Hastings' friend and subordinate, John Shore, who was appointed to the Supreme Council the year after Hastings' departure from India, and now, six years later, became Governor-General, and was at the same time created a Baronet.

THE MARQUIS CORNWALLIS.

Five years more, and Sir John Shore was raised to the peerage of Ireland, as Baron Teignmouth. To him succeeded, in the following year, the Earl of Mornington, who was created Marquis Wellesley—also in the peerage of Ireland—and Knight of the Garter. Lord Cornwallis was then prevailed upon, against his better judgment, but in obedience to a lofty sense of public duty, to accept the risk of going out a second time, and he died in office, and statues in his honour were erected in St. Paul's Cathedral, London, and in Calcutta, Madras, and Bombay. To him succeeded Baron Minto, in the peerage of Great Britain, who was created Viscount Melgund and Earl of Minto, in the peerage of the United Kingdom, for his services in India. Then followed the Earl of Moira, in the peerage of Ireland, who, for his services in India, was created Viscount Loudoun, Earl of Rawdon, and Marquis of Hastings, in the peerage of the United Kingdom, Knight Grand Cross of the Bath, and Knight of the Garter.

But not only were the five successors of Hastings in the Governor-Generalship advanced in rank in virtue of their services in that capacity, but conspicuous honours were also conferred during his lifetime on three Governors of Madras—Lord Macartney; Robert, Lord Hobart; and Edward, Lord Clive.

THE MARQUIS WELLESLEY.

The first-named had, by the force of his own abilities in the diplomatic service, been raised to the Irish peerage before he proceeded to India, where he served under Hastings, from 1781 to 1786, with so much credit to himself that the Court of Directors offered him the succession to the Governor-Generalship on Hastings' retirement. He declined the promotion, returned to England, and shortly afterwards was created Viscount and Earl Macartney, in the peerage of Ireland, for his services in Madras and elsewhere; and three years later—or in the year of Hastings' acquittal—Baron Macartney, in the peerage of Great Britain, for his services in China. Robert, Lord Hobart, son of the third Earl of Buckinghamshire, was Governor of Madras from 1794 to 1798; and, on his return to England, was called up to the House of Lords in his father's lifetime, as Baron Hobart, which position he held until he succeeded to the earldom, on his father's death, in 1804. As for Edward, Lord Clive, in the peerage of Ireland—the son of Robert, Lord Clive, the hero of Plassey, who died in 1774—he was, in 1784, created Baron Clive of Walcot, in the peerage of Great Britain; he became Governor of Madras in 1798; and, on his return home in 1804, he was created Baron Powis of Powis Castle, Baron Herbert of Cherbury, Viscount Clive of Ludlow, and Earl of

THE MARQUIS OF HASTINGS.

Powis, all in the peerage of the United Kingdom, partly on account of his services in India, and partly also because of his marriage with the sister and heiress of the last Earl of Powis of the family of Herbert.

These numerous creations were calculated to set Hastings thinking that he had received less than his reasonable deserts from the Crown, or that he had not been elevated to the social distinction which would have appropriately rewarded his services. This feeling peeps out in the letter, quoted on another page, to the Clerk in Chancery to the Chaptered Order of St. Joachim, dated 28th July, 1806, in which he alludes to his "present undignified condition of life," and to his "acceptance of any title of honour from a foreign state" being liable to injurious constructions. The Prince of Wales professed to be desirous to serve him; but years passed, and he did nothing; so at length, in March, 1806, Hastings resolved to approach His Royal Highness on the subject. An interview was accorded him at Carlton House.

Hastings recorded the following account of the interview in his diary :—

ROBERT, LORD CLIVE.

14th March. Thanks, &c. Since the great changes which have taken place in your administration of this country I have purposely forborne to intrude myself on your R.H.'s notice, fearing to appear importunate, and mistrustful of your R.H.'s remembrance of me. But it has been suggested to me that this caution, if extended too far, would render me liable to the imputation of disrespect by marking a seeming indifference to your R.H.'s gracious intentions towards me. Under this influence, but not quite satisfied that I have done right in yielding to it, I have ventured to solicit the honour of presenting myself to your R.H.; but claiming nothing and expecting nothing, till your R.H., in your own time, shall do me the honour to make me the subject of your direct and effectual consideration.

To the Prince's question, "What were the specific objects that I looked to?" I answered: "My first object has been employment (*i.e.*, as explained by his R.H. himself), either the Board of Control or Government of India"; but of this I now relinquished all thoughts—perhaps I ought not to have entertained them. My next view was to obtain a reparation from the House of Commons, for the injuries which I had sustained by their impeachment of me. Though acquitted, I yet stand branded on their records as a traitor to my country, and false to my trust. (This point I left unconcluded.) The third point principally regards the expectations which your R.H. yourself has excited in the breast of the person in the world, whose wishes I have ever preferred to my own. Though the best, the most amiable of women (the Prince said courteously, "She is so"), she is still a woman, and would prefer her participation in a title to any other benefit that could be bestowed upon me. (These last were not the words; I have forgotten them.) The

CARLTON HOUSE.

Prince cordially assenting, but (I thought) not as a thing to be done, but to be tried, said I must employ Lord Grenville and Lord Moira to effect it; and, on my expressing a wish to owe the execution of it to Lord Moira, after some further discussion, he desired me to go immediately to his Lordship, and tell him that he desired me. The Prince took my hand, and professed his regard for me with so much fervour, that I could not help exclaiming impulsively: "Sir, I know not how it is, but I have never yet parted from your R.H. without added sentiments of gratitude and attachment."

Hastings called upon Lord Moira immediately after he had taken leave of the Prince. Lord Moira was not at home. Hastings then wrote to Lord Moira "desiring to wait upon him at any appointed hour." Lord Moira immediately replied, and invited Hastings to call on the following day, which he did, when "I informed him," Hastings noted in his journal, "of my conversation with the Prince of Wales and my own expectations. He gave me the most cordial assurances, but pointed out the difficulties." On the 29th Hastings called again on Lord Moira, and entered the following account of the conversation that passed in the appendix of his journal:—

29th March. I expressed my regret and compunction for the part which I had been imperceptibly led to take in my conversations with his Lordship

KING GEORGE IV.

and the Prince of Wales on the 14th. When his R.H. drew from me the exposition of the specific point which I wished to obtain, I thought only of receiving it from his unparticipated bounty. Nor had I any other conception during my subsequent conversation with your Lordship. I was indeed a little startled, and ought to have been awakened to a sense of the danger into which I was precipitating myself by an allusion to your Lordship. You expressed a doubt whether some of the members of the Cabinet would be brought to give their assent to any public act in my favour which might imply a condemnation of their former behaviour towards me. It is evident that, as the concurrence of these is necessary, they cannot yield it even to his R.H.'s injunctions without a sacrifice of their sentiments respecting me, nor in short without conferring a favour on me, though yielding only to the request of his R.H. Notwithstanding this obvious conclusion, I still recurred to my first deception (*sic*), and thought no more of these persons than as the instruments of his R.H.'s purpose, not of mine. But I now see my error. My Lord, I never will receive a favour without an acknowledgment, much less will I accept a favour from men who have done me great personal wrongs, though the act so construed should be the result of their submission to a different consideration. I beg, my Lord, that the affair may go no further. I am content to go down to the grave with the plain name of Warren Hastings, and should be made miserable by a title obtained by means which would sink me in my own estimation.

(This is the substance and nearly, but not quite literal, of what I said.) His Lordship replied, that he perfectly conceived my feelings, but begged that I would not give up the point, but confide in him, and he promised that he would take care that nothing should pass that should reflect the smallest discredit on me, or wound my feelings, either in the way which I had mentioned, or in any other.

In the conversation, Lord Moira interrupted me, and said, he did not know that these gentlemen retained their prejudices against me. He had only supposed it as an effect of the human passions; they might cheerfully give their assent, which would be an indication that they no longer considered me in the light they had done formerly. I answered that this made no difference. I should still in the case supposed accept an obligation from men who had grossly wronged me; and in allusion to something more said by his Lordship, which I have forgotten, that the atonement ought to precede my acceptance of anything like a favour from them if in any case it could be justified. I expressed at parting my gratitude to him, for the sincerity of which he would give me credit, after the manner in which I had expressed my objection to acknowledgments made in which my heart did not participate. The whole discourse occupied about five minutes.

The affair went "no further," and Hastings may have regretted that he was so emphatic in his communication to Lord Moira. Seven years more passed, and public opinion, which had once regarded Hastings as a misdemeanant whom it would have been base flattery to call a statesman, underwent so great a reaction in his favour, that when, in 1813, he was examined as a witness in connection with the renewal of the Charter of the East India Company, he was received with acclamation by the House of Commons and the House of Lords, and as he retired, the members rose and uncovered. He made these entries with reference to these incidents in his diary:—

March 30th. I attend House of Commons at 4. Was called in about 6, and underwent an examination of 3½ hours. All the members on my dismission with heads uncovered.

April 5th. I attend the Committee of the Lords. Was examined. Was allowed a chair. Not usual. On my departure the Lords all rose, as the Commons had done, with their hats off. The Duke of Gloucester called at ¼ past 11. Took me with him. Sat with me in the usher's room. Conducted me into Committee room, and left it with me, walking with me to his carriage, ordered it to re-convey me, which it did, to my door. He afterwards called to report my reception, and his own approbation of my evidence.

Shortly afterwards the University of Oxford conferred upon him its degree of Doctor of Laws. The Prince Regent was then prompted to admit him to the Privy Council. On the 5th May, 1814, Hastings received a letter from Mr. James Buller, acquainting him, by desire of the Lord President, that a meeting

THE OLD HOUSE OF COMMONS.

of the Privy Council was to be held the following day at Carlton House, and requesting his attendance in order that he might be sworn in. "In the evening I received," he noted in his diary, "a similar command in the name of the Prince Regent from Lord Sidmouth, courteously expressed." On the following day: "At 3 I went to Carlton House, and was soon after called into the Council Chamber, took the oaths, kissed the Prince Regent's hand, was seated, and was dismissed, and departed. I was (long after) admitted to a private audience, and returned home a little before 6." In another part of his diary he stated that at the private audience he congratulated the Prince Regent "on the wonderful turn of affairs"—consequent on the abdication of the Emperor Napoleon during the immediately preceding month. On the 9th May he wrote to the Earl of Liverpool, the Prime Minister, to whom, he was informed, he was indebted for the original proposition for his admission to the Council. He said that his sense of obligation was increased by the report that, "I was honoured with the suffrage of your judgment in my favour at a time—now far distant—when your

THE OLD HOUSE OF LORDS.

opinion of such a person, and such a mind as your Lordship's was an essential support to my character."

Hastings received, docketed, and preserved until his death the following copy of the text of the oath of a Privy Councillor which he took on being sworn in :—

You shall swear to be a true and faithful Servant unto the King's Majesty as one of His Majesty's Privy Council. You shall not know, or understand of any manner of thing to be attempted, done, or spoken, against His Majesty's Person, Honour, Crown, or Dignity Royal, but you shall lett and withstand the same to be revealed to His Majesty Himself, or to such of His Privy Council as shall advertise His Majesty of the same. You shall in all things to be moved, treated, and debated in Council, faithfully and truly declare your Mind and Opinion according to Your Heart and Conscience, and shall keep secret all matters committed and revealed unto you, or that shall be treated of secretly in Council. And if any of the said Treaties, or Councils, shall touch any of the Counsellors, You shall not reveal it unto him, but shall keep the same until such Time as by the consent of His Majesty, or of the Council publication shall be made thereof. You shall to your uttermost bear Faith and Allegiance unto His Majesty, and shall assist and defend all Jurisdictions, Pre-eminences, and Authorities granted to His Majesty, and annexed to the Crown by Act of Parliament, or otherwise, against all Foreign Princes, Persons, Prelates, States, or Potentates. And, generally in all Things, you shall do as a faithful and true Servant ought to do to His Majesty. So help You God and the holy contents of this Book.

In the following month, as has been stated on a former page, the Prince Regent presented Hastings at the Guildhall, London, to the Emperor of Russia and the King of Prussia. According to a memorandum in Hastings' diary, the Prince described him in English and French to their Majesties "as the most deserving, and at the same time one of the worst used men in the Empire. I have made a beginning, and shall certainly not stop here. He has been created a Privy Councillor, which he is to regard as nothing more than an earnest of the esteem in which I hold him; he shall yet be honoured as he deserves." But nothing further was done; and, a few days before his death, Hastings said: "I wish the Prince, for his own sake, had abstained from making that display of his good intentions; I was a Privy Councillor at the moment; it was not worth while to speak of more, when more, as the event has shown, was not intended."

Like the great majority of Britons who, having lived a very active life as officials in India, return to their native land, and find themselves doomed to an inactivity that is uncongenial to their habits, Hastings would have been glad, notwithstanding the charm of Daylesford, of employment in England, suited to his experience and attainments, had it been offered to him; but he was conscious that he lacked the interest to overcome the prejudice excited by his trial. Writing from Daylesford to Mr. Thompson, he remarked: "To have governed the first and only valuable portion of the British Empire in India thirteen years; to have received at my departure and since the fullest assurance of my carrying with me the regrets and affection of my fellow-servants and countrymen there; and to find myself without interest with those whom I had successfully served, might have been a subject of mortifying reflection to a mind even less susceptible than my own"; but "it has had less influence on mine by my incessant care to preclude, or run away from it." In a later letter to the same friend, he said: "There is certainly some mysterious spell put upon me, for I

LORD SIDMOUTH.

cannot otherwise account for the utter neglect of me even by those who proclaim their belief of my past services, and subsequent retention of what talents I formerly possessed."

Hastings was on intimate terms with half of the statesmen who formed the "Ministry of All the Talents" that came into office on the death of Pitt; but the presence of Mr. Fox in the Cabinet, as Secretary of State for Foreign Affairs, probably hindered his friends from serving him. The Ministry being, as he said, "made up of discordant ingredients," and having "promised so much, performed so little, and undone so much," soon forfeited public confidence, and a "new perspective" was suggested by Mr. William Scott to Hastings, who said, in reply :—

To the question which Lord Selkirk did me the honor to propose to you, and in which you express so partial an interest, which I feel very sensibly, I answer without hesitation, that in the event which you suppose, I should be most happy to participate in any way that would do me credit, by being rendered suitable to what remains of my capacity for official employment, for I would rather give my gratuitous services to Lord Sidmouth than be the mercenary associate of any statesman now in being.

Nothing, however, came of this proposition.

On the 15th May, 1812, Hastings, who was then in his eightieth year, wrote the following letter to the Prince Regent :—

SIR,—When the Kingdom is threatened with external dangers, and disturbed by internal convulsions, it becomes the duty of every loyal subject, be his condition of life what it may, to endeavour to contribute to its defence. To this principle I join an ardent desire to prove my personal zeal and attachment to your Royal Highness. I beg leave, therefore, most humbly, and, I hope, not improperly, to make an offering of my services thus directly to your Royal Highness, to be employed in any way which your Royal Highness may think it proper to command them.

I have the honor, etc.

The Prince Regent did not see his way to avail himself of this patriotic offer, which was Hastings' last attempt to obtain employment.

CHAPTER XI

SOME OF HIS FRIENDS

WARREN HASTINGS possessed in an eminent degree the art of making friends, for he had many engaging characteristics, and he was habitually mindful of the little courtesies of life that have so much to do with the retention of friendship. He had borne himself with heroic dignity during the fiery trial in Westminster Hall; and, according to Wraxall, he neither carried his "political vexations into the bosom of his family," nor mixed in society as a man suffering under unmerited ill treatment, but "as a youth on whom care never intruded." He preferred to dispense rather than to receive hospitality; and his friends readily fell in with his partiality for his home, and its beautiful surroundings. He could never have been a dull, or uninteresting host, for he was full of sympathy for his guests; he adapted himself with facility to their company; and he was "playful and gay." It might be hazardous to say who among his many intimate friends occupied the largest place in his regard; but there is reason to suppose that long and close association conferred that position on Sir Elijah Impey.

Impey was born at Hammersmith six months before Hastings saw the light at Churchill; and his father, an East Indian and South Sea merchant, who resided at Hammersmith, put him, at the age of seven, at the preparatory branch of Westminster School. In May, 1747—as has been said on a former page—Impey competed for election as a King's Scholar, and his name occupied the fourth place on the list of successful candidates. Hastings was removed prematurely from the school; but Impey remained there for two years after his friend's departure for India, and he then proceeded to Trinity College, Cambridge, where, in due course, he took a good degree, and was elected a

Fellow. In 1758 he was called to the bar at Lincoln's Inn; in 1766 he was appointed Recorder of Basingstoke; in 1768 he married a daughter of Sir John Reade, Bart; and in 1772 he was retained as counsel for the East India Company, and discharged his duties in that capacity with so much industry and skill, that, in the following year, when the Regulation Act for the better government of India was passed, he was, on the recommendation of Sir Edward Thurlow, then Attorney-General—afterwards Lord Chancellor—appointed, at the age of forty-one, the first

SIR ELIJAH IMPEY.

Chief Justice of the Supreme Court of Calcutta. He left England at the same time as Francis, but in a different ship; and for the rest of his life he had bitter cause to regret that Francis ever set foot in India. He remained in India only nine years, and was, during almost the whole of that time, regarded as the intimate friend, and by Francis as the tool of Hastings. It was he who tried and condemned Nuncomar for forgery, and sentenced him to be hung; and he also tried Francis for adultery with Madame Grand—who subsequently married Talleyrand, to the disgust of Napoleon—and awarded her husband Rs. 50,000 damages. Francis preceded him to England, and succeeded so well in playing on the imagination and prejudices of Burke and others as to bring about the recall of Impey in 1783. The impeachment of Hastings having been arranged, it was proposed to bring Impey also to trial; and he was summoned before a Committee of the whole House of Commons to answer the allegations which Sir Gilbert Elliot, afterwards Earl of Minto, brought against him. It was alleged among other things that he had been, in effect, the agent and advocate of Hastings, and had pronounced a charge when he summed up the evidence on the Nuncomar trial, "with the most gross and scandalous partiality, dwelling on all the points which appeared favourable to the prosecution, and either omitting altogether, or passing lightly over, such as were favourable to the prisoner, and manifesting throughout the whole proceedings an evident wish and determined purpose to effect the ruin and death of the said Maharajah."[1] But he made a powerful speech in his defence, and satisfied the majority of the members of the Committee that it would be inexpedient to proceed with his impeachment. In 1789 he resigned his appointment; and, in the following year, he entered Parliament as member for New Romsey. He was mostly a silent member until 1796, when Parliament was dissolved, and he did not seek re-election. Though town-born and town-bred, he was fond of rural pursuits, and having purchased the estate of Newick, in Sussex, he found agreeable occupation in farming, as well as in travelling. He was a frequent, and a most welcome guest at Daylesford, where he could not have been at a loss for conversation with his host and hostess about old times, and mutual friends and enemies.

Impey had five sons. The eldest, a Major in the 66th Foot, was killed in a duel with a brother officer of his regiment; the second attained the rank of Admiral in the Navy; and the remaining three were—like their father before them—elected King's Scholars at Westminster.

Exactly forty years after Impey's death his memory was ruthlessly assailed by Macaulay, who was not only one of the

[1] Sir James Stephen, writing in 1885, when he was one of the Judges of the High Court of India, Queen's Bench Division, declared that "every word of this appears to me to be absolutely false and unfounded."

greatest rhetoricians and historians of modern times, but also the most notable of the several able men who have filled the office of Legal Member of the Government of India. In this eminent censor's judgment Impey was nothing less than a vile man. "No other such judge," said Macaulay, "has dishonoured the English ermine since Jefferies drank himself to death in the Tower. . . . Impey, sitting as a judge, put a man unjustly to death, in order to serve a political purpose."

The eldest of the trio of Impey's sons who were educated at Westminster sprang forward gallantly to the defence of his father's memory, and compiled an elaborate biography which did his heart, if not his literary skill much credit; but he was not a David to slay the literary Goliath with a sling and a stone, and Impey remained under the gibbet of Macaulay's essay until 1885, when Sir James Stephen, who succeeded his friend Macaulay in the Law Membership of the Government of India, and had thence been raised to the bench of the High Court of England, published a masterly work,[1] in which he expressed the conviction, "after the fullest consideration of the whole subject, and in particular of much evidence which Macaulay seems to me never to have seen," that the "dreadful accusations" of the latter are "wholly unjust."

It appeared to Sir James Stephen that Impey "owed his moral ruin" to a "literary murder," of which Macaulay "probably thought but little when he committed it"; and that the essay on Hastings in which that murder was perpetrated, "was a mere effort of journalism hastily put together from most insufficient materials." For his own part he formed this estimate of Impey :—

I have read everything I could find throwing light on Impey's character, and it appears to me that he was neither much blacker nor much whiter, in whole or in part, than his neighbours. He seems to me to have resembled closely many other judges whom I have known. He was by no means a specially interesting person, and was in all ways a far smaller man than Hastings. He seems to have had an excellent education, both legal and general, to have been a man of remarkable energy and courage, and a great

[1] The *Story of Nuncomar and the Impeachment of Sir Elijah Impey*, by Sir James Fitzjames Stephen, K.C.S.I., 1885.

deal of rather common-place ability. I have read through all his letters and private papers, and I can discover in them no trace of corruption. Though he had a strong, avowed, and perfectly natural anxiety about his own interests, he seems to have had a considerable share of public spirit. He was obviously a zealous, warm-hearted man, much attached to his friends, but not the least likely to be a tool of, or subservient to any one, and certainly not to Hastings, with whom at one time he had a violent quarrel. There was nothing exceptionally great or good about him, but I see as little ground from his general character and behaviour to believe him guilty of the horrible crimes imputed to him as to suspect any of my own colleagues of such enormities. When his conduct in the different matters objected to is fully examined, I think it will appear that, if the whole of his conduct is not fully justified, he ought at least to be honourably acquitted of the tremendous charges which Macaulay has brought against him.

Thus has Impey, in these latter days, been vindicated; and thus has Macaulay been indicted as a literary murderer, by an eminent master of the law of evidence.

Sir Elijah Impey died at Newick, on the 1st October, 1809, after a month's illness, and was buried in the family vault of the old parish church of Hammersmith, which was within a few yards of Butterwick House,[1] on the opposite side of the high road, where he was born. A memorial tablet was placed near his resting-place, bearing the following inscription :—

In the family vault beneath this chapel are deposited the remains of

SIR ELIJAH IMPEY, KNT.,

who closed his mortal career on the 1st day of October, 1809, aged 77 years.

He was distinguished through life by a superiority of nature and acquired talents, which elevated him to a station of primary rank and importance in the legal profession. On the establishment of the Supreme Court of Judicature over the British provinces in the East Indies, he was the first appointed to preside at that tribunal, a trust which he executed with integrity, and resigned with reputation. Besides those qualities which eminently marked his public life, he was endowed with a rectitude of principle, and a liberality of action which, added to the graces of a cultivated mind, constituted his character as a gentleman and a scholar, and which, combined with a peculiar tenderness of disposition in the nearer relations of society, rendered him while living beloved, and when dead lamented, as a kind master, a steadfast friend, an indulgent father, an affectionate husband.

In pious remembrance of his virtues, and in sorrowful testimony of her attachment, this monument was erected by his affectionate widow.

---

[1] This house was at one time the residence of the Earl of Mulgrave and

Lady Impey survived her husband nearly nine years; she then died, and was also buried in the family vault. Another tablet was added to the left of the tablet of the Chief Justice, and the two tablets bear a resemblance to the tablets of Elizabeth and Sir Philip Francis at Mortlake Church. The second tablet has the following inscription:—

In the same vault, and close to his beloved remains, are deposited those of

DAME MARY IMPEY,

widow and relict of Sir ELIJAH IMPEY, Knt.

To him she was a most faithful and affectionate wife, to their joint and numerous issue the tenderest of mothers. Pious to God, and benevolent to mankind, in reverence for religion, in diffusion of charity, in meekness of spirit, in singleness of heart, she lived and died a true Christian. Born on the 2nd of March, 1749, deceased on the 20th of February, 1818.

This tablet was erected in filial respect to her memory by her afflicted offspring.

The old church at Hammersmith was demolished about nine years ago, and replaced by the present fine building, and all trace of the Impey vault, which was filled up with concrete, has been lost.

Sir John Hadley D'Oyly, 6th Baronet, and his two sons, Sir Charles D'Oyly, 7th Baronet, and Sir John Hadley D'Oyly, 8th Baronet—all of the Bengal Civil Service—were included among Hastings' most intimate friends during the best years of their lives. They were descended from William D'Oyly, M.P. for Norfolk, who was created a Baronet, in 1663, by King Charles II., for services rendered to the Royal cause previous to the Restoration. The first-mentioned Sir John Hadley D'Oyly was born in 1754; and, at the age of ten, he lost his father, the Rev. Sir Hadley D'Oyly, M.A., and succeeded to the title. The family had once been, but was not now in affluent circumstances; and Sir John was at first destined for the honour-

Baron Butterwick, who died here in 1646. In 1666 it was purchased by the Ferne family, from whom it passed early last century into the possession of Mr. Elijah Impey (father of the Chief Justice), who died in 1750, leaving a considerable fortune.

THE OLD CHURCH AT HAMMERSMITH.

able, but not lucrative appointment of Page of Honour to the Royal Family, as the stepping-stone to other employment at the Court. It was hoped, however, by such friends as he had that if he were sent to India, he might succeed in repairing the fortunes of his family by giving a vigorous shake to the "pagoda tree" which still flourished in that land. Accordingly, at the early age of sixteen, with an imperfect education, and little knowledge of the world at large, he was shipped off to the far East. It must have been with no little regret that he turned his back on his native land, and set sail, not in a floating palace, served by steam and electricity, but in a little tub of a wooden ship, for the El Dorado beyond the seas to which social derelicts were too often banished. How he, and lads like him, contrived to kill time, and drive dull care away during the weary monotony of a six months' voyage by the Cape route, cannot be easily imagined by persons who go down to the sea in P. and O. ships, and have every luxurious want anticipated during the few days of their journey.

But, whatever were his intellectual resources, and however ill-found his ship may have been in light literature and other means of amusement, he duly arrived in Calcutta, where, three years later, he made the acquaintance of Hastings, shortly after the latter had arrived from Madras, and assumed the office of Governor-General. Hastings always cherished a fellow-feeling for lads who reached Hindustan, as he himself had done, friendless, and perchance forlorn; and he promptly offered a cordial welcome to D'Oyly, and interested himself in his advancement.

It does not appear that D'Oyly was actually appointed to the service of the East India Company before he left home; but in those good old days the public service of India was not a close preserve, enclosed by the barbed wire of regulations, and showing a sign-board bearing the strange device: "No outsiders need apply!" as is now the case; and gentlemen who succeeded in winning their way to positions of comparative eminence in India, had a way of thrusting friends and relatives into neat billets regardless of the periodical injunctions of their "honourable masters," not to intercept the flow of the patronage of the India House. It was a far cry in those halcyon times from Leadenhall Street to Calcutta, and when there was the will little difficulty was experienced in discovering the way to serve a friend. Thus it was that Hastings succeeded in providing very comfortably for the young Baronet. D'Oyly had been caught young, and he took very readily to the life in India. He soon found that the lot of an official was not a hard one, and that there were abundant opportunities for making money during the intervals of official business. His "most intimate and kindest friend" in Government House, Calcutta, aided him in mounting the official ladder, and eventually appointed him President of Moorshedabad. In 1780, after nine years' residence in India, and at the age of six-and-twenty, he married Diana Rochfort, widow of William Coles, of Calcutta, and niece of the 1st Earl of Belvedere. Five years later—by which time he had been but little more than fourteen years in the country—he found himself possessed of what in those days was regarded as a "princely fortune." Thereupon he took leave of India, which had befriended him so handsomely in his need, and returned with Lady D'Oyly to his native land, where perhaps he had never been missed.

Shortly after his arrival in England D'Oyly made a pious use of some of his fortune. His father had died in embarrassed circumstances twenty-one years previously, leaving creditors in Suffolk who had long ago written off their claims against him in their books. Sir John D'Oyly diligently sought out these creditors, or their representatives, and paid their claims in full. The recipients of the windfall were not slow to appreciate the filial devotion and other virtues of the young "Nabob," who had suddenly appeared in their midst, intent on clearing the reputation of his father, whose existence they had almost forgotten; and his conduct attracted so much favourable comment, that five years later he was urged to present himself as a candidate at the General Election for the suffrages of the free and independent electors of Ipswich. He seized this chance of entering public life; and, after a hot contest, which, in the fashion of those days of bribery and corruption, involved a large outlay, he was triumphantly returned to St. Stephen's. It thus came to pass that he was a member of the House of Commons during the greater part of the trial of Hastings, and he did all in his power to help and console his old friend during the cruel ordeal to which he was subjected. At length Hastings was acquitted, and D'Oyly gave a grand entertainment in honour of the event, invitations to which were (according to the *Annual Register*) "sent by newspaper to Scotland and Ireland." Hastings was very sensible of D'Oyly's goodness to him during his protracted adversity; and, in token of his gratitude, he presented him with a small oval box of black wood, mounted in silver, with a cornelian seal, which I have sketched on page 226, inserted on the lid. The seal bears an inscription in Persian, the interpretation of which is: "This affliction has also passed away." On one side of the box is a silver plate on which these words are engraved :—

This seal was
Presented by the Right Honble. Warren Hastings
Governor-General of India,
to his devoted friend, Sir J. H. D'Oyly, Bart, M.P.,
in token of the unfailing support afforded him
during his memorable trial by the House of Lords,
which lasted seven years, and ended in an
honourable acquittal, on the 23rd April, 1795.

This interesting souvenir is now in the possession of General Sir Charles D'Oyly.

In 1798 Hastings presented D'Oyly with a book, which I have failed to trace; but I have found in Hastings' diary that he wrote the following inscription in it :—

To my dear friend, Sir John H. D'Oyly, I give this book, in confidence that it will be preserved as a lasting deposit in his family, and that in the descendants of his line, which I fervently pray may be extended through endless generations, I shall never want an advocate warmed with some portion of the spirit and benevolence of their virtuous progenitor, should a name so humble as mine, but connected with one great public event, which must give it a fixed place in the annals of this kingdom, ever require it. London, 27th January, 1798.

Sir John D'Oyly purchased a large estate, near Lymington in Hampshire, called Newlands (now owned by Mr. Cornwallis West); and he acquired later on another estate, not far distant, which he named D'Oyly Park. He had a passion for bricks and mortar, and he loved to be his own architect in designing what he regarded as "improvements." He had little occasion to cultivate thrift in India; on the contrary, he acquired expensive habits during the most susceptible period of life, and unfortunately he brought these habits home with him. He was much given to hospitality, and being also generous to a fault, and fond of a large establishment, his fortune—which, regarded from the standpoint of a century later, may not have been a colossal one—became seriously impaired; and in 1797, when he was on the point of sending his eldest son Charles to India, he began to think of resigning his expensive seat in Parliament, realizing his properties, and returning to Bengal.

On the 12th April, 1797, he wrote a long letter[1] from Newlands to Hastings, in the course of which he said :—

I plead guilty to the general charge of extravagance, but trust I can bring such pleas in palliation as to common minds might have excused a friend in treating it with somewhat less leniency. Thrown early in life into a society where even the name, much more the practice of economy was unknown, and where the means of profusion were unbounded, I adopted the habits of that society, and unfortunately, I allow, brought them with me to a country, the manners of which are as dissimilar as light from darkness. In this country I was placed with, if you please, a "princely" but unrealized fortune. At this period (indeed at what period is it not?) a sensible, judicious friend, experienced in the ways of this country, would have been a treasure to me. I had none such. Such a friend, instead of arrogantly dictating to me, or proudly resenting the errors I naturally fell into, would have calmly reasoned with, and by every conciliatory mode have endeavoured to set me right. I meant not (as you have stated) to exalt myself above my equals, but to live in that state of life which I conceived my fortune entitled me to. I soon found I was mistaken in my calculations on this head, and that the expenses of this country much exceeded what I had imagined. I also felt the great disadvantage of leaving the most material part of my property in India, being thereby obliged then, and for many years afterwards, to live on ways and means, and I believe it is a known and undisputed fact that a person lives with more economy upon a certain fixed income than upon a fluctuating one. What was my conduct upon this discovery? An immediate determination to give up my house in town, and to live entirely in the country. This, at least, did not show that I was obstinately fixed in error, and although from an unfortunate passion for buildings and improvements, added to the still remaining habits of extravagance acquired in India, and the unfortunate contest at Ipswich (for which at the time you condemn me you should recollect how many men, with much more experience, have fallen into the same error), this plan did not answer better than the former, yet a more candid judge might have made some allowance for.

Hastings, in reply, urged D'Oyly to abandon the idea of an immediate return to India, and at the same time said that he did not approve of his "laboured apology for personal extravagance, which is the least of your faults, and would have been none had you committed no other." Six days later he wrote :—

I repeat, that your domestic expenses since your return to England were at no time so great as to deserve the reproach of extravagance. I, there-

[1] This letter is included among the Hastings collection in the British Museum.

fore, put the excess (as I believe many of your other friends have done) to the account of your liberality transgressing the bounds of discretion.

Early in the following month D'Oyly asked Hastings to favour him with letters of introduction for his son Charles, who was Mrs. Hastings' godchild. He received the following reply, which Hastings copied into his diary :—

I have been not a little embarrassed to answer your wishes with respect to recommendations for Charles. After twelve years' absence from Bengal have you any personal friends left there? I have none. With Sir J. Shore I have kept up a correspondence. To Chapman I have made a promise, or rather, a declaration, that I never would give any one recommendations to him. A similar assurance I gave to the former, when he went abroad ; but having in two instances broken it, I should not forgive myself if I adhered to it on the present occasion. I have written to him in terms the most likely to ensure his friendship to your son, if he retains any for me. To Chapman I mentioned him in a letter written to him a month ago, which will be as effectual as one delivered to him in form by Charles himself, and its operation will be free from restraint. To Mr. Speke I have never before written ; but I am confident that my letter to him will be of service ; and he is a man whose good will, both on account of his rank, and the probity of his character, I should wish that Charles would cultivate. In my letter to Belli, I have desired him to take your son by the hand, and introduce him to the most respectable of his acquaintance. My letter to General Morgan is written in terms equally strong with the rest. In these I have gone to the utmost extent of my present acquaintance in Bengal, at least of such as I could write to for such a purpose. Mrs. Hastings desires me to express her regret that she cannot write ; for, excepting Mr. and Mrs. Chapman, she literally knows nobody to whom her introduction could be of any use. Julius is not in that rank in the service which could enable him to offer more than the terms of equal acquaintance and friendship. To him Mrs. Hastings has written long ago to apprise him of the claim which Charles will have to both, as the son of two friends whom we both dearly love. She desires me to present her affectionate remembrance to yourself and Lady D'Oyly, and love to Charles, and I pray you to add mine.

In February, 1798, Sir John D'Oyly remarked, in a letter to Hastings, that he had lately been prompted by the example of Sir Charles Reed, to devote part of every day to the superintendence of some of the studies of his daughters ; and he added :—

Will you oblige me by pointing out such books as you would recommend them to study, so as to read and speak with propriety, together with a knowledge of geography that will fall under my department to teach them ?

Hastings replied :—

I am greatly delighted with your plan of superintending the education of your daughters. I had it once or twice on my mind to recommend it to you ; but I was not sure of the propriety of it, and therefore deferred rather than relinquished the design. I do not think myself qualified to give you a list of books suitable to the instruction of young ladies of their age, and I doubt whether such a collection, though it has been often called for, though it is so essentially necessary, and even promised (if I recollect right), either in the Guardian, or some other of Addison's periodical writings, has never yet been formed. I will, however, mention such as I at present recollect, and think more immediately necessary. For history, Rollin, Verliot's Revolutions, Dr. Gillio's history of Greece, Fergusson's of the Roman Republic, Russell's ancient and modern history (an excellent work though written in the finical form of letters, and an abridgement), Hume's history of England, and Velly's of France. For poetry, Milton, Pope, Prior (to be read with your own selection), Parnell, Gay's fables, Goldsmith, and Gray—and (how came I to forget him ?)—all Shakespeare. For ethics, all Addison's Spectators, Guardians, and Tatlers, with the exclusion of all papers written in them by others, the Rambler, Adventurer, and Paley's Philosophy, also Aunt Kitty's Theology—pray do not forget that. For style and elegance of composition Molinoth's works, Mrs. Montague's observations on Voltaire's censure of Shakespeare, and Madame Sevigné's letters. I recommend that when they read, it should be aloud, and to you, and that you should read at least as much to them as they to you, both to give them a good tone, and accustom them to attention. I do not think a looking glass a bad assistant in this part of discipline, as a pleasing, but unaffected countenance adds infinitely to a graceful elocution, and young people fall naturally into the habit of contracting their brows, and setting their features to a form of constraint when they read. But enough of this. Your own better judgment will add to these crude surmises, and correct them, for they need it.

In the year 1802, Sir John D'Oyly resigned his seat in Parliament, and he may have totalled up the expenditure that he had incurred during ten years in connection with it, and have arrived at the not unusual conclusion that "the game was not worth the candle." In 1803 his wife died. In the following year he placed his younger son under the care of Hastings and Henry Grant; and, accompanied by his two daughters, he carried out his project of returning to India, and re-entering the Civil Service of the East India Company. He was appointed Collector of Calcutta and of the twenty-four Pegunnahs. Later on he became Postmaster-General and Senior Merchant on the Bengal Establishment. His second period of service in India extended, like his first, to about fourteen years. Unfortunately he did not achieve his object of returning to spend the residue of his days in his native land, for he died in Calcutta, in 1818, the year also of Hastings' death, aged sixty-four. An admirable portrait of him, by Sir Joshua Reynolds, is now in the possession of his grandson, General Sir Charles D'Oyly. According to Mr. W. D'Oyly Bailey's history of the D'Oyly family,—

> He was distinguished not only as a man of education, taste, and refinement, but as a sincere philanthropist. Were the objects of his benevolence, humanity, or pity, public or private, his exertions to do good were equally strenuous, while by his industry and integrity he restored the family from the ruined condition in which his predecessors had left it, and gained for it an importance and influence in the East Indies perhaps as valuable to it as its lost landed interest in England.

Charles, his elder son, who succeeded him in the title, was born in India in 1781, and, after being educated in England, was admitted to the Civil Service of the East India Company, and returned to Bengal in 1797, at the age of sixteen. He was appointed Assistant Registrar of the Court of Appeal in Calcutta in 1798; Keeper of the Records in the Governor-General's office at Calcutta in 1803; Collector of Dacca in 1808; Collector of Customs and Town Duties in Calcutta in 1818; Opium Agent at Behar in 1821; Commercial Resident at Patna in 1831; and Senior Member of the Board of Customs, Salt, and Opium, and also of the Marine Board at Calcutta in 1833. He had put in nearly twenty-one years of service—less such leave as he may have taken, and which, under the indulgent old regulations, did not count as service — when his father, and official superior, died. He was a genial man; and being wise enough to make the best of life in India, he was treated well by that sunny land of his birth. Having completed forty years' service, he took his well-earned pension, and returned to Europe. He was twice married; but, as he had no family to educate and start in life, he was free to choose his place of residence; and being endowed with a taste for fine art which he had successfully cultivated in India, he was led to take up his abode in Italy, where he spent the greater part of the seven remaining years of his life, and produced numerous drawings and paintings (now in the possession of his grand-nephew and namesake), that are remarkable for their atmospheric effects and high finish. Bishop Heber—one of Hastings' many champions—said of Charles D'Oyly, that he was the "best gentleman artist I ever met with." In 1845 D'Oyly died at Ardenza, near Leghorn, and was regretted by his former associates in India as a man who was "distinguished for benevolence and hospitality even in a country far-famed for those virtues."

As an amateur artist of high merit Charles D'Oyly is chiefly

BISHOP HEBER.

remembered in connection with his admirable series of drawings entitled the "Antiquities of Dacca." On the 11th May, 1815, Hastings wrote to him as follows :—

I was extremely gratified by the receipt of a letter from you yesterday, dated the 10th of last October ; and avail myself of the friendly offer of Mr. Barwell, who is on the point of his departure on his return to India, to reply to it. I have another letter, if not two, yet unacknowledged ; for the natural infirmities incident to my time of life have pressed upon me during the course of the last year with a weight so disproportionate to their gradual progress, that it has become a painful employment to express my thoughts, sometimes on the most simple occasions, in the distrust of my natural powers. To this disability the recent financial regulations have contributed ; for I am not sure, that in their present incomplete state this letter may not render me liable to the penalties denounced on the breach of them . . . I have received, and thank you for the beautiful drawings of the ruins of Dacca. They excel even those which you formerly presented to me. Give my love, and my dear Mrs. Hastings', who charges me with it, to your father, and our fervent wishes for the long continuance of his life, health, and happiness. With the same to you, and our added blessing, I am, my dearest Charles, your truly affectionate friend.

Engravings from the drawings of Dacca to which Hastings referred in the above letter were published in four large folio parts by John Landseer,[1] Engraver to the King. The first part appeared in the year 1814; the second in 1817; the third in 1826 or 1827, and the last in 1827 or 1828. In each of three of the parts four large steel-plate engravings were given; and the remaining part contained three plates. There were, consequently, twenty-three plates in all. The majority of them were engraved by John Landseer, but in the production of the others the aid of J. Scott, W. Finden, S. Middman, and G. Cook was enlisted. There were a few vignettes in the letterpress by G. Chinnery. Each plate was "inscribed" or "dedicated" by Sir Charles D'Oyly to a friend. One of them was "most affectionately inscribed" to his father; another was "inscribed with the most grateful respect" to Warren Hastings; a third was dedicated to the Countess of Loudoun and Moira; a fourth to the Marquis of Hastings, K.G., G.C.B., Governor-General and Commander-in-Chief of India. Other plates were inscribed to Lady Mawbey, "in gratitude for her friendship to departed Excellence"; to Sir John Malcolm, Bart., G.C.B., Governor of Bombay; to Edward Strachey, "late of Dacca, etc." The original drawings must have been executed with great taste and care; and the engravings are fine examples of an art that is threatened with early extinction by the combined agency of photography and electricity.

Sir Charles D'Oyly also furnished the illustrations, drawn by himself on lithographic stone, for a book illustrative of the then

[1] John Landseer died in 1852, aged eighty-three. He was the father and first instructor in art of Thomas Landseer, a clever engraver, who died in 1880, aged eighty-five; of Charles Landseer, R.A., who died in 1879, aged eighty; and of Sir Edwin Landseer, R.A., the famous animal painter, who died in 1873, aged seventy-one.

New Road from Calcutta to Gya. The work was issued by the Asiatic Company's Press, Chowringhee, Calcutta. He also drew the landscapes, while Christopher Webb Smith depicted the birds in an illustrated monograph on the *Feathered Game of Hindostan.* He provided numerous coloured lithographs for a book published by Ackerman, in London in 1828, entitled *Tom Raw the Griffin*, and described as a "burlesque poem in twelve cantos" illustrative of "the adventures of a cadet in the East India Company's service from the period of his quitting England to his obtaining a staff situation in India." The poem was written by "A Civilian," and is rather poor stuff. The sketches are humorous, and are suggestive of Rowlandson's illustrations of Dr. Syntax's famous journey in search of the picturesque. Better examples of Sir Charles D'Oyly's genius are to be found in the coloured plates of a volume entitled *The European in India*, which was published by Edward Orme, of Bond Street, London, in 1813.

Upon the death of Sir Charles D'Oyly the title passed to his brother, John Hadley, who was left in England in 1804, under the care of Hastings and Henry Grant, as has been related on a former page. On the 8th February, 1806, Hastings, being then in London, visited, as he noted in his diary, Mr. and Mrs. Grant, and "appointed to call upon them on Monday at quarter-past ten, to accompany them to Pentonville, to see Mr. Lendon and his school there."

> At half-past ten, I accompanied Mr. and Mrs. H. Grant to Mr. Lendon's, at 6, Rodney Street, Pentonville, where we agreed to place John D'Oyly, and to carry him there on Friday. Terms, 80 gs. per annum, entrance 5 gs. to instruct him in English, Greek, Latin, and Geography; Writing and Arithmetic, extra 5 gs.; French and dancing (if taught) 5 gs each, with entrance.

On the 14th—

> I went with Mrs. Grant and J. D'Oyly to Mr. Lendon's, paid 5 gs. entrance, and left the boy with him.

That Hastings was not a merely nominal guardian of the lad is shown by the following extracts from a letter (which he copied into his diary) that he wrote at Daylesford, on the 14th October, 1807, to Sir John D'Oyly at Calcutta:—

I think your son much improved. He passed his summer holidays at Daylesford. The first fortnight was granted as an extra grace, as the school did not break up till the end of the month, and I engaged to keep him to his daily exercises during that time, which I did; nor was his vacation, which I think too long, unprofitably employed. Besides his tasks he went through the construction of B' and Ph' in Ovid, and got it completely by heart. He is indeed much improved. He reads better than many grown men. . . . I am thus minute in detailing his accomplishments because I hear through the medium of Mrs. Patlock to Mrs. Motte, that you were displeased with his letters for their deficiency in neatness, grammar, and spelling. Recollect that his mind has been totally uncultivated for two entire years; that the arrears of intellectual progress at the age of eleven are not recoverable but by slow gradation; and that when he wrote to you he could not have been more than half a year with Mr. Lendon. It is true that his handwriting is yet a bad one, and that his words are not so correctly put together as they should be; but this is the case with all schoolboys, and of those especially who follow the discipline of Westminster School, where the English language is never taught. Yet I must say, that his letters to me are far from being ill-written. I have received one from him written on his return to school, with which I was much pleased, but you will hear from him yourself, and you should read his letters with the allowance due to the considerations which I have advanced. In addition let me inform you that your son possesses by nature, apparently improved by habit, an equality aud gentleness of temper, in which he can scarcely be exceeded; and to these qualities he joins the attention and courtesy of a gentleman. He always went to his studies without reluctance, and without bidding, and much oftener reminded me of them, when his exercises were to be shown to me, or repeated by heart, than I had occasion to put him in mind of them. It was rarely that he had playfellows at Daylesford, but he was never at a loss for amusement; busying himself with his own inventions, which were all of the taste and kind which used to occupy the mind of his brother when he was of the same age; and in these he shows great ingenuity. You may trust me that this report is not partially delivered; nor my judgment of him deceived; nor do I mean that he is advanced so far in knowledge as another boy of equal natural parts would be at the same age who had prosecuted his studies in uninterrupted progression. He has yet a large arrear to bring up, and he will recover it.

This is a remarkable letter for a childless man of seventy-five years of age to write about a lad, who was not a relation of his, to the anxious father in India. Forty-nine years had passed since Hastings was bereaved of his own little son; but the parental instinct was strong within him; and, notwithstanding his advanced age, he could enter as a father into the feelings of a father who was also a dear friend, and show at the

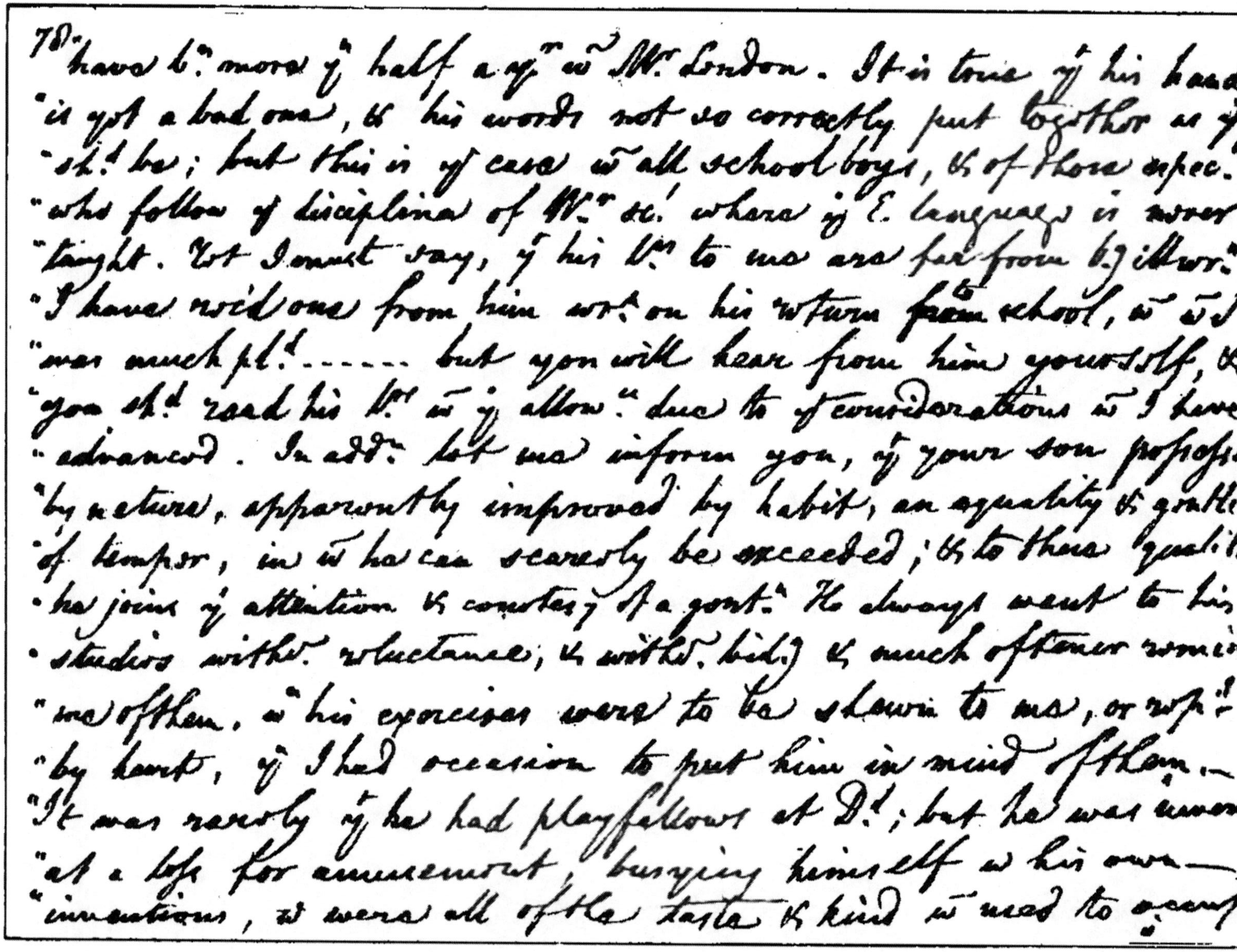

78 "have b. more ȳ half a yr in Mr. London. It is true ȳt his hand
"is yet a bad one, & his words not so correctly put together as ȳ
"sh.d be; but this is ȳ case wth all school boys, & of those espec.y
"who follow ȳ discipline of Wr. &c. where ȳ E. language is never
"taught. Yet I must say, ȳ his lrs to me are far from b. illwr.
"I have recd one from him wrt on his return to school, wh wd
"was much pl.d ...... but you will hear from him yourself, &
"you sh.d read his lrs wh ȳ allow.ce due to ȳ considerations wh I have
"advanced. In add.n let me inform you, ȳt your son possesses
"by nature, apparently improved by habit, an equality & gentl.s
"of temper, in wh he can scarcely be exceeded; & to these qualities
"he joins ȳ attention & courtesy of a gent.n He always went to his
"studies witht. reluctance, & witht. bidg & much oftener reminded
"me of them, wn his exercises were to be shown to me, or rep.d
"by heart, ȳ I had occasion to put him in mind of them.—
"It was rarely ȳ he had playfellows at D.l; but he was never
"at a loss for amusement, busying himself wh his own
"inventions, wh were all of the taste & kind wh used to occupy

FACSIMILE OF A PAGE OF THE APPENDIX OF HASTINGS' DIARY,

Containing part of his copy of the letter to Sir John H. D'Oyly, printed on page 210.

[*Face page 210.*

same time that, so far from being bored by the presence of a boy at Daylesford during the holidays, he regarded him with affectionate interest for his father's and his own sake, and readily acted not only as a companion, but also as a tutor to him. The lad was destined by his father for the Civil Service of Bengal, and was in due course placed at Haileybury College,[1] near Hertford, which had just been opened for the training of youths for the service of the East India Company. The Pro-

OLD HAILEYBURY COLLEGE.

fessors of the College were new to their work ; and the students included some lively spirits who regarded them as their natural enemies, and indulged in acts of insubordination which so offended the Court of Directors that it was resolved to make

[1] Previous to the year 1800 the lads who were sent out by the East India Company as Civil Servants were not required to undergo any special training before they took up their appointments ; and probably their seniors in the Service on whom they were inflicted, "licked them into shape" without too tender a regard for their susceptibilities. The Marquis Wellesley then founded a Training College for Civil Servants at Calcutta. His scheme was not wholly approved by the Court of Directors ; and in 1804 a College was opened provisionally in Hertford Castle, near the town of Hertford, for Indian students. In 1805 the Haileybury estate, two miles from Hertford, was acquired by the East Indian Company for £5,000 ; and College build-

examples of the ringleaders by expelling them. Young D'Oyly had not aided, or abetted, the disturbance, but he had witnessed it, and seen who were the chief culprits. He was called upon to give up their names; but this he declined to do, and he then wrote to Hastings as his guardian, and solicited his advice. Hastings wrote the following letter in reply, and made a copy of it in his diary:—

19th November, 1811. I have received your letter, and read it with great sorrow. The reason which you assign for being present in the late riot does not satisfy me, and I much fear it will not exculpate you with those who are to decide on your conduct. If the Court is to meet on this day for the purpose of enquiring into the business, it will be of no avail to give you the advice which you desire; and your own judgment, honour, and conscience will be your best advisers. But it is not a matter of advice; for advice implies the right of choice, and you have none. But I will tell you what you ought to do, and knowing that you must do it, with a total disregard of all the consequences of it. This, then, is what you ought to do.

If with a clear conscience you can say, "I was not privy to the design of the rebellion—I was not consenting to it, nor consulted upon it—I was in no wise concerned in it, that I was passively present, and the cause of my being so was that I was unable to sleep for the noise that was being made, and went out, certainly with no intention of joining in any act of mischief; I neither fired a pistol, nor blew a horn, nor encouraged, or took part, by word or action in the riot which I saw passing"—say so, or say whatever variation from this may be the stricter truth.

But accuse no one. If any questions are put to you, unless in such a way as the laws of your country require, concerning what others did, desire respectfully to decline the office of an informer; if pressed, refuse it, and persevere in the refusal, even though dismission from the College shall be threatened to be the consequence. By the expression which I have used, of "such a way as the laws of your country may require," I mean your being put to your oath before a magistrate. In that case you will be compellable to answer, and, I need not add, to answer according to truth. But I do not suppose that that will, or can be legally done, unless a criminal information be laid against persons actually named, and a judicial process instituted upon it.

---

ings were erected thereon, at a cost of £50,855, from designs by W. Wilkins, of Caius College, Cambridge, the architect of the National Gallery, and of the façade of the East India House, Leadenhall Street. The students moved into Haileybury College from Hertford Castle in 1809. See *Memorials of Old Haileybury College*, London, Archibald Constable & Co., 1894.

Young D'Oyly followed his guardian's advice, which, doubtless, coincided with his own views of honour, and declined to inform against the chief participators in the riot, whereupon the Court of Directors resolved to punish his contumacy by inflicting upon him the disgrace of expulsion from the College, which involved his perpetual exclusion from official employment in India. Hastings noted in his diary :—

23rd November, 1811. John D'Oyly dismissed from the College.

24th (*Sunday*). I sent to J. D'y a draft of a letter to the Court of Directors, with a long letter of instructions to him, to send the letter or its substance immediately, to show it to Mr. Partington, and amend it with his advice, if it exceeds, or falls short of the truth ; and to Mr. G. Baring, if without delay, but peremptorily to write to-morrow.

The following is the draft referred to :—

HONORABLE SIRS,—I humbly beg leave to appeal to your honourable Court against a general sentence of dismission from your College, in which I am involved, on the ground of my refusal to give information against the ringleaders of the mutiny in the College, on the night of the   instant.

It would be disrespectful in me to vindicate an act to which your Court has attached the sense of criminality, but as it is considered in a very different light by those with whom I have lived in society, and (as I am assured) by the bulk of mankind, so that if I were to purchase your forgiveness by affording that test of my obedience which you require, I should enter your service in the character of an informer ; I humbly hope that you will be pleased to relax of your severity for this sole offence, and allow me to lay before you my exculpation against the severer charge of rebelling against the authority of those whom your honorable Court has appointed to be our instructors, and of making an ungrateful return to your bounty in the institution established for our benefit.

In the first place, I declare upon my honor, that I was not a party to any design of that kind, nor privy to it before it took place ; that though I was present during the existence of the riot, my presence was purely accidental, and occasioned by my being deprived of my sleep by the noises which I heard, and more by my fear than curiosity to know what was passing ; and that I neither blew a horn, nor fired a pistol, nor did any other act by which I could be justly charged as an accomplice.

In the second place, I beg leave also to appeal to the Masters and Professors of the College for my general conduct, which I am sure they will deliver in my favor, because I am conscious that I merit it.

I have the honor to be with great respect, &c.

The letter had the desired effect of inducing the Court of Directors to reconsider its hasty judgment, and, on the 31st

January, Hastings had the satisfaction of recording in his diary: "Colonel Toone wrote: 'Young D'Oyly has permission to proceed to India, with loss of rank.'" On the 24th of the following month young D'Oyly arrived at Daylesford, stayed five days with his guardian and Mrs. Hastings, and then left. Shortly afterwards, or in the year 1812, he proceeded to India, where the episode at the College which nearly wrecked his prospects did not hinder his steady advancement in the service.

He returned home in 1842, after a service of thirty years. He married twice, his first wife being a daughter of Mr. George Nesbit Thompson, Private Secretary to Hastings, while the latter was Governor-General of India; and his second wife (born in 1795, the year of Hastings' acquittal) was a daughter of Mr. John Fendall, a member of the Supreme Council at Calcutta. He died in 1869, aged seventy-five; and his widow died in 1886, at the advanced age of ninety-one. He left two sons, the elder of whom, now General Sir Charles Walters D'Oyly, late Bengal Army, was for five years on the personal staff of Lord Dalhousie, Governor-General of India, and subsequently served with distinction throughout the Indian Mutiny campaign. The younger son, Warren Hastings D'Oyly, retired lately from the Bengal Civil Service. It is worthy of remark that General Sir Charles D'Oyly has a genius for painting similar to that possessed by his uncle, the former Sir Charles D'Oyly; and there is much reason to believe that had he adopted art, instead of arms, as his profession, he would have attained considerable eminence as an artist. It is gratifying to be able to add that time has not deprived his sword-hand of a skill in depicting the beautiful in Nature that must be almost unique in a General Officer of any army.

Among the individuals for whom Hastings cherished an affection that did not cool as the years rolled by, a prominent position must be assigned to Mr. Nathaniel Brassey Halhed. This gentleman was at Harrow with Sheridan, whose acquaintance he dropped after the latter had shown his unbridled rancour against Hastings. From Harrow he proceeded to Oxford; and, after a short residence at Christchurch, he accepted the offer of a writership in Bengal, to which was attached a small salary, coupled with the privilege of private trading. He arrived in Calcutta in 1772, and in the following year he made the acquaintance of Hastings, who, as the first Governor-General, was the observed of all observers in the Anglo-Indian metropolis. He was much impressed by the character of his official chief; and he was not slow in forming an admiration for him that he retained for nearly fifty years. Those were halcyon days for the enterprising official in India who had an eye to business; and, young and inexperienced as Halhed was on his arrival, he turned to such good account the opportunity afforded him of shaking the pagoda tree, that, in the extraordinarily short period of six years, he amassed a competency. Little is known about his merits as a public functionary. The duties that devolved on a young official in his time were light, for law-makers and law-menders had not yet made a hunting-ground of India, and the natives were left severely to themselves, so long as they paid rent and taxes with punctuality, and kept the peace. But, if he was no more than an average servant of "John Company," Halhed was by instinct and cultivation a linguist. At Harrow and at Oxford he studied Greek and Latin to good purpose; and in Bengal he took up with zest the study of Persian, Sanscrit, and local dialects. Being a man of simple tastes and moderate ambition, he determined, in 1778, to take his fortune to England, and remain there for the remainder of his life. Accordingly he returned home.

But, either he discovered that it was more expensive to live comfortably in England than he, with his small experience, had imagined; or England offered no scope for the exercise of his abilities; or he made injudicious investments that suggested to him the desirability of supplementing his capital; for, after he had passed six more or less unprofitable years at home, he was induced to seek and obtain permission to return to Bengal in an official capacity. His re-appearance in Calcutta may have surprised some persons who had envied his good luck in being able to "cut the country," but he must have missed his revered friend in Government House. He settled down to the old life expecting to spend several more years in the protection of the Company's, and the promotion of his own interests; but, within a year, the climate told so severely upon him that he found it necessary to take final leave of India, and to be content with such means as he had acquired. So, in 1779, he was back again in London.

Parliament was then almost the only avenue to distinction that was open to the retired Anglo-Indian; and Halhed succeeded in inducing the electors of Lymington, in Hampshire, to return him as their representative. It was not yet expected of a Member of Parliament that he should efface himself, and enact the part of an automaton; so, as Halhed was a scrupulous man, who placed *patrie* before party, he voted not to order, but according to his conscience, without obtruding himself on the notice of the House. From time to time he published translations from Persian and Sanscrit works which brought him into contact with a select class of learned men; and he acquired familiarity with several modern languages; but he was, for all his commercial experience in India, deficient in financial and political foresight; and yielding to too sanguine a view of the prospects of France, he made such hazardous investments in the French funds that he lost £30,000, which formed nearly the whole of his resources. His circumstances then became much straitened; and he was compelled to grasp the helping hand of Hastings, which was readily held out to him. He did not, however, as borrowers have from time immemorial so often done, forfeit the friendship of the lender, for Hastings was unremitting in his practical kindness to him, and continued to show him and Mrs. Halhed much hospitality both in London and at Daylesford. The high esteem which Halhed had long entertained for Hastings was now increased by a grateful recognition of him as a friend in need; and he found expression for his ardent feelings in the occasional production of odes in his honour, which he presented to Hastings on his arrival at, or departure from London, and on other occasions. These friendly efforts to give him pleasure were much appreciated by Hastings, who, in one of his letters of acknowledgment, remarked to the bard: "Praise from the heart is always pleasing, but when adorned with the brightest graces of poetry, and blended with philosophy (and that of a Reshee could not be better expressed than yours), it is most delightful."

For several years Halhed endured with fortitude a hard struggle for existence; for, being afflicted with the infirmity of deafness, he could not secure remunerative employment. The attitude of his mind is shown by the following lines of his:—

> I ask not life, I ask not fame,
> I ask not gold's deceitful store;
> The charm of grandeur, wealth, and name,
> Thank Heaven! are charms to me no more.
>
> To do Thy will, O God, I ask,
> By faith o'er life's rough sea to swim,
> With patience to work out my task,
> And leave the deep result to Him.

Halhed was always mindful of the birthdays of "my dearly loved friend and patron," as he was wont to style Hastings. In 1808, for example, when Hastings completed his seventy-fourth year, Halhed wrote:—

> On Hastings, then, ripe wisdom's meed we fix,
> From youth maturing up to seventy-six.

And in a letter to Hastings he remarked: "Oh! would it were seventy-six ten years hence; but then I could hardly live to see what a divine old man you would make at eighty-six." He did, however, see Hastings at eighty-six. Eventually, Halhed obtained a well-paid Secretaryship in the India Office, and he promptly repaid the loans that Hastings had made to him.[1]

In April, 1812, Hastings presented to Halhed a "bound book of testimonials" containing the following inscription, which he entered into his diary:—

> To Nathaniel Brassey Halhed, Esq., I present this book, and request his acceptance of it as a memorial (poor as it is) of the high estimation in which I hold the unchanged friendship which I have experienced from him through a long course of years, of mine for him, of my respect for his moral character, and my admiration of the versatility of his talents.

[1] I am indebted to Dr. J. Grant's article in the *Calcutta Review*, March, 1856, on "Warren Hastings in Slippers," for most of the information that I have given about Halhed.

Halhed died in 1830, aged eighty-four, having survived the "divine old man" twelve years.

An equally amiable and constant, but much more distinguished friend of Hastings was the Duke of Gloucester. This little-remembered Prince was the only son of William, Duke of Gloucester and Edinburgh, and Earl of Connaught, the third son of Frederick, Prince of Wales, father of George III. He was, therefore, a nephew of that monarch. His mother was Maria, daughter of Sir Edward Walpole, K.B., and widow of James, Earl of Waldegrave. He was born at Rome, in 1776, the sixteenth year of the reign of his uncle, and was educated at Cambridge. He entered the Army as a Captain in the 1st Foot Guards, and with the rank of Colonel, in his thirteenth year. In 1794, at the age of eighteen, he went on active service to Flanders; and, having shown gallantry in the field, was appointed to the command of the 115th Regiment. In the following year he was promoted to Major-General, and was appointed Colonel of the 6th Regiment. In 1799 he had command of a brigade under his cousin, the Duke of York, and took a distinguished part in several engagements. In November of that year he was promoted to Lieutenant-General, he being then twenty-three years of age; in 1808 he was advanced to General; and in 1816 he was gazetted Field Marshal. He succeeded his father in 1805, and his allowance was then increased by Parliament to £14,000 a year. In 1811 he was elected Chancellor of the University of Cambridge. He was created a Knight of the Garter in 1814, and a Knight Grand Commander of the Bath and of the Hanoverian Order in 1815. He was Governor of Portsmouth, Ranger of Bagshot Park, LL.D. and F.R.S.

He married his cousin, Princess Mary, the fourth daughter of King George III. and Queen Charlotte. She was born in 1776, the year of the birth of the Duke, and cherished an attachment for him from an early age; but, when each was one-and-twenty, Princess Charlotte, daughter of the Prince Regent and the Princess of Wales, was born, and "as it soon became understood that there would be no heir apparent if the Princess of Wales lived," as that lady was practically separated from her husband, "the necessity was admitted of keeping Prince William single, to marry Princess Charlotte, the presumptive heiress to the throne, in case of no eligible foreign Prince appearing for that function. For twenty of their best years, therefore, Prince William and Princess Mary were kept waiting" (*Annual Register*). But in 1816 Princess Charlotte was united to Prince Leopold of Saxe Coburg; and Prince William—now Duke of Gloucester—and the Princess Mary were allowed to marry. Each was now forty years of age, and the bride had lost the charm of youth; yet, according to Lord Malmesbury, she was "all good humour and pleasantness"; her "manners are perfect"; and "I never saw or conversed with any Princess so exactly what she ought to be." They lived together happily and usefully for eighteen years. The Duke then died without issue; and the Duchess survived him twenty-three years, living in "much retirement, doing good when she could, and universally beloved." She died at Gloucester House, Park Lane, London, on the 20th April, 1857, aged eighty, being the last survivor of the fifteen children of George III.

Hastings' intimacy with the Duke of Gloucester extended over many years, and it was marked by much courtesy and good feeling on both sides. On the 12th January, 1807, Hastings wrote to the Duke from Daylesford:—

SIR,—I am infinitely obliged to your Royal Highness[1] for the letter which you have done me the honor to write to me. For the portrait my thanks are due to your Royal Highness for your acceptance of it, and I am proud that you have thought it deserving of that distinction.

Your Royal Highness has dignified me with the appellation of your friend, and given me credit for the sincerity which appertains to that relation. The pleasure which I received from this assurance is yet mingled with a sense of regret that I must continue to owe to your generous construction of my attachment that conviction which I should deem it the most fortunate circumstance of my life to be able to establish by proof.

You have furnished me with the strongest inducement to visit London. My first object then will be to pay my respects to your Royal Highness.

---

[1] As the Duke's mother was not of Royal birth, he was given the title of Royal Highness in courtesy only previous to his marriage in 1816, when it was definitely conferred upon him by his uncle and father-in-law, King George III.

Mrs. Hastings desires me to make her grateful acknowledgments for your remembrance of her, and to assure your Royal Highness of her respectful attachment.

I have the honour to be, with very great respect,

Your Royal Highness's most obedient friend and devoted servant.

In September, 1807, the Duke sustained the loss of his mother, and Hastings offered his condolences, which the Duke promptly acknowledged. Hastings then wrote :—

SIR,—I return your Royal Highness my grateful thanks for the honor of your letter, and for the gracious manner in which you have been pleased to signify your approval of my participation in your Royal Highness's affliction.

Permit me, Sir, at the same time, to express my admiration of the just and truly religious sentiments which your letter conveys. These, aided by the lenient hand of time, will, I trust, soon tranquillise your mind, and leave only the fixed principle of affection, and the soothing remembrance of well acquitted duties. Sorrow so associated and attempered is the only tie that can connect our present existence with those whom we have loved and lost in this world, and is (may we not so hope ?) the pledge of our reunion in a better.

I am grieved that any cause should have affected your Royal Highness's health ; and devoutly pray that the retirement which you have chosen may contribute to its speedy restoration, and to that of your Royal sister.[1]

Mrs. Hastings desires me to offer to your Royal Highness her dutiful respects and best wishes.

I have the honour to be your Royal Highness's

Faithfully devoted, and most humble servant.

The Duke paid several visits to Hastings and his wife at Daylesford. The first of these was in October, 1809. He arrived at six in the evening of the 10th, attended only by Captain Curry, his equerry. On the 11th he rode, accompanied by Captain Curry, to Sesencot to make a call, and in the evening he was met at dinner at Daylesford by Sir Charles and Lady Cockerell, Mrs. Barton, Miss Rushout, and Mr. and Mrs. Leigh. On the 12th Hastings walked with the Duke round by Cornwell Knarefield, the garden, and park. Lord Redesdale, Sir John, Lady and Miss Read, and Mr. Penyston "dined with us." At eleven on the following morning the Duke left Daylesford. No mention is made of his having beguiled the time by

[1] Princess Sophia of Gloucester, Ranger of Greenwich Park, who died unmarried in 1844.

shooting. In the following February Hastings paid his usual visit to London, and waited upon the Duke, who promptly invited him to dinner, at which Hastings met the three members of the Duke's staff, Sir Francis and Lady Baring, Sir George Shee, Mr. Wombwell, and another gentleman, whose name he did not catch. The Duke "invited me," says Hastings, "to call on him on Sunday at a quarter before 11, to accompany him to his church" (St. George's, Hanover Square), "to dine with him on Tuesday at 5, and to go afterwards to Covent Garden Theatre to his private box." Hastings fulfilled

THE DUKE OF GLOUCESTER.

these engagements. This was the first of many occasions on which Hastings accompanied the Duke to the church referred to. Sometimes Hastings was indisposed, and the Duke immediately called to see and cheer his elderly friend. Occasionally the Duke himself was on the sick list, and then Hastings exhibited every solicitude for him. But Hastings did not presume on his intimacy with the Duke. He was a ceremonious man, with a deep respect for dignities, and he never forgot the Prince in the guest. This is well shown by the following letter which he addressed to the Duke on the 26th September, 1811 :—

Mrs. Hastings and myself are grateful for the honour that your Royal

Highness has announced to us of your intention of being our guest on Thursday, the 10th of October. The hour of dinner—as your Royal Highness has with your accustomed goodness been pleased to allow us to fix it—will be 6 o'clock. I hope I shall not trespass too much on your Royal Highness's indulgence in expressing the wish, that in the arrangement of your future movements, you will extend the honour of this visit to as great a length as you can without inconvenience to yourself afford it. I shall obey your Royal Highness's commands in abstaining from my purpose of paying my personal respects to you at Cheltenham. For this purpose I had ordered horses to be in readiness for me to-morrow, and had intended to execute it yesterday, had not the severity of the weather prevented it. I am always glad to meet Captain Curry, and shall be happy to receive him, and any other person or persons whom your Royal Highness may bring with you. Mrs. Hastings charges me to present her respects, and to say everything that can attest her grateful sense of the very kind manner in which your Royal Highness has expressed your remembrance of her, and of your interesting enquiry concerning her health, which, I am happy to be able to announce, is perfectly re-established.

The Duke "arrived to dinner" on the 10th October, accompanied as before by Captain Curry, and was met by Mr. and Mrs. Penyston, and Mr. and Mrs. Beach. On the 11th "our company was Mr. Bowles, Lady Northwick, and Sir Charles Cockerell." On the 12th the guests at dinner were Mr., Mrs., and Miss Dawkins, and Mr., Mrs., and Miss Leigh. The following day was Sunday, and "we all went to church; had the Adlestrop band. Marian's birthday. No company except Colonel Shaw, who arrived about noon, and staid." On the 14th Hastings accompanied the Duke to Northwick Park, and rode with him, and with Lord Northwick, Miss Rushout, and Mr. Bowles round the Park. He then took leave of the Duke, and returned to Daylesford. During the following twelve months he met the Duke frequently in London, called upon him, received his calls at Fenton's Hotel, Portugal Street, or elsewhere; dined and walked with him, and accompanied him to church. In October, 1812, the Duke paid his third autumnal visit to Daylesford, and Hastings invited the following ladies and gentlemen to meet him at dinner: "Lady Northwick, Miss Rushout, and Mr. Bowles, Sir Charles and Lady Cockerell for the 5th—five persons; Lord and Lady Redesdale, Miss Milford, Mr., Mrs., and Miss Talbot for the 6th—six persons; Mr., Mrs., and Miss Dawkins, Mr. and Miss Penyston for the 7th—five persons; and Mr. and Mrs. C. Pole for the 8th—two persons." The Duke duly arrived; gave, as usual, little trouble; and was content with the society of his host and hostess and their friends.

In December, 1812, Hastings was in London, and he made these entries in his diary:—

Portugal Street, 4th Dec. At about 11 we left Daylesford.

5th. The Duke of Gloucester called, and invited me to dine with him next Saturday. Promised to call to-morrow, and take me to church.

6th. The Duke called, etc. I returned in his coach, which he left to walk.

9th. I wrote my name at Princess Sophia's of Gloucester. We both dined with the Duke of Gloucester, and came home about 1. Princess Sophia, Lady Wilymer, Lady Mary Wedderburn, Sir George and Lady Warrender.

12th. I dined at the Duke of Gloucester's. Lord Sidmouth, Mr. Van Sittart, Mr. Cooper, Mr. Wilberforce, etc.

13th. I accompanied H.R.H. to St. George's church, he calling for me.

14th. I went with H.R.H. to the Levée.

17th. My 80th birthday. The Duke of Gloucester came to congratulate me upon it.

20th. I went with the Duke of Gloucester to St. George's church.

25th (Christmas Day). We both dined with the Duke of Gloucester, Princess Sophia, and his own household.

Hastings was back in his old quarters in Portugal Street in the spring of 1813.

3rd March. The Duke of Gloucester dined with us, and Lord and Lady Ellenborough, Mrs. Motte, Sir H. Inglis, Colonel Toone, Colonel Dalton, and Captain Curry.

17th March. I dined with the Duke of Gloucester, Bishops of Chester and Norwich, Law and Bathurst.

5th April. I attended the Committee of the House of Lords. The Duke of Gloucester called at 11¼, took me with him, sat with me in the Usher's room, conducted me into the Committee Room, and left it with me, walking with me to his carriage, ordering it to reconvey me, which it did, to my door. He afterwards called, to report my reception, and his own approbation of my evidence.

3rd May. In consequence of a message from the Duke of Gloucester yesterday by Colonel Higgins, I wrote to Mr. Baber, Mr. Auriol, and Mr. Chamier, calling on the two last, requesting them to accommodate H.R.H. by voting to gravel Piccadilly and Park Lane instead of paving it.

On the 15th July, 1814, Hastings, who was again lodging in

Portugal Street, called on the Duke of Gloucester, "who," he recorded, "engaged himself to us at Daylesford, the 1st of October—condition, no other company. I was admitted to the presence of the Princess Sophia of Gloucester." Accordingly, on Saturday, the 1st October, the Duke arrived at Daylesford. On Sunday Hastings took his Royal guest to the little church near the park, but Mrs. Hastings remained at home, as she was indisposed. On Monday, in the afternoon, the Duke left for Sesencot, where he was joined the following day by Mr. and Mrs. Hastings. The party at Sesencot included Lord and Lady Redesdale, Lord and Lady Ducie, Lady Cockerell, Mr. and Mrs. Dutton. Mrs. Hastings returned home in the evening; but Hastings remained two days at Sesencot, when he returned to Daylesford with the Duke, "who sat an hour with us, took leave, and proceeded to Stowe."

27th June, 1816. I received a message by Colonel Higgins from the Duke of Gloucester to call upon him to-morrow between 12 and 1.

28th June. I waited on H.R.H. His marriage not fixed, but will take place between the 15th and 18th July.

5th February, 1817. I wrote my name at the Duke of Gloucester's at Carlton House.

7th March. I dined with the Duke of Gloucester "to meet the Prince Regent"; presented to the Duchess.

8th March. I visited Princess Sophia of Gloucester, was admitted, the Duke came. At 4 we received a visit from the Duke.

12th March. We attended a numerous party at the Duke of Gloucester's.

24th March. Visit of H.R.H. the Duke of Gloucester. Last night the Duchess's party.

18th April. I called at Gloucester House, and was received by the Duke and Duchess in her Royal Highness's apartment. Mrs. H. and Lady Imhoff went to the Duchess's party.

21st April. I sent to H.R.H. the dimensions of his portrait.

5th May. I wrote to H.R.H. announcing our departure, and praying an appointment to wait on him to-morrow.

6th May. At 12, I called by appointment on the Duke of Gloucester, to take leave, who came at three for the same purpose.

7th June. I went to Cheltenham to pay my respects to the Duke of Gloucester, and returned the same day bringing with me *Junius Identified*. lent by H.R.H.

17th June. I returned the book lent by H.R.H. with a letter.

On the 7th June Hastings wrote to the Duke, "accepting his intimation of a promise to come to Daylesford from

Cheltenham." But a week afterwards, on account of the commencement of Hastings' last illness, Mrs. Hastings wrote an excuse, and the Duke never saw his old friend again.

Hastings was always ready to give recommendations to men who had rendered good service as his subordinates in India. The following letter, written from Daylesford on the 26th April, 1805, to one of them, is as courteous as it is considerate :—

I beg you to believe, as I can with truth assure you, that my having so long delayed to answer your letter has not been owing to any indifference with respect to the subject of it, but to the reluctance which I felt to answer it in terms not adequate to the expectation which you had formed when you wrote it. With more leisure, and my mind less occupied than when I received your letter, I am sorry that I am unable to reply to your appeal by more than a general attestation of your merits and services, as they remain impressed on my memory, without the recollection of any specific acts which have contributed to produce it. Indeed, the nature of your official functions does not in itself admit of much specification, consisting only of promptness of attention, diligence in execution, and correctness and perspicuity in composition. To your possession of these qualities I can conscientiously give my testimony, though the degree in which I may have originally estimated them must have been somewhat effaced by a lapse of more than 21 years. I will add, that I retain as much of esteem for your private character as to suffer much regret that I can only offer this very imperfect effort to do you justice.

He was also very courteous to young men of merit, and they were duly respectful to him. On one occasion he presented a "sett of classics," as he described the collection in his diary, to a Mr. Frith ; and his gift was accompanied by the following letter, which he copied into his diary :—

I request your acceptance of a selection of classical books, intended as a pledge of my regard for the son of an honoured and most esteemed friend. As such, I beg you to preserve them for my sake ; and, for your own, I earnestly recommend to you to make a perusal of them a part of your daily occupation, by allotting if it be but five minutes of every morning, to regular and connected study of any one of them ; until by your easy practice the Latin poetry shall be so familiar to you as to become an amusement. If you follow my advice the time will come, if it pleases God to grant you life, when you will feel a sense of obligation to me for having given it. I most sincerely pray for your health and success.

But sometimes Hastings' good nature was over-taxed. For example, in September, 1807, a lady invited him in respectful terms to permit her to dedicate a forthcoming book of hers to him. He declined the compliment in the following letter :[1]—

So much use, and so much more of abuse, has been made of my name, that I never see it in print, but with painful sensations ; and this renders me the more tender of obtruding it upon the public on occasions not necessarily demanding it ; and, for a stronger reason, on any occasion which of itself might subject me to blame. I think I should deservedly expose myself to blame if I should directly authorise my name to be prefixed to a literary composition which I had never seen, in a character which, so placed, would imply a recommendation of it. But I have not only not seen your book, but (pardon me, Madam) I have only a faint conjecture that I recollect the name and person of the author. I think I do recollect both, and if I am right in that recollection, I am not sure that my vanity might have got the better of my discretion, and inspired me with a feeling of pleasure, if by chance I had met with such a distinction paid to me in it, without having been directly instrumental to it. But the question becomes very different when I was called to give my express authority for it ; or if I were in any way to predeclare my assent to it.

PERSIAN SEAL.

(*Presented by Warren Hastings to Sir John H. D'Oyly.*)

[1] Historical MS. Commission, 6th Report.

CHAPTER XII

THE CLOSING SCENE

It was not until his eighty-second year that the health of Warren Hastings began to decline. He started in life with a very poor chance of becoming an octogenarian. His father was a reckless person, who is believed to have passed away at an early age; his mother died a few days after giving him birth; he was nurtured in infancy under harsh conditions; he had few relatives to minister to his comfort, and safeguard his health during his youth; he went out to India with an unformed constitution; he spent fourteen consecutive years in the steamy plains of Bengal, without any change; and, after four years in England, he served two and a half years in Madras, and thirteen more years in Bengal. Those thirteen years were years of almost incessant worry and mental strain, yet his health never gave way seriously. He returned home at last, looking thin, bald, and delicate, but placid and strong notwithstanding; and he kept his health during the long preparation for, as well as throughout the seven years' torture of his trial. He then retired to the country to rest, but not to rust. He did not fish, hunt, or shoot, but he was at no loss for congenial occupation in his library, garden, and farm. His had been a very chequered and stormy career, that would have killed many a man with a far finer physique than he could boast of; but the sunset of his life was full of brightness and peace. He owed his longevity primarily to his temperate and regular habits. He had a good appetite, but he was a small eater, as he had a poor digestion; he drank a little Madeira when he was in India, but he was a total abstainer by choice after his return to England; he was always a good sleeper; and he took much, but not violent exercise. Moreover, he lived a full life, and having much ambition, fortitude, and self-reliance, he was braced up rather than depressed by opposition, and he was cheered by the belief that posterity would do him justice. Directly and indirectly, he owed much to his wife, Marian. His married life with her of forty-one years' duration was one long honeymoon. "Of the ingredients of happiness, which I once enumerated in rhyme," he wrote to a friend, "I possess all (and the catalogue is pretty large) but one. . . . my beloved wife is what she was in her moral and spiritual substance, and I should and ought to be perfectly contented if her health was more stable." She thoroughly reciprocated his affection, sympathised with his joys and sorrows, identified herself with his pursuits, and watched carefully over his health with the devotion of a true helpmeet. In his eyes, as he wrote to her son when she was nearly sixty years of age, she continued "even in beauty to exceed every woman who comes within my observation"; and to the last he held her judgment, taste, and tact in the highest respect. She was, according to Miss Fanny Burney, "lively, obliging, and entertaining, and so adored by her husband that in her sight and conversation he seems to find a recompense, adequate to all his wishes, for the whole of his toils and long disturbances and labours."

On the 14th January, 1814, "I was," he noted in his diary, "seized about three with a total loss of articulation, and want of power in my right hand for the first time." But he soon recovered. His health was variable during the three following years. He suffered at times from toothache; at other times from spasms and languor; but for an octogenarian he was unusually active and hearty. He was periodically troubled by weakness of the eyes. In a memorandum he referred to "a sensation like that caused by a hard substance enclosed between the eyelid and the back of the eye, the left eye more affected than the right. I have suspected that this complaint has its seat in a cause as remote as the 23rd of August, 1782, originating in a very severe fever." In another memorandum, also without date, he noted that: "My eyes have always more or less been subject to inflammation, if their affection do not rather proceed from the lids, being a complaint similarly inherent to the maternal branch of my family. For some years past I have been in the daily habit of embrocating the adjacent parts with a lotion of zinc and elder-flower water, but without any certain conviction of its efficacy. . . . In the autumn of 1784 I was seized by a violent fever while I was in India, which hung upon me in a variety of forms during many subsequent years." He also mentioned that after this fever he was periodically subject to a swelling in both his legs; and that on the 22nd of March, 1800, while "in London, and at table, in a large company, but unperceived by any part of it," he was conscious of "a numbness and disability. It consisted in a partial deprivation of my powers of speech, and a torpid sensation in my right hand, frequently and variously recurring." He added that he was subject to these ominous sensations at irregular intervals, but "they seem to have totally left me for some years past."

On the 18th January, 1818, he remarked, in a letter to a friend, that his "mind was so worn, that it cannot be sure of spelling a word of four syllables without losing one of them by the way." The following entries in his diary have a melancholy interest:—

Jan. 19th, 1818. I have laboured for near a fortnight with an inflammation in the roof of my mouth, and inability to eat solid food, and since last night with a violent cold.

Feb. 19th. I visited Adlestrop and my neighbours, and returned by Daylesford church, not apparently worse; but after dinner my cough caused incessant irritation.

March 6th. At 7 I arose, having passed the whole night almost without coughing.

7th. I have passed a second night without coughing.

8th. And a third, but my strength not advancing proportionately.

April 20th. I took my first airing in the coach with no sensible effect. This is the thirtieth day since my confinement.

May 8th. At 20 minutes past 8 Mrs. Hastings departed for London, the day overcast, but clearing; her intention to make but one journey. About noon I walked round the garden, came in greatly fatigued.

In a long letter to Mr. Halhed, he remarked:—

I am much gratified by your approval of my decision to let Mrs. Hastings depart, and leave me behind. I have the conscious satisfaction of having throughout allowed a bias in favor of every wish and opinion of hers in preference to my own; and, after the age of four-score, I believe it is the wisest resolution as well as the most virtuous that a man can come to. I almost regret her absence, as it deprives her of the new beauties of the spring, which is bursting upon us with all the arrears of delight which we have been so long neglecting.

On the 29th he noted in his diary:—

Mrs. H. still convalescent. Went to the party of the Duchess of Gloucester, with Sir Charles and Lady Imhoff, and in her reception from the Princess, and a gracious remembrance of the Queen, found a preservative against all that her health would have suffered from such a trial.

May 9th. The last week employed in arranging the library. My health equable, and rest good, generally to 5; my strength on a level floor good, ascending bad; appetite from the 1st, perfect; memory variable.

12th. My legs much swelled, the left most. Doctor prescribed the camphorated liniment 10 or 15 minutes morning and evening. Mrs. Hastings well.

15th. I went to the farm and garden in the gig: my first airing. I suffered only and but little by a short walk in the kitchen garden.

21st. Heated, and my nerves shaken by walking. This is the third day that I have been affected with the confused sound of distant multitudes.

22nd. I have been visited by confused and individual sensations as of the sounds of distant multitudes. I date their first perception from the 20th. At times resembling slow music.

31st. I went to church, and came home well, though a little exposed to the sun.

June 2nd. Mrs. Hastings appointed to come to-day; prevented by an invitation of the Prince Regent to the family, and waits to Thursday.

4th. At past 9 Mrs. H. arrived, having waited half an hour at Oxford for horses; proceeded with tired ones. She was neither heated nor fatigued.

7th. I wrote to the Duke of Gloucester accepting his intimation of a promise to come to Daylesford from Ch'n.

9th. His answer promising it for one day next month.

On the same day he concluded a long and chatty letter to Mr. Halhed as follows:—

You will rejoice to hear that my dear wife, after all that she had encountered of tumult, parade, and festivity, and some sickness in London, with added inflammation, dust, and jaded horses in her departure from it, returned to her own comfortable abode in perfect health and gaiety of spirits, and found me as glad without going so far for it.

Ten days later he resolved to go to London for advice about his eyes:—

June 19th. Since about a fortnight past my eyes have been much inflamed, with a movable sensation of some internal irritation. Last night, near its close, I awoke with an acute heat in the eyelid. The left eye the

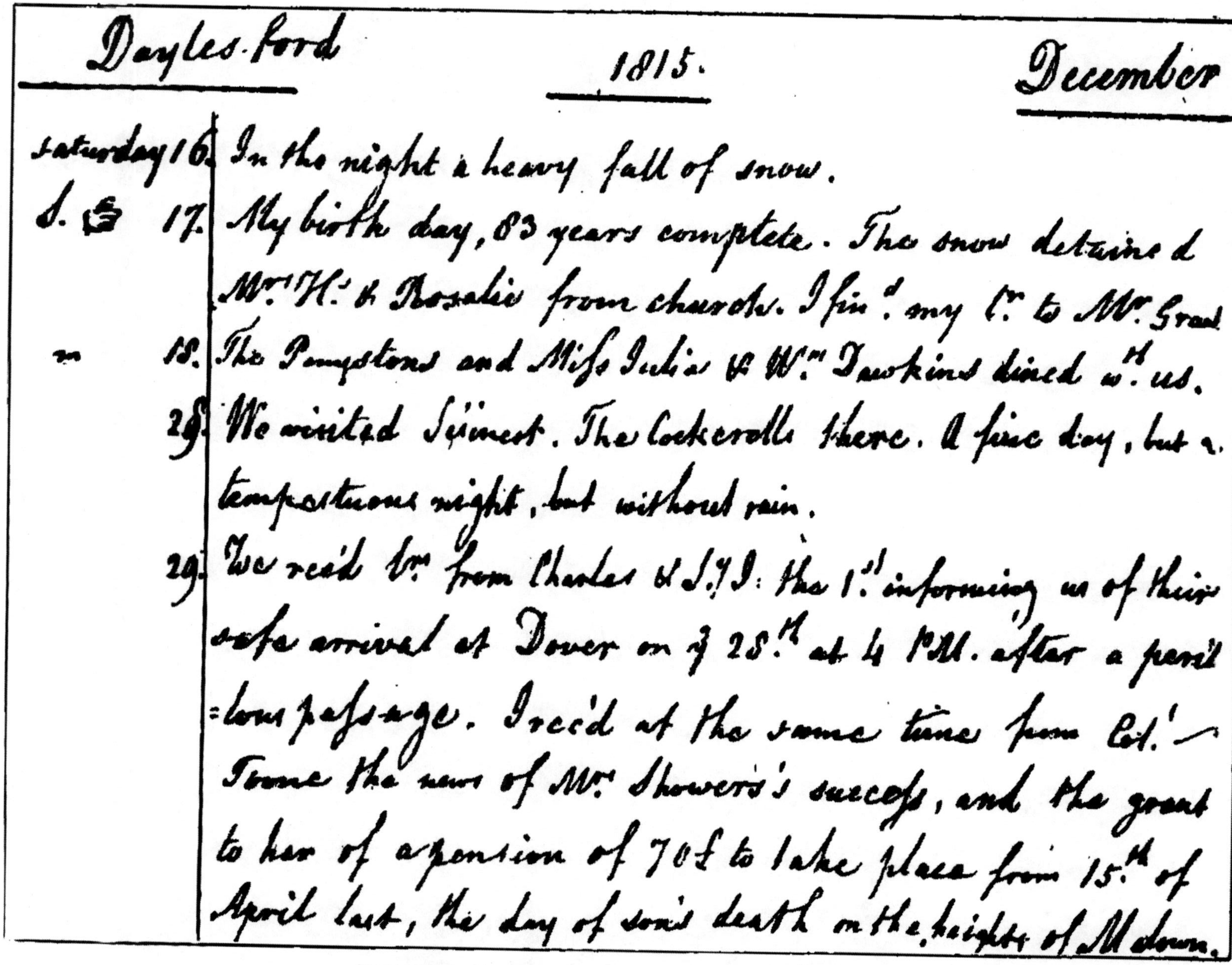

Daylesford 1815. December

saturday 16. In the night a heavy fall of snow.

S. 17. My birth day, 83 years complete. The snow detained Mrs. H. & Rosalie from church. I fin.d my L.r to Mr. Grant

18. The Pengstons and Miss Julia & Wm. Dawkins dined w.th us.

28. We visited SeSinect. The Cockerells there. A fine day, but a tempestuous night, but without rain.

29. We rec'd L.rs from Charles & S.T.I: the 1st informing us of their safe arrival at Dover on y 28th at 4 P.M. after a peril=lous passage. I rec'd at the same time from Col. Toone the news of Mrs. Showers's success, and the grant to her of a pension of 70£ to take place from 15th of April last, the day of son's death on the heights of Malown.

FACSIMILE OF A TYPICAL PAGE OF HASTINGS' DIARY.

[Face page 231.

immediate seat of the complaint. I formed the plan of going to-morrow to London, if not better, and wrote accordingly.

20th. I slept well, and awoke free from any new pain, and relinquished my intention of going to London.

July 13th. I took an airing after dinner in the coach with Mrs. Hastings; in leaving it I was seized with staggering. I sent for Mr. Haynes, who took from me about 7 ozs. of blood. The bandage loosening, I lost much more. After the operation I slept a little, and awoke in great and universal agitation, which ceased on the second discharge of blood. I slept well, and awoke as usual, but with additional weakness.

14th. Mrs. Hastings wrote an excuse to the Duke of Gloucester, who was engaged to come on Thursday.

17th. I passed an unquiet night, and arose with my limbs weak and shaken.

19th. My health better, but strength much diminished. I sat in the great chair much of the middle of the night, and afterwards in the bed lay till late.

20th. I awoke with my throat much swelled, and a difficulty of swallowing at breakfast continued unabated at dinner, which I took alone, but without pain, and my appetite the same as it had been, unchanged through all other variations. . . . I cannot recollect the loss of time, but ascribe the past events of the day to . . .

This unfinished entry closed the diary that he had kept in eleven neat little volumes since the 18th January, 1784, the day before Mrs. Hastings left Calcutta for Europe. It is reasonable to assume that he had been in the habit of keeping a diary for many years previously; but, if such was the case, the earlier volumes were not preserved. They might have proved of great value to the historian.

He died at Daylesford on the 22nd August after six weeks' illness, surrounded by the nearest and dearest of his friends. He once reminded his wife, in a letter dated Lucknow, 13th August, 1784, of how often she had "heard me declare in the most resolute terms that I never would be seen by you under the disgusting circumstances of a state of sickness"; and Gleig states in his memoir that, just before he expired, Hastings drew a cambric handkerchief over his face, and when those who were weeping near him found that he suffered it to remain there some time, and gently raised it, they found that he was dead. Thus, like Job, he "came to the grave in a full age, as a shock of corn cometh in his season." He was buried near his mother, and among his ancestors, in a new vault, close to the chancel of the little church which he rebuilt; and when that unassuming edifice gave place to the present handsome structure, care was taken to retain for the vault its original position. The tomb is marked by a pillar, crowned by an urn on which his two names —or his "conjoint appellative" as he styled it—are inscribed, and Mrs. Hastings placed within the church a plain tablet bearing the following inscription :—

In a vault just beyond the Eastern extremity of this Church lies the body of the Right Honourable Warren Hastings, of Daylesford House, in this parish, the first Governor-General of the British Territories in India, a member of His Majesty's Most Honourable Privy Council, LL.D., F.R.S., the last public effort of whose eminently virtuous and lengthened life was the re-erection of this sacred edifice, which he superintended with singular energy and interest to its completion, and in which, alas! the holy rites of sepulture were very shortly afterwards performed over his mortal remains. He died 22nd August, 1818, aged 85 years and 8 months. "Lord, now lettest Thou Thy servant depart in peace."

Hastings gave proof of his unbounded affection for, and confidence in his wife by his will, of which I have obtained a copy from Somerset House. It is dated the 27th of July, 1811, or seven years before his death :—

I, Warren Hastings, Esquire, late Governor-General of Fort William, in Bengal, being in my perfect and sound mind, do make and declare this to be my last Will and Testament. I give, devise, and bequeath unto my dear wife, Anna Maria Apollonia Hastings, all my estates both real and personal, all the debts which are or shall be due to me, and all my rights of property, to hold to her, her heirs, executors, administrators, and assigns, according to the nature of such estates, with power to give, devise, and bequeath the same to whomsoever she shall think proper. And I appoint her sole Executrix of this my Will, and hereby revoking all former Wills, I declare this alone to be my last Will and Testament. In testimony whereof I have hereunto set my hand and seal this twenty-seventh day of July, one thousand eight hundred and eleven.

There were spots on his fame, but so splendid was that fame that it would, says Macaulay, "bear many spots," and his administration "gives him title to be considered as one of the most remarkable men in our history." He was responsible for abuses, but he "never had a share in the worst abuses" of those old times. He might easily have become enormously rich had he been guilty of cruelty or fraud; but far more than Clive might he have been "surprised" in his retirement by his "moderation." He was "neither sordid nor rapacious." In a letter to the Editor of the *Edinburgh Review*, Macaulay said:—I think Hastings, though far from faultless, one of the greatest men that England ever produced. He had pre-eminent talents for government, and great literary talents too; fine taste, a princely spirit, and heroic equanimity in the midst of adversity and danger." Professor Wilson maintained that "there were defects, no doubt, but there were no great crimes and misdemeanours to justify his impeachment. . . . The safety and honour of British India were manifestly the motives of all his actions. Whether he was not at times less unrelenting than the occasion called for may admit of conjecture; but undoubtedly the times were critical, great firmness was demanded, and its excess was a venial error, when its deficiency would have been an inexpiable crime." Sir James Stephen arrived at the conclusion that:—"If a man's ability is measured by a comparison between his means of action and the results of his action, Hastings must be regarded as the ablest Englishmen of the eighteenth century"; and Colonel Malleson maintains that "no nobler son ever devoted to his country's interests a life more pure, a prescience more profound, talents more commanding than did" Warren Hastings.

Hastings was not bred to public affairs. In the answer that he made to the indictment of the House of Commons he complained that a "state of perfection" was expected from "a man who was separated, while yet but a schoolboy, from his native country, and from every advantage of that instruction which might have better qualified him for the high offices and arduous situations which it became his lot to fill." He proceeded to say, and "with strict truth" so far as Sir James Stephen could judge:—

> Every division of official business which now exists in Bengal, with only such exceptions as have been occasioned by the changes of authority enacted from home, are of my formation. The establishment formed for the administration of the revenue, the institution of the courts of civil and criminal justice in Bengal and its immediate dependencies, the form of government established for the province of Benares, with all its dependent branches of revenue, commerce, judicature, and military defence; the

arrangements created for subsidy and defence of the province of Oude, every other political connection and alliance of the Government of Bengal, were created by me.

"He owed," says Sir Alfred Lyall, "nothing to the study of text books, nothing to accepted usage, official precedent, professional tradition," or the pressure of public opinion. He "had been shipped out to India a raw lad, and had been left to gather his experience among the extraordinary incidents of Anglo-Indian politics in their earliest, roughest, and most rudimentary stage." Burke characterised him as "a bad scribbler of absurd papers who could never put two sentences of sense together"; and Macaulay alleged that "gentlemen in the Indian services write above their abilities," are "too much of essayists," and that Hastings "gave the character to Indian official writing which it now bears." But Francis, implacable foe though he was, admitted that there was no contending against the pen of Hastings, whose "power of making out a case, of perplexing what it was inconvenient that people should understand, and of setting in the clearest point of view whatever would bear the light, was incomparable." In the fragment of the autobiography to which I have already alluded, Hastings refers to himself as a man who had been "placed by His will who governs all things in a situation to give birth to events that were connected with the incidents of nations; which were invariably prosperous to those of his own; but productive to himself of years of depression and persecution, and of the chances of want only relieved by occasional and surely providential means, though never affecting the durable state of his mental tranquillity."

He inspired all classes in Bengal with confidence and attachment. He enjoyed a popularity among the natives "such as no other Governor has been able to attain." The Civil Service felt an affection for him that was constant through all his disasters; and the Army revered him as a chief who was well worthy of support. He was considerate towards religious and race prejudices, and he gave Bengal a peace such as it had not previously known. His temper was calm, and, according to Macaulay, "equal to almost any trial. Quick and vigorous as his intellect was, the patience with which he endured the most cruel vexations, till a remedy could be found, resembled the patience of stupidity. He seems to have been capable of bitter and long-enduring resentments; yet his resentment so seldom hurried him into any blunder that it might be doubted whether what appeared to be revenge was anything but policy." He had "the full command of one of the most fertile minds that ever existed," and "no complication of perils and embarrassments could perplex him, but for every difficulty he had a contrivance ready" that "seldom failed to serve the purpose for which it was designed." In private life, according to the *Annual Register* of 1818, "he is painted as the most amiable of human beings, with a nature 'full of the milk of human kindness,' and without a tincture of gall in its composition."

The *Gentleman's Magazine* of September, 1818, contained a sketch of the life of Hastings by "One who knew him well," in which the author remarked :—

> Mr. Hastings possessed a mind which has been figuratively but truly said to have been cast in a heroic mould—noble, brave, generous, and sincere. It was equal to any occasion that called it into action; no dangers appalled it; no difficulties perplexed it; by the dint of its own energies it surmounted them all whenever they arose. Ample proofs of this have been given in various instances during his long and arduous government, when dangers and difficulties pressed on every side, and when every mind but his was alarmed and confounded. But, on no occasion was his fortitude ever more severely tried than on that of his impeachment; when, for seven tedious years he bore with unparalleled patience the grossest abuse, and the most malevolent invectives. An elevated mind, conscious of its own innocence, was his great support. It was not only a brazen wall to him, but a shield of virtue on which the shafts of malice fell harmless and impassive. The sentence of acquittal which the Lords passed afterwards did not redound more to his praise than did his enduring patience, his dignified comportment, and his undisturbed temper during the protracted trial. In private life he was one of the most amiable of human beings. He was the most tender and affectionate husband; he was the kindest master; he was the sincerest friend. He had "a tear for pity, and a hand open as day for melting charity"; his generosity was unbounded in desire, and did not always calculate on his means of indulging it. He had that true equanimity which elevated him above all selfish considerations or personal resentments. His own private interest was always lost in his regard for the public welfare, and to those who had been his most implacable enemies he was ever ready to be reconciled.

Hastings was described by one lady as the "indulgent friend

FLAXMAN'S STATUE OF WARREN HASTINGS.

and parent of my life"; and by another as a "sincere angelic friend"; for he was blessed with a disposition that endeared him to all his friends, and enabled him to bear up under trials that would have crushed the spirit of an average man.

There was an interval of thirty-three years between the date of Hastings' resignation of the Governor-Generalship and that of his death, and he consequently survived almost all his contemporaries. But when he died, people were reminded of what he had been; and five years after his death the Directors of the East India Company marked their respect for his character, and their gratitude for his services, by erecting a white marble statue of him by Flaxman within the precincts of their House.[1] That famous head-centre of the administrative machinery of India, with its labyrinthine corridors, wainscoted rooms, wide staircases, and old-world air, disappeared soon after Parliament required the Company to resign its authority to the Crown; and the statue was removed from Leadenhall Street to the new India Office in St. James's Park, where it now occupies a conspicuous position in a hall close to the Secretary of State's rooms.

[1] It is remarked by Mr. William Foster, B.A., in his catalogue of the Paintings, Statues, and Prints, in the India Office, that:—"Hastings died on the 22nd August, 1818. At a General Court held on the 22nd September in the following year, the Chairman of the Company notified his intention of moving that a statue of the deceased statesman be placed in the General Court Room. The motion did not come on, however, until the 12th January, 1820, and then it met with some ungenerous opposition. But in the end the Chairman's proposition was declared carried, and it was formally resolved:—'That as the last testimony of approbation of the long, zealous, and successful services of the late Right Honourable Warren Hastings, in maintaining without diminution the British possessions in India against the combined efforts of European, Mahomedan, and Mahratta enemies, a statue of that distinguished servant of the East India Company be placed among the statesmen and heroes who have contributed in their several stations to the recovery, preservation, and security of the British power and authority in India.' Eight months later the Chairman informed the Court that John Flaxman had been chosen as the sculptor, and that the price agreed on was one thousand pounds. Flaxman seems to have worked upon it leisurely, for it was not until April, 1823, that he was able to report that the statue was completed. He was then permitted to send it to the Royal Academy of that year, and it must therefore have been the latter part of 1823 before the memorial was in position at the India House."

It is surprising that the Directors did not raise a monument in Hastings' honour in Westminster Abbey, where, according to Trikell, who was buried in the Poets' Corner :—

> Along the walls the speaking marbles show
> What worthies form the hallow'd mould below ;
> Proud names who once the reins of empire held,
> In arms who triumph'd, or in arts excell'd ;
> Chiefs, graced with scars, and prodigal of blood :
> Stern patriots, who for sacred freedom stood ;
> Just men, by whom impartial laws were given ;
> And saints, who taught, and led the way to Heaven.

A monument was erected in the Abbey by the Company in 1758 to the memory of Admiral Watson, as a "grateful testimony of the signal advantages which they obtained by his valour and prudent conduct" in recovering Calcutta after the Black Hole catastrophe, in the immediately preceding year. Close to it is another large monument, that was erected by the Company to the memory of General Sir Eyre Coote, Commander-in-Chief in India, who repeatedly defeated the French and Hyder Ali in the Carnatic. In the nave is a monument that was erected by the Company in honour of General Stringer Lawrence, "in testimony of their gratitude for his eminent services in the command of the forces on the Coast of Coromandel." The Earl of Minto, Governor-General of India from 1807 to 1813, who pre-deceased Hastings, was buried in the Abbey ; and his brother, the Honourable Hugh Elliott, Governor of Madras from 1814 to 1820, was placed some years later by his side. For Sir Archibald Campbell, Governor of Madras from 1786 to 1790, a resting-place was found in the Poets' Corner. In later years the Abbey received the remains of Sir John Malcolm, Governor of Bombay ; Sir Herbert Edwardes, the hero of Multan ; Earl Canning, and Lord Lawrence, Viceroys of India ; Sir George Pollock, of Afghan fame ; Lord Clyde, and Sir James Outram, Commanders-in-Chief in India, etc. The white marble statues of Lord Canning and Sir John Malcolm are among the finest in the Abbey ; and the monuments of some other eminent men who have been named attract attention. At St. Paul's Cathedral there are memorial statues of Middleton, the first Bishop of Calcutta; of Heber, his immediate successor; of Sir William Jones, Orientalist and Judge; of the Marquis Cornwallis, twice Governor-General; of Mountstuart Elphinstone, Governor of Bombay, and historian of early India; of Sir Henry Lawrence, the hero of Lucknow; of Sir Charles Napier, Commander-in-Chief in India; and of General Robert Gillespie; not to speak of the Duke of Wellington, the hero of Assaye and a hundred other battles. There are bronze statues of Lord Napier of Magdala, Lord Lawrence, Lord Clyde, and Sir George Pollock, in Waterloo Place; of Sir Henry Havelock and Sir Charles Napier at Charing Cross; of Sir James Outram and Sir Bartle Frere on the Thames Embankment; of Lord Clive in the market-place at Shrewsbury; and of Lord Strathnairn at Knightsbridge; but in death, as in life, Warren Hastings received less than his deserts as compared with the public recognition of the services of other men who once occupied high rank in India.

As the Directors did not move in the matter, Mrs. Hastings charged herself with the duty of placing in the Abbey a memorial of her husband, consisting of a tablet surmounted by a bust. The tablet bears the following inscription:—

Selected for his eminent talents and integrity, he was appointed by Parliament, in 1773, the first Governor-General of India; to which high office he was thrice re-appointed by the same authority. Presiding over the Indian Governments during thirteen years of a most eventful period, he restored the affairs of the East India Company, from the deepest distress, to the highest prosperity, and rescued their possessions from a combination of the most powerful enemies ever leagued against them. In the wisdom of his councils and the energy of his measures, he found unexhausted resources, and successfully sustained a long, varied, and multiplied war with France, Mysore, and the Mahratta States, whose power he humbled, and concluded an honourable peace; for which, and for his distinguished services, he received the thanks of the East India Company, sanctioned by the Board of Control. The kingdom of Bengal, the seat of his Government, he ruled with a mild and equitable sway, preserved it from invasion, and, while he secured to its inhabitants the enjoyment of their customs, laws, and religion, and the blessings of peace, was rewarded by their affection and gratitude; nor was he more distinguished by the higher qualities of a statesman and a patriot, than by the exercise of every Christian virtue. He lived for many years in dignified retirement, beloved and revered by all who knew him, at his seat of Daylesford, in the county of Worcester, where he died in peace in the 86th year of his age, August the 22nd, in the year of our Lord 1818.

Beneath the inscription it is stated that :—

This memorial was erected by his beloved wife and disconsolate widow, M. A. Hastings.

When the news of Hastings' death reached Calcutta a public meeting of the inhabitants was held, and it was resolved to

BUST IN WESTMINSTER ABBEY.

request the Marquis of Hastings, then Governor-General, to allow a statue of his eminent predecessor to be erected in that city. The Marquis had, as Earl of Moira, been one of Hastings' judges ; and, after expressing his concurrence in the proposed tribute of public respect, he stated that he had been most punctual in his attendance at the trial of Hastings ; that he had conscientiously pronounced a verdict of acquittal ; and that all which he had learned since his arrival in India had testified to the justice of that finding.

"Madame" Hastings, as she was called at Daylesford long before and after her decease, was in her seventy-first year when she lost her husband, yet she survived him nearly twenty years; and there are a few old folk still living at Daylesford who cherish a personal and a grateful recollection of her. She completed her ninetieth year on the 2nd February, 1837; and on the 20th of the immediately following month she passed away. Her will, dated the 29th March, 1830, commenced with an expression of her devout thanks to the Almighty for granting her strength of mind to dispose of her affairs, and of her desire to be laid beside her beloved husband in the vault in Daylesford churchyard, from whence, she trusted, they would rise together to that blessed abode which God, in His infinite mercy, had promised to those who did His will. It directed that the burial was not to take place within ten days of her demise; that it was to be conducted very privately; and that no man was to be allowed to touch her body. It stated that she had deposited with her bankers £6,000 to pay off a mortgage raised by her husband on the estate.[1] It proceeded to say that she left £13,900

[1] The total value of Hastings' estate was inconsiderable, for the maintenance of the position of a hospitable country gentleman entailed an expenditure which his income did not enable him to meet with facility. He never forgot that he had been Governor-General of India, and though it cannot be justly alleged that he affected a style of living that was extravagant, yet he appears to have thought that he could not without derogating from the dignity of that office, be as thrifty as he might otherwise like to be. He said to Lord Castlereagh, the Court of Directors, and others :—"My expenses are none of them such as deserve the character of extravagance, yet I cannot conform to that strict line of economy which another might, who possessed by inheritance an income of the same measure as mine, and had formed the habits of his whole life to it. This was not to be expected from a man who had passed all the active part of his life in the hourly discharge of public duties, which allowed him little leisure, or thought to attend to his own affairs, or to care about them.' It must be admitted that he did not "cut his coat according to his cloth"; but his establishment at Daylesford was always on a modest scale, judging from the enumeration of his servants in his diary, and he kept few horses and carriages. His periodical visits to London and his intimate association there with the best society of the day refreshed his mind and kept him in agreeable touch with the Court and with public affairs, but they added to his expenditure. He was moreover very generous to needy friends and relatives. But all the time he was almost wholly dependent on the liberality of the Court of Directors, and he was

in Consols; directed the distribution of this sum among her nieces and grand-nieces; and ordered the payment of £1 to each man, woman, and on behalf of each child on the estate. It gave her son, Sir Charles Imhoff, the free use of the house and estate during his life, with the rents and profits arising therefrom; and it provided that, should he not care to reside at Daylesford, then the house was to be let exactly in the condition as to furniture in which it had been left by her husband and herself. It required her executors to sell the house and estate after her son's death, and to divide the proceeds between her nieces, Mrs. Woodman and Miss Marian Chapuset, and her grand-nephew, Mr. W. H. Woodman. It apportioned the residue equally between these three relatives, another niece, and Lady Imhoff, and directed that, in the event of Lady Imhoff's death, her share should be divided equally among the other participators in the residue.

Sir Charles Imhoff (who was appointed Lieutenant-Governor of Jersey in 1814, and was promoted to the rank of General in the British Army in 1846) attained the same age as his octogenarian step-father, and survived his nonagenarian mother by sixteen years. He died at Daylesford on the 14th February, 1853. By his will, dated the 10th August, 1847, he left legacies amounting to £22,500. He directed that, in the event of his dying in London, he was to be buried beside his wife—who predeceased him—in Kensal Green Cemetery; but should he die at Daylesford, then his body was to be laid beside that of his mother in Daylesford churchyard. He bequeathed £1,000 to his half-sister, the daughter of his father, Baron Imhoff, by his second wife; and divided the rest of his property among his first and second cousins. A marble tablet in the church is—

> In memory of General Sir Charles Imhoff, K.J., who departed this life 14th February, 1853, aged 86. According to his express desire he was interred by the side of his beloved Mother, Anna Maria Apollonia, relict of the Right Honourable Warren Hastings.

He left no children, and the estate being offered for sale,

---

confident that "your Honourable Court will not suffer me to descend to the grave with my last moments embittered with the prospective horrors of an insolvent debtor."

under Mrs. Hastings' will, was purchased by Mr. R. N. Byass, by whom it was sold to Mr. Harman Grisewood, of Hill Street, Berkeley Square, London, who held it until his death in London

NEW DAYLESFORD CHURCH. *(Hastings' Tomb.)*

in 1870; and in 1873 it was acquired by Mr. C. E. Baring Young, son of a former partner in the firm of Baring Brothers. Mr. Grisewood marked his tenure of the property by adding to the embellishments of the house, and enhancing the beauty of the grounds, and also by rebuilding the few cottages forming the village, and by substituting a gem of a Gothic church for the unpretentious edifice which Hastings had caused to be erected. He had the last-named fact recorded in the following inscription on a tablet which was placed immediately under the tablet that Hastings erected in commemoration of the reconstruction of the old church :—

> This Church, which was rebuilt by the Right Honourable Warren Hastings, in the year of our Lord 1816, as is recorded in the foregoing inscription, having been found too small to accommodate the increasing number of the inhabitants of the parish, was taken down, and the present edifice erected on the same site by Harman Grisewood, Esq., in the year of our Lord 1860.

Mr. Grisewood was buried in the adjoining churchyard, which, with its closely mown grass, its beds of bright flowers, its well-arranged tombs, its neat walks, its yew and walnut trees, its ivy-clad walls, and its picturesque lych gate, does honour to the Rev. Arthur Grisewood, the present Rector, nephew of the late lord of the manor, and is a worthy resting-place of him who, in the words of Macaulay, was the "greatest man who ever bore the ancient and widely extended name" of Hastings.

APPENDIX

PORTRAITS AND OTHER MEMORIALS

THE late Sir George Scharf, K.C.B., the Director of the National Portrait Gallery, was so obliging as to draw up for me the following list of painted and engraved portraits of Warren Hastings :—

Oil painting, when young, by Sir Joshua Reynolds, in the possession of Lady Northwick. Engraved in 1774 by T. Watson. Wearing his own dark hair, seated at table cross-legged, nearly full length.[1]

Oil painting by Tilly Kettle, in the National Portrait Gallery, to waist ; red coat, full face, left hand to cheek. Engraved by Angus.

Oil painting, full length, life size, seated, by A. W. Devis, now in the National Portrait Gallery, formerly in Government House at Calcutta.[2] Lent by the Secretary of State for India. Sprig-patterned waistcoat. A marble bust of Clive is seen behind in a circular niche on the wall. Engraved by Hudson.

Oil painting, full length, standing figure, hands joined in front, dark buttoned coat, full face. In the Council Chamber at the India Office.[3]

---

[1] A photogravure of the engraving, executed for this book by the Swan Electric Engraving Company, is given opposite p. 36.

[2] Macaulay refers to "the face pale and worn, but serene, on which was written as legibly as under the picture in the Council Chamber at Calcutta, '*Mens æqua in arduis.*'" There is a copy of the picture both in the Council Chamber at Calcutta and in the Council Chamber at Madras.

[3] The painter is unknown. The picture was bequeathed in 1800 to the East India Company by Mr. William Larkins, and it now hangs behind the chair of the Secretary of State. It is described as follows by Mr. William Foster, B.A., in his catalogue of paintings, statues, and prints, in the India Office :—"A full-length, life-sized portrait, painted evidently in later life, representing Hastings standing in an easy attitude, with hands clasped in front, and right leg slightly advanced. The face, close shaven, is turned partially towards the left ; but the dark eyes look directly at the spectator. The head, slightly bald, is fringed with silvery hair, fuller over the ears than elsewhere. The costume is very plain, consisting of a white cravat, dark double-breasted coat with gold buttons, black silk breeches, white stockings, and shoes with plain gold buckles."

Oil painting by Masquerier; holding a letter in the right hand and spectacles in the left. Presented in 1815 by Sir Charles Forbes, Bart., to the Oriental Club, Hanover Square, London. Engraved by T. Watson.[1]

Oil painting by Sir William Beechey, R.A., kit-cat size, now in the possession of General Sir Charles D'Oyly, at Blandford, Dorset. Engraved in 1817 by W. Skelton.

Oil painting, half-length, in a black coat, by Sir Thomas Lawrence, in the National Portrait Gallery. Painted in 1811 for the wife of Colonel Barton, aide-de-camp to Warren Hastings. Inscribed with Hastings' name and age, 79. Exhibited at the Royal Academy in 1811, and at the Manchester Art Treasures, 1857, where it was attributed to Sir Joshua Reynolds. Engraved by W. Say in mezzotint.[2]

SIR THOMAS LAWRENCE.

A picture in sprigged waistcoat, like the full length by Devis, was exhibited in 1879 by Colonel Davies at Burlington House, and was attributed to Zoffany.

A picture on twilled canvas, probably by Abbot in the collection of Mr. Passmore Edwards, was sold at Christie's 11th July, 1885. It had formerly belonged to Mrs. Plumer.

A picture by G. Stubbs, an equestrian portrait, was sold at Christie's a few years back.

Engraving (B.M.) by G. T. Stubbs, bust to left, in a hat, published 1795.

Engraving, in Evans's Catalogue, "printed in colours."

[1] An engraving of this picture appears on p. 164.

[2] A photogravure of this mezzotint, executed for this book by the Swan Electric Engraving Company, is given as a frontispiece.

Engraving (seen privately) after Zoffany, plain dress, white shirt front, cloven chin. Frontispiece to *Memoirs Relative to State of India*, by Warren Hastings, published by John Murray, Fleet Street, 1786.

Engraving (B.M.) after Ozias Humphry, arms folded. Engraved by Greatbach, published by Bentley, 1841.

Engraving (B.M.) after Zoffany, by Brittridge, published at Calcutta, 1784.

Engraving (B.M.) in Jerdan's National Portrait Gallery. To the waist, nearly full face ; after Reynolds or Mathir Brown ; engraved by H. Robinson, in stipple ; appears also in a re-issue of the work by Fisher, and text by Taylor.

Engraving (B.M.) after J. T. Seton, by J. Jones, in mezzotint.

Engraving (B.M.), marble bust in niche, after T. Banks, by T. Gaugàin, in stipple.

Engraving (B.M.), bust, to the left, after R. Fulton, by W. Nutter, in stipple, published 1801.

Engraving, 8vo, in oval face, three-quarters to the right, published in 1795 by Crosby.

Folio, within an oval resting on a square tablet, with his name, and a full length standing Hindoo figure on each side. Painted by Stothard, engraved in 1797 by Bromley.

To this list should be added an admirable oil painting by L. J. Abbot, which was presented by Hastings to Mr. David Anderson, and is now in the possession of Miss Winter. It represents a very benevolent and tranquil face, with much earnestness of expression. Hastings was prompted by this picture to write the following lines at the expense of the managers of the trial :—

A mouth extended fierce from ear to ear,
With fangs like those which wolves and tigers wear ;
Eyes whose dark orbs announce a sullen mood,
A lust of rapine, and a thirst of blood—
Such Hastings was, as by the Commons painted
(Men shuddered as they look'd, and women fainted)
When they display'd him to the vacant Throne,
And bade the Peers the labour'd likeness own ;
And such in all his attributes array'd
Behold him here on Abbot's canvas spread !
'Tis true, to vulgar sense they lie conceal'd,
To Burke, and men like Burke, alone reveal'd.
They, their own hearts consulting, see him here
In lines reflected from themselves appear ;
With metaphysic eyes the picture scan,
Pierce through the varnish, and detect the man.

To Burke it shows a soul with envy curst,
Malignant, mean, and cruel when he durst;
To Sheridan, a foe to shame, untrue
To every kindred tie, and social too;
To Fox, a shuffling knave, with false pretence;
Michael alone descried his want of sense;
And all in avarice agreed to find,
Or make, the ruling passion of his mind.
Yet he has friends! and they—nay, strange to tell,
His very wife, who ought to know him well,
Whose daily suff'rings from the worst of men
Should make her wish the wretch impeach'd again—
Believe him gentle, meek, and kind of heart.
O, Hastings, what a hypocrite thou art!

On the 22nd January, 1797, Mr. Anderson wrote from Edinburgh to Hastings:—

The present which you have sent me will afford me more real happiness than any gift that Fortune could bestow. To nine-tenths of the world a portrait of you, drawn from the life, would be highly valuable. What must it be to one who can look back to twenty years of uninterrupted friendship, and who owes to your kindness much of the comfort I have enjoyed, and to your distinguished attention perhaps all the share of fame that I possess! I shall preserve it as a sacred memorial of our friendship, and transmit it to my descendants as an object of veneration and an incitement to virtue.

The picture reached its destination safely, and Mr. Anderson wrote on the 3rd February:—

Your picture is arrived, and I am delighted with it beyond expression. It is not only a fine painting, but, what is infinitely more valuable, it is the strongest resemblance I ever saw. I could almost imagine when I look at it that you were present, and speaking to me. Mrs. Sands and many of your friends have been here to see it, and every one admires it more than another. I do not know how to thank you sufficiently for this valuable portrait. Mrs. Anderson is almost as proud of it as I am.

Several busts of Hastings were executed during his lifetime, including, according to Sir George Scharf,—

Bronze bust by Thomas Banks, R.A., in the National Portrait Gallery; bare neck, drapery round shoulders. Engraved by Condé, 1792.

There is a copy of this bust, in plaster, at the India Office.

In the year 1800 Major John Osborne, an "old Indian acquaintance," who was one of Hastings' guests on the day of his acquittal, and who, according to Mr. E. B. Impey, "was remarkable for his attachment to Mr. Hastings and my father," erected on his estate at Melchet, Wiltshire, a small temple, after the Hindu style of architecture, for the reception of a bust of Hastings. The building was designed and built under the superintendence of Thomas Daniell, R.A. A bust rested on a pedestal surmounted by the sacred flower of the lotus, and bearing the following inscription :—

THE HASTINGS TEMPLE AT MELCHET.

Dedicated to the Genii of India, who from time to time assume material forms to protect its nations and its laws, particularly to the immortal Hastings, who in these our days has appeared the saviour of those regions to the British Empire.

Major Osborne sent two copies of an engraving by Daniell of the temple to the Court of Directors, and requested that they might "have a fit place" in the Company's newly erected Library. The gift was accepted, and one of the engravings is now hung in the India Office. I am informed by the Rev. A. Gay, rector of Plastford, near Romsey, Hampshire, that "it is forty-five years since the temple was removed in consequence of continual robberies from it at midnight. For a time a few of the statuettes were to be seen knocking about the Park, but these were taken by one person after another, until all trace of them has disappeared."

INDEX